China's Economy

China's Economy

A Collection of Surveys

Edited by Iris Claus and Les Oxley

WILEY Blackwell

This edition first published 2015

Originally published as a special issue of the *Journal of Economic Surveys* (Volume 28, Issue 4)

Blackwell Publishing was acquired by John Wiley & Sons in February 2007. Blackwell's publishing program has been merged with Wiley's global Scientific, Technical, and Medical business to form Wiley-Blackwell.

Registered Office
John Wiley & Sons Ltd, The Atrium, Southern Gate, Chichester, West Sussex, PO19 8SQ, United Kingdom

Editorial Offices
350 Main Street, Malden, MA 02148-5020, USA
9600 Garsington Road, Oxford, OX4 2DQ, UK
The Atrium, Southern Gate, Chichester, West Sussex, PO19 8SQ, UK

For details of our global editorial offices, for customer services, and for information about how to apply for permission to reuse the copyright material in this book please see our website at www.wiley.com/wiley-blackwell.

Library of Congress Cataloging-in-Publication data is available for this book.

ISBN 9781118982471 (paperback);

Cover image by Main image © Natalie Chun. Background image . . . . . (istock); Falling Economy Background © LPETTET/iStockphoto

A catalogue record for this book is available from the British Library.

Set in 10/12pt Times by Aptara Inc., New Delhi, India
Printed and bound in Malaysia by Vivar Printing Sdn Bhd

1 2015

CONTENTS

1

THE CHINESE ECONOMY, PAST, PRESENT AND FUTURE

Iris Claus and Les Oxley
University of Waikato

Since initiating reforms in 1978 China has experienced an unprecedented rate of economic growth and development to become the second largest economy in the world after the United States. Yet there is so much that we do not know about the internal workings and operations of the Chinese economy, in part, because the available English-language literature is but a fraction of the scholarly work on China. English-speaking scholars, business people, analysts and policy makers are typically excluded from Chinese-language scholarship, analysis and commentary, or are often limited to 'executive summary-type' articles from 'business-literature' outlets. We hope to fill at least part of the gap in the story of *China, past, present and future* with nine up-to-date surveys on some of the critical issues facing China, which have been written by leaders in the relevant fields of scholarship.

China's rapid economic growth and development was reinforced by industrialization, mainly driven by export-oriented and labor-intensive industries in Eastern China's coastal cities, and urbanization. Between 1990 and 2011, urban areas expanded 3.4 times and the urban population increased 2.3 times (CSY, 2012).[1] This fast urbanization proceeded despite stringent constraints imposed by a household registration system, the *Hukou* system. A survey by Wang (2009) and PTSPLT (2011) discovered that approximately 220 million people of the urban population are rural migrants living in cities without having obtained the formal status of urban household registration. Migrants without urban registration only have limited access to most welfare entitlements and basic public services, like education for their children, and are excluded from many urban jobs. This differentiation between migrants and native urbanites is creating serious social problems and contributing to China's rising inequality. Many argue (e.g. Xia and Liu, 2012) that China's current urbanization exhibits a relatively low quality of life, fails to fully play its role in creating market demand and supply and, due in part to the effects of the *Hukou* system, creates an environment that is not well integrated with national social and economic goals and responsibilities (Ba, 2013). Moreover, industrialization and urbanization have proceeded without agricultural modernization, which is contributing to a

China's Economy: A Collection of Surveys, First Edition. Edited by Iris Claus and Les Oxley. Published 2015 by John Wiley & Sons, Ltd.

large and growing urban–rural income gap (Wang, 2011). For example, by a comprehensive evaluation based on eight indicators (e.g. labor productivity, land output and mechanization), Yin (2011) finds that China's agricultural modernization ranks 51st in the world.

China's industrialization has also occurred in an economy with a relatively low level and growth rate of informatization and the extent to which China is becoming information based lags behind other countries. Since 2003, China's industrial value added has accounted for over 45% of total gross domestic product (GDP), which by Chenery's (1979) criterion suggests that China has entered the middle and late industrialization phases. China's course of industrialization exhibits quantitative expansion with excess productive capacity (Xu and Zheng, 2011), while informatization is still in its growth phase, mainly limited to investment, and its effective integration with industrialization is impeded by technological bottlenecks and interregional barriers (Guo, 2013). Furthermore, according to a survey by Akamai Technologies US, in the fourth quarter of 2011, the world average Internet speed was 2.7 Mbps, while in China it was 1.4 Mbps, leaving China ranked 90th in the world.

The nine papers presented here discuss in detail some key aspects of the Chinese economy, *past, present and future*. They survey the present and future challenges of the Chinese economy, based upon a rich (ancient) past, yet contested (recent) history, and identify some common themes, such as the household registration system, urbanization, demographic transition, inequality and the sustainability of economic growth.

In terms of *China's past*, the first article by Deng (2014) presents *A Survey of Recent Research in Chinese Economic History*, which argues that differing views on China's more ancient economic history have started to converge to a consensus view. However, parts of China's economic history, in particular the more recent history, remain unknown or unresolved to some extent due, in some cases, to taboos. As a consequence, we do not have clear statements to make or analysis to cite relating to the effect that China's more recent history has had on current outcomes. Knowing more about what conditions were important for China's modernizations is important, not only for China, but as potential lessons for other countries and Deng appeals for more work on China's economic history.

For *China's present and future*, the central government has proposed a goal of 'economic and social development'. In October 2010, the 5th Plenum of the 17th Central Committee of the Communist Party of China (CPC) outlined China's 12th five-year plan and proposed *Three Modernizations Coordination*, targeted at agricultural modernization synchronized with industrialization and urbanization (Xu, Duan and Liu, 2012). Two years later, in November 2012, the Report of the 18th CPC National Congress explicitly announced a new, grand policy orientation of *Four Modernizations Synchronous Development* (FMSD), which is aimed at synchronously developing industrialization, informatization, urbanization and agricultural modernization – all with Chinese characteristics. As previously the CPC indicated the need for a significant transition to achieve the goal of economic and social development (Ren, 2012). Secretary General Xi Jinping stated that, within a century of the establishment of the People's Republic of China the goal of economic and social development is to build a modernized socialist China that is prosperous, strong, democratic, culturally advanced and harmonious. A central driver to achieve this goal is the *Four Modernizations Synchronous Development*. Secretary General Xi Jinping acknowledges that the FMSD will be a long process with contributions over several generations, a 'two-century' timeline, divided into several stages based on the developing speed and complexity of the problems to be resolved.

Some of the critical issues facing modern day China are addressed in the papers presented here. In the second article *Demographic Transition and Labour Market Changes: Implications for Economic Development in China*, Du and Yang (2014) discuss China's demographic transition, which has been influenced by strict population control policy and coincided with rapid economic growth. However, China's changing age structure, i.e. a declining fertility rate and an ageing population, is occurring at a much faster pace than was projected by the government and has led to labor market shortages and rising wages. Population control policy is not the only influence in families' decisions to have children but other factors, such as income growth, increased educational attainment and urbanization, also have been important and the impact of these effects likely has been underestimated in government population projections. A further challenge facing China is that its population has started ageing while China remains a middle-income country without a comprehensive social protection system to support the elderly.

Pension reform, which became a prerequisite for restructuring state-owned enterprises and labor market reform because of the lack of portability of pension benefits, has been on-going since the late 1980s and, as Cai and Cheng (2014) discuss in *Pension Reform in China: Challenges and Opportunities*, a three-part pension system was introduced in 1997. The first part of the pension system is a basic pension plan, which provides employees with a defined benefit. The second part consists of a defined contribution system under which employees and their employers contribute to individual accounts and the third part is voluntary pensions. However, despite three decades of reform China's pension system remains incomplete. Critical issues that need to be addressed are that the current system is only available to urban workers and local government employees in rural areas, its operation is fragmented by decentralized financial and administrative management, it is fiscally unsustainable in part because of low compliance and faster than expected population ageing, and individual accounts earn low rates of return mainly due to investment restrictions and underdeveloped capital markets in China.

Another cornerstone of China's reforms was housing. Housing reform was launched in 1978 and centered on rent reform, the privatization of public housing and the build-up of a housing market. *The Evolution of the Housing Market and its Socio-economic Impacts in the Post-reform People's Republic of China: A Survey of the Literature* is the focus of the fourth article by Chen and Han (2014). As one might expect, the housing sector has been growing rapidly coinciding with sustained high economic growth, internal migration and expanding urban centers. News coming from many local and international sources suggest that the Chinese housing market has entered a bubble-period of price growth, partly as a result of government policies and incentives and/or supply side factors. However, Chen and Han find that empirical evidence on whether or not China has a housing bubble is inconclusive and conclusions largely depend on the definition of what constitutes a bubble that is applied. They suggest that more work is required in this area before a bubble phase can be confirmed – a difficult effect to isolate in any economy and not just China.

Urbanization, which has been a fundamental driving force behind the evolution of China's housing market, is considered in more detail by Lu and Wan (2014) in *Urbanization and Urban System in the People's Republic of China: Research Findings and Policy Recommendations.* The household registration or *Hukou* system has been a major issue in China and as Lu and Wan discuss has led to lagging urbanization as well as efficiency losses arising from too many small cities and larger cities not being large enough. The authors, among other things, propose a quota system under which long-term migrants convert their rural residential land to construction-use land, which is transferred to the city of their employment for urban expansion. Such types of proposal will be important to consider if the known inhibitors to the success of the *Four Modernizations Synchronous Development* are to be removed. The *Hukou* system is one such impediment to the future, equitable growth of China's economy and society, yet like many other challenges facing China, it is a fundamentally difficult one to resolve.

The *Hukou* system has also been contributing to rising income inequality as discussed by Wang, Wan and Yang (2014) in *Income Inequality in the People's Republic of China: Trends, Determinants and Proposed Remedies.* A large proportion of China's population still lives in rural areas and the *Hukou* system prevents many potential migrants from sharing the growth dividends in urban or coastal areas. The urban–rural gap is in fact the dominant component of overall inequality in China and while there is consensus that the *Hukou* system must be reformed, as highlighted in the *Decision on Major Issues Concerning Comprehensively Deepening Reforms*, adopted at the 3rd Plenum of the 18th Central Committee of the Communist Party of China, comprehensive reform at the national level remains a daunting task. Moreover, reform of China's fiscal system is considered by Wang, Wan and Yang to be another important driver of positive change.

China's industrialization has largely been led by labor intensive and export-oriented industries in urban and coastal areas. However, industrial production, which is the main source of local and global pollution, has been shifting since the mid 2000s with rising labor and land costs in coastal cities. In *The Evolving Geography of China's Industrial Production: Implications for Pollution Dynamics and Urban Quality of Life* Zheng, Sun, Qi and Kahn (2014) analyze the effects of China's changing industrial geography. In particular, the authors highlight the current trend to shift industrial production from the original coastal preference to inland cities, which, to some extent, has helped reduce regional inequality. It has also lowered the Pigouvian social cost of industrial production in terms of pollution in China, with consequent quality of life effects. More people have benefitted from a reduction in pollution than have suffered from an increase as coastal areas tend to be more densely populated than inland cities. Moreover, the use of cleaner, internationally sourced technology has resulted in some reduction of emissions, however, the overwhelming dependency on coal as a major energy source, especially to produce electricity, remains a concern for the future. Reducing the use of this cheap source of energy, which is fuelling China's industrial production, in order to meet international pressures for lower emissions, will continue to be a source of tension.

China's economic growth over the past decades has been spurred largely by economies of scale in labor-intensive industries rather than through invention and innovation. However, with demographic transition and rising labor costs innovation capability is becoming a more critical factor for sustaining economic growth and it is the topic of discussion by Fan (2014) in *Innovation in China.* Fan demonstrates that although China's innovative capacity is now growing rapidly, the spatial distribution of capabilities remains uneven across China's regions. Moreover, the rapid catching-up of China to be, in some areas, competing directly with established, innovative intensive countries is quite different from other newly industrialized economies. The Chinese approach seems to have initially involved significant in-house research and development (R&D), to be replaced now by a much more globally integrated approach, particularly in the area of telecommunication equipment manufacturing. Like many of the surveys presented in this book, the call from Fan is for further study and research and one particularly interesting and important example, but yet largely neglected issue, relates to the impact of international labor migration and Chinese returnees.

China's industrialization policy, which typically has favored exports of manufactured goods and heavy industries, has started to encourage high-tech manufacture and services and *China's Service Trade* is the topic considered by Chen and Whalley (2014). In this final article, the authors argue that although the development of China's service trade still lags behind merchandise imports and exports, despite high growth rates recently, service trade already has had large effects on China's economic growth, employment and technology diffusion. Even more major impacts are expected in the future and growing service imports and exports are projected to significantly affect global trade and foreign direct investment. According to Chen and Whalley, liberalization of service trade has the potential to lead to considerable increases in China's and the world's gross domestic product and the international migration of people is becoming an increasingly important aspect of trade in services.

The nine surveys presented here fill some gaps in the story of *China, past, present and future*. However, much more analysis and research on the Chinese economy is needed to help avoid some of the negative consequences of rapid economic growth in particular, growing income and spatial inequality.

Note

1. Land urbanization and construction have grown faster than the urban population (Ba, 2013) leading to many 'dead cities' nationwide.

References

Ba, S. (2013) Agricultural population urbanization is the first priority. *China Economic Times* 4: 12 (in Chinese).

Cai, Y. and Cheng, Y. (2014) Pension reform in China: challenges and opportunities. *Journal of Economic Surveys* 28(4): 636–651.

Chen, H. and Whalley, J. (2014) China's service trade. *Journal of Economic Surveys* 28(4): 746–774.

Chen, J. and Han, X. (2014) The evolution of the housing market and its socio-economic impacts in the post-reform People's Republic of China: a survey of the literature. *Journal of Economic Surveys* 28(4): 652–670.

Chenery, H.B. (1979) *Structure Change and Development Policy*, New York: Oxford University Press.

CSY (2012) [China Statistical Yearbook], Beijing: China Statistics Press (in Chinese).

Deng, K. (2014) A survey of recent research in Chinese economic history. *Journal of Economic Surveys* 28(4): 600–616.

Du, Y. and Yang, C. (2014) Demographic transition and labour market changes: implications for economic development in China. *Journal of Economic Surveys* 28(4): 617–635.

Fan, P. (2014) Innovation in China. *Journal of Economic Surveys* 28(4): 625–645.

Guo, X. (2013) To strengthen the integration and interaction, promote the "four modernizations synchronization" development. *Agricultural Economics and Management* 1: 5–6 (in Chinese).

Lu, M. and Wan, G. (2014) Urbanization and urban system in the People's Republic of China: research findings and policy recommendations. *Journal of Economic Surveys* 28(4): 671–685.

PTSPLT (2011) [Project Team of Studying Problems of the Rural Labor Force Transfer in the Process of Urbanization]. Rural labor transfer in the process of urbanization: strategic choice and policy thinking. *Chinese Rural Economy* 6: 4–14 (in Chinese).

Ren, Q. (2012) The synchronisation of four modernizations is the cognitive leap of information. *Journal of the Party School of Tongren Municipal Committee of CPC* 4: 22–25 (in Chinese).

Wang, S. (2009) Capital advantage: the core advantage of economic development in Beijing. *Expanding Horizons* 5: 57–60 (in Chinese).

Wang, Y. (2011) On the coordinated development among the industrialization, urbanization and agricultural modernization in central plains' region. *Academic Journal of Zhongzhou* 3: 73–76 (in Chinese).

Wang, C., Wan, G., and Yang, D. (2014) Income inequality in the People's Republic of China: trends, determinants and proposed remedies. *Journal of Economic Surveys* 28(4): 686–708.

Xia, C. and Liu, W. (2012) The empirical study of coordinated development between modernization of agriculture with urbanization and industrialization. *Agrotechnical Economics* 5: 79–85 (in Chinese).
Xu, D., Duan, S. and Liu, C. (2012) Research on the internal mechanism of interaction and synchronous development among coordinated industrialization, urbanization and agricultural modernization–based on the theory of synergetic and mechanical design. *Issues in Agricultural Economy* 2: 8–13 (in Chinese).
Xu, G. and Zheng, J. (2011) Research on the strategies and countermeasures to promote the integration of information technology and industrialization. *New Century Library* 10: 3–6 (in Chinese).
Yin, C. (2011) Rational thinking and strategies to promote the synchronization of three modernizations: report on the 2011 Annual Conference of Chinese Agricultural Economic Association. *Issues in Agricultural Economy* 11: 8–12 (in Chinese).
Zheng, S., Sun, C., Qi, Y. and Kahn, M. (2014) The evolving geography of China's industrial production: implications for pollution dynamics and urban quality of life. *Journal of Economic Surveys* 28(4): 609–624.

2

A SURVEY OF RECENT RESEARCH IN CHINESE ECONOMIC HISTORY

Kent Deng

London School of Economics

1. General Introduction: The Field of Economic History of China

China's recent economic performance has transformed a visibly traditional economy, in which over 70% of the country's work force was employed by the farming sector at the point of Mao's death in 1976, beyond recognition within just two generations. With its unbroken economic growth for three decades, China has also become the largest exporter and the second largest economy in the world. China has now become more industrial, more commercial, more urban and more affluent since her glorious 'Song Economic Revolution' in the 10th to 11th centuries. In this context, not only do outsiders want to know more about China and its long history, but also Chinese themselves become more and more motivated to understand their own past.

Looking back, China attracted research interests in the West as early as the time of Jesuit missionaries during the late Ming Dynasty (Ming: 1368–1644). Marco Polo aside, at the early stage what appealed to the outsiders like Matteo Ricci (1552–1610), Giulio Aleni (1582–1649), Sabbatino de Ursis (1575–1620), Johannes Schreck (1576–1630) and Johann Adam Schall von Bell (1592–1666) was undoubtedly China's unique culture, its stable state and its liberal and well-to-do economy. The early reports by these missionaries on China served as a source of aspirations for the European elite.[1]

China's prestige was tarnished from the late 19th century onwards by which time the Jesuits had long stopped operating on China's soil (following the 1733 order of Pope Clement XIV). China's old positive image of confidence and tranquillity was steadily replaced by a new negative one of conservatism, corruption, arrogance, ignorance, incompetence and chaos, which in turn altered China's impression on the international stage from the 'Wonder of the Orient' to the 'Sick Man of Asia'.[2] From then on until the end of the twentieth century, there was a consensus that a European model of growth and development – be it Adam Smith, Bismarck, Peter the Great, or Lenin and Stalin – was needed to save China from alleged cultural, political, territorial and economic bankruptcies.[3] Indeed, the vast majority of Chinese

China's Economy: A Collection of Surveys, First Edition. Edited by Iris Claus and Les Oxley. Published 2015 by John Wiley & Sons, Ltd.

reformers and 'revolutionaries' from the late 19th until the late 20th centuries were brought up in some 'anti-traditional' and 'Eurocentric' ways.[4]

The fundamental reason for this new attitude to occur was the adoption by the Chinese elite of the seemingly scientific ideology of Social Darwinism, which justifies 'social struggle' and radical changes/revolutions. This ideology was closely entwined with another European idea of 'nationhood' or 'nationalism' which linked social struggle and revolutions directly to China's territorial unification and integrity.[5] Among that generation of the Chinese elite, the main issue was how to make China another Europe.

In this context, why China failed (or why China did not progress from its archaic success) in accordance with a 'universal' (synonymic for 'European') standard has become the repertoire topic in Chinese economic history. There have been two main debating points here. The first is 'Needham's Puzzle' in regard to science and technology; and the second, 'budding capitalism' (or 'sprout of capitalism') in terms of unfavourable socio-political and economic systems for a full-blown capitalism.[6]

'Needham's Puzzle' stems from Joseph Needham's multi-voluminous *Science and Civilisation in China* in which China seems to have been a centre of creativities, inventions and innovations for a long time.[7] How China was able to get there and what China did with her inventions and innovations in history have been debated.[8] Here, the puzzle is deeply rooted in the general and normative impression that a traditional agrarian economy should be subsistent (or 'Malthusian'), backward, conservative and ignorant. It produces no science. Indeed, most Marxists and a great many traditionally trained historians believe that the social conditions in traditional China such as Confucian ideology (either classical Confucianism or 'neo-Confucianism'), education for bureaucrat recruitment examinations, government rent-seeking, landlordism, low wages, and so forth were incompatible with the sort of achievements in science and technology portrayed by Needham. On the other hand, if China was so ahead of the rest of the world, why China stopped and did not enter modernity. This is baffling from a Eurocentric perspective.[9]

In tackling this puzzle, arguments are often circular: for example, China failed because it lost all its wars with invaders (until 1945); China lost, because it did not have modern technology; China did not have modern technology, because China was unable to develop them. Such logical plight shows rather accurately the state of the play in Chinese economic history.

Related to Needham's Puzzle is the notion of 'budding capitalism' in traditional China. China's markets, moneys, bills of exchange, merchant capital, business contracts, wage labourers, profit making and so forth have all been counted as 'capitalistic'.[10] The vision of budding capitalism is deeply rooted in the Marxian notion of linear and teleological 'development stages' which China never followed historically: by 1950, China's 'national bourgeoisie' counted for less than 0.2% of China's total population.[11] China's alleged slavery and feudalism has turned out to be groundless.[12] The problem here is if China only managed to have the sprout of capitalism over a millennium since the Song period (960–1279), that sprout may have not been 'capitalistic' at all. Discussions have usually ended with a list of defects and constraints in China's indigenous mindset, institutions and resource endowment that stopped China from becoming another Europe.[13] External shocks and destruction from the Mongols during the 13th century and from modern powers after 1840 have also been attributed to.

Karl Marx himself at least had the decency to admit that his developmental stages did not apply to Asia. Thus, he created the 'Asiatic Mode of Production'. What he did not realise is the fact that with one of the largest political units and populations in world history China should be the developmental norm instead of a developmental exception.[14] Historically speaking, Europe indeed once modelled after China, not the other way round.[15] That China was no longer viewed as a role model by Europe came rather late.[16] Moreover, capitalism was transplanted in Asia, China included.[17] The best example is Tokugawa Japan where a full-grown feudalism did not lead to capitalism until the visit by Commodore Matthew Perry in the mid-19th century.

Another problem was that Eurocentric ideas (Social Darwinism, 'revolutions', and so forth) did not fare all that well in China. Maoism (1949–1976) was littered with power struggle among communist leaders and mismanagement of the economy by a party-state in obvious cases such as the 1959–1962 Great Leap Famine and the 1966–1976 Great Proletarian Cultural Revolution.[18] The debate is still going strong with the increasing amount of de-classified materials for the Mao's era.

2. New Development During the Last Two Decades

Coincided with China's recent phenomenal economic growth spurt, the most noticeable development since the 1990s has been the rise in studies of 'one period' and 'two approaches'. The 'one period' is that of post-1750 when Western Europe succeeded in industrialisation. The two approaches are 'global' and 'Sinological'. The former accepts China conceptually as a global norm, parallel with the West;[19] and the latter bends towards 'China exceptionalism'.[20]

2.1 *Re-thinking China in Global History of Post-1750*

China's achievements in the pre-Industrial Revolution era have long been viewed as largely 'unexplained' from an idiosyncratically agrarian society. Such a verdict seems to be out-dated in the wake of the emergence of the 'California School'.[21] In a nutshell, the California School argues that pre-modern China was more socially mobile and better governed than Western Europe. After all, China was where the globally circulated silver went in exchange for China's unique products of silk, porcelain and tea. So, it was not teleologically inevitable for Western Europe to catch up with and then surpass China. Rather, it was to a great extent accidental: because of the European processions of unique resources, known as the 'coal and colonies thesis'.[22]

The California School challenges the very cornerstone of Western economic thinking, which places production efficiency (which is a supply-side story) or productivities (labour, capital and total factor) at the very centre of all intellectual inquiries, and offers an alternative parameter such as living standards, which are a demand-side story. The methodology of the California School is simple: 'a country was what it ate'. From the viewpoint of final consumption of the population, China was on a par with Western Europe until 1750, the California School has concluded. Such a shift in parameter is very innovative, shedding new light on many old issues of growth and development in human history. Inevitably, questions and doubts have been raised on samples and data used by the California writers.[23] But, on the whole, the new framework has been well accepted.[24] It created a shock wave known as the 'Great Divergence Debate' in the past decade. The ripple of the debate can be felt in China where the academia has been trailing the debate with enthusiasm.[25]

In the mid-2000s, the debate took a direction known as the 'real wage divergence' led by Robert Allen. The new debate sticks to the Great Divergence label; but the similarity stops there. Real wage analyses intentionally produce various league tables of 'earning power' of the unskilled labour in different economies. This is unmistakeably a return to the neo-classical tradition of productivity and production efficiency. Not surprisingly, the Real Wage School has reached conclusions that real wages in Western Europe were persistently higher than in China from very early on.[26] With the help of historical national income reconstruction,[27] the Real Wage School has gained a great deal of millage.[28] The California School has been on the defence lately.

2.2 *'Sinological Approach' Regarding China's Own Performance in Post-1750*

Together with the onset of the Great Divergence debate, an increasing number of historians have departed from the Marxian unilinear framework in the past two decades. Such a trend has yielded a range of new works on China done in the West. Firstly, there is the 'Frank-Flynn Thesis' on a silver-cum-world economy in which Ming-Qing China was positioned in the very heart of a global market exchange.[29] From 1560 AD onwards, over a period of 250 years, large quantities China-made luxury goods – porcelain, silk and tea – were exported to the rest of the world in exchange of large quantities of silver which China did not produce.[30] This new insight seriously undermines the notion that China was insulated from the outside world and trapped in a growth impasse.[31] Rather, China ran an open and dynamic market economy, which interplayed actively with the West.

Secondly, there is a trend to re-calculate China's growth performance.[32] It has been suggested that China was once a global economic superpower in GDP terms.[33] There has been a renewed effort to calculate China's national income, a tradition which began in the 1940s.[34] Many new works are linked to the Great Divergence debate.[35] There was also the debate of living standards *per se*.[36]

This new development has given many scholars, especially those inside China, newfound confidence. Among historians inside China, the focus has increasingly been placed on conduciveness of China's indigenous institutions and incentives for growth and development. In the past two decades, research by the Chinese academia has taken in two directions. One is that of positivism to replace the dogmatic Marxian normativism or Eurocentrism. Works are more willing to show achievements made by the Empire of China instead of miseries caused by alleged class suppression and exploitation. Three successful dynasties, the Song (960–1279), Ming (1368–1644) and Qing (1644–1911), have now received the renewed attention. Scholars now argue that Song China made so many breakthroughs in farming, mining, metallurgy, manufacturing, media, commerce, urbanisation, social mobility, governance, consumption and living standards that Song society looked rather modern.[37] These findings justify the notion that China was a genuine donor of technology and institutions to the outside world.[38]

The other direction is to re-investigate and re-interpret China's political economy and performance of the economy in the late Qing Era when China allegedly went downhill. A path-breaking work by Gao Wangling argues that the rent level in late Qing China was low and the notion of excessive rent-seeking by the landlord class was groundless.[39] His evidence comes from well-entrenched customary practices in rural China where rent obligation was relevant only to officially registered land (*zhengtian*). Crops from hill sides and riverbanks or incomes from by-employment and market exchange (e.g. sales of home-made textiles, home-grown vegetables and domestic animals) paid no rent. Moreover, only the main crop bore rent. The second crop was rent free (typically winter wheat and the second cropping of rice in autumn). Furthermore, tenants' housing provided by the landlord was free. Therefore, although the nominal rent rate was commonly stated as 50–60% of the tenant's output,[40] this was by no means the real rent burden. In real terms, the tenant retained 70% of his total annual output, not counting his free housing. The notion of excessive exploitation by the landlord class collapses.

In addition, there was a common practise of 'rent paid in advance' (*yazu*). The old Marxian School views it as the hard evidence for landlords taking advantage over poor and powerless tenants. The new findings indicate that tenants were willing to make such rent advance not because of the exploitive pressure from greedy *rentiers* but because it was a good business deal for the tenants: by paying the annual rent up front, the tenants made a capital loan to landlords. The latter had to either pay an interest of 12–14% a year to the tenants,[41] or reduce the tenants' rent by half.[42]

This new insight explains well the lasting puzzle that life style of the average tenant was very similar to that of an owner-tiller in the late Qing, known as 'tenants becoming middle-income peasants (*zhongnong*)'.[43] The traditional Marxian historians always firmly deny such a trend not because the middle-income tenants never occurred but because their prejudice against the landlords does not allow tenants to be well off.

Research has also indicated nuances regarding the term 'landlords' thanks to China's sophisticated sub-division of freehold rights of the same plot. Under sub-division arrangements, there was the 'pseudo-absentee landlord' who possessed the 'subsoil' (*tiandi*) and the 'pseudo-tenant' who owned the 'topsoil' (*tianmian*) and ran the farm. The former, often an absentee, had no power to interfere in the business of the latter.[44] The key issue is why farmers (here 'topsoil owners') wanted to sell the 'subsoil' to a stranger. The Marxian explanation has always been poverty suffered by the former. It has now been clear that many topsoil owners were not poor. They allowed outsiders to purchase the subsoil as a way to attract urban capital investment, similar to a company's offering shares to the public. To protect their control of the farmland, the price for topsoil ownership was much higher than that for the subsoil ownership of the same plot.[45] In this duel ownership, the absentee investor, often urban, was able to expect an annual dividend from his capital investment in the farm at about 10% of the output which was still called 'rent'. The output retention rate for the topsoil-owner was 90%.[46] There was no obvious reason for the two business partners to engage in class struggle of the Marxian type. All these new findings of the Qing rural economy fundamentally challenge the very core of the dogmatic interpretation of the political economy of rural China as 'feudal' and the allegation of excessive rent seeking by landlords.

Similarly, new findings by Lin Wenxun on the well-to-do stratum (*fumin jiecen*) show that there was no definite link between private wealth and political privilege from the Tang to the Qing.[47] It is compatible with various studies of China's low tax regime under the empire system that allowed ordinary citizens to accumulate personal wealth.[48]

Meanwhile, research into China's demography gained its momentum in the past two decades.[49] It has become clear that rational choices prevailed at the household level regarding the number of children a family was prepared to raise, successfully argued by James Lee and Wang Feng.[50] Li Bozhong went a step further to argue that Chinese families practised the prevention check with methods and approaches not too different from what are available in the modern world today.[51] Such studies challenge the stereotype that all traditional societies were ignorant and thus suffered from their own miscalculations between their population sizes and their resource bases.

The most significant progress by far has been made in the regional growth performance in China. It has been argued that during the Qing Period when large quantities of luxuries were exported from China in exchange for foreign silver, the Yangzi Delta moved steadily towards a mixed economy of farming, manufacturing and services.[52] This view is echoed by a case study in North China, which shows that the delta was not alone.[53] Economy-wide, China was clearly moving towards modernity.[54] Such studies are highly compatible with the literature on China's top-down 'Westernisation Movement' of the late Qing. Now, whichever way one looks at the late Qing economy, there has been little evidence so far for the Maoist claim that China was 'poor and bleak' (*yiqiong erbai*).

Remarkable progress has also been made in the study of 20th century China. Four sub-periods have received most attention: the Nanjing Decade (1927–1937), Japanese Manchuria (or 'Manchukuo', 1931–1945), the Maoist Period (1949–1976) and the post-Mao era (post-1976) with three major issues. First, economic performance during the Republican rule is no longer so politicised. A fast growth during the Nanjing Decade is revealing in a combination of private initiatives and government promotion, including the restoration of China's customs autonomy.[55] There can be little doubt that if China had continued without the Japanese destruction, the country would have reached full modernity by the 1960s.

Some modern growth occurred in Japan-controlled Manchuria.[56] But such growth was achieved at the expenses of resources and human lives in that region. In other words, it was a false economy, very similar to the growth in Nazi-controlled Europe. So, there is a serious moral issue whether one should romanticise such a growth pattern any longer.[57] The issue of the aftermath of the growth in Manchuria is no longer a taboo. It is now openly discussed how the Soviet Union became the main beneficiary of the Japanese investment in Manchuria. It was no secret that Stalin's Red Army stripped Manchuria of much of its industrial assets worth a total of US$ three billion (at 1945 prices).[58] So, growth had to start in Manchuria all over again.

There has been a tendency to de-politicise and de-glorify economic performance under Mao's rule. Unnecessary social and private costs incurred under Mao's rule have been open to scrutiny, regarding the destruction of China's human capital during the Great Leap Famine in which 30–40 million died,[59] during the political purges from the 1950s to 1970s in which intellectuals were systematically targeted, and during the Cultural Revolution when high schools and universities were all shut down.[60]

The notion that Maoism laid the political, ideological and physical infrastructure for China's economic take-off under Deng Xiaoping has also been challenged, when one takes into account of the absence of economy-wide technological progress and the lack of capital depreciation in China's industries.[61] The truth has come out that China's growth performance under Mao's rule was both wasteful and unstable.[62] The most powerful evidence is from investment performance of the Maoist economy. It was documented that under Mao the amount of annual investment was a quarter of China's GDP. It was also claimed that after 1957 one *yuan* investment would yield one *yuan* worth of GDP.[63] If so, over 25 years from 1952 to 1977 China's capital stock should have grown 264.7 times of its starting size (i.e. from 24.1 billion *yuan* to 6379.3 billion *yuan*). However, the registered state-owned fixed capital assets (*guding zichan*) in 1978 were mere 448.2 billion *yuan* (constant price).[64] This means that the investment waste rate was a staggering 90%. As a result, by the end of Mao's rule, the structure of the Chinese economy was still traditional with the primary sector as the main provider of employment according to the official statistics (% in total).[65]

	1952	1957	1962	1965	1970	1975
Primary sector	83.5	81.2	82.1	81.6	80.8	77.2

One also faces statistical discrepancies when comparing Mao's employment structure with China's GDP structure: the industrial sector allegedly produced 49% of China's total GDP (as in 1978),[66] but Mao's 'modern industrial workforce' never exceeded 7% of China's total population and its growth rate was lower than China's population, suggesting that China's industrialisation process stalled.[67]

	Industrial workforce (I)	Total population (II)	I/II (%)
1959	45.5 million	672.1 million	6.8
1974	59.1	908.6	6.5
Annual growth (%)	1.76	2.03	

Similarly, China's urbanisation level dropped by 1.8% from 1960 to 1978.[68] Does this suggest that Mao's industrial workforce was so productive that it performed 700% above China's national par? Or, does this 49% GDP share merely come from 'creative accounting'?

An increasing number of works have re-examined other aspects of Mao's economy. It has become clear that Mao's government was excessively rent seeking for 'primitive accumulation of capital'. The main device was 'scissors pricing' which intentionally inflated China's industrial GDP and deflated its agricultural GDP to make the economy look industrialising on paper. The monopolistic rent between the two scissors prices served as a stealth tax. Only the rural sector bore that tax. Estimates made by Chinese scholars indicate the total gain by the Maoist state from the scissors prices was astonishing (in billion *yuan*):[69]

	Wen	Li	Wang and Zhang	Cui	Zhang *et al.*
1952–1986	–	–	–	–	582.4
1953–1978	800.0	337.6	949.5	–	–
1955–1978	767.8	–	–	–	–
1960–1984	–	–	–	428.3	–

Given that from 1952 to 1978 the net increase in the Maoist state-owned capital stock was 424.1 billion *yuan* (or 448.2 billion *yuan* at current prices), the entire capital stock of the Maoist economy had to come from the peasantry.

The direct impact of Mao's rent seeking was the concentration of wealth in the hands of the state on one hand and widespread poverty in society on the other. Evidence comes from changes in bank deposits (% shares):[70]

	State deposits	Citizens' deposits
1979	76.5	23.5

By 1978, about half of all households in China were below the official poverty line; in the rural sector, the proportion was 65%.[71] Moreover, the agricultural sector suffered from deep recession, which jeopardised China's food security:

	Agricultural GDP in the 1952 price (in billion *yuan*)[72]
1952	41.7
1977	29.0
Gross annual growth%	−1.4
Net annual growth%	−3.4 (after population growth)

	Food imports (in 10,000 tons)[73]		
	South China	North China	China as whole
1956–1960	–	472.0	–
1976–1978	22.8	1106.4	1129.2

Furthermore, the decline in China's input in science and technology lowered the technological content of China's physical capital. By the time Mao died, much of the capital stock was made of 'junk capital' with little market value. In a survey of 50,000 state-owned firms conducted in 1992, 62% lost part of their capital value, and 23% only had negative equity.[74] By 2000, the state sector had still remained the least efficient in the economy: its productivity was 60% lower than the non-state sector's.[75] Mao's state-run industrial growth was far from being a success story.

Finally, in terms of a 'human development index' (HDI), Maoism did not score high, either. In terms of mass education, the best record under Mao was 1964 when only 0.6% of the population received some forms of tertiary education; 34% remained illiterate.[76] Only after 2000, were over 90% of the rural Chinese able to read and write.[77] Mao's China had a very high infant mortality rate: in 1965, China's infant mortality rate was 165 per 1000.[78] The same level of infant mortality applied in 2004 only to the poorest countries on earth with low life expectancies of around 40, including Afghanistan, Angola, Liberia, Niger, Sierra Leone and Somalia.[79] To reach life expectancies over 60 years, something that Mao's regime boasted to reach, a country has to sustain an average of 26 hospital beds for every 10,000 people.[80] But by 1981, China had just two million hospital beds and 1.2 million registered medical doctors.[81] On average, there were five hospital beds and three doctors for every 10,000 population, hence putting Mao's China on a par with less developed countries such as Afghanistan (as in 2001), Cambodia (2004), Guatemala (2003), Myanmar (2000), Somalia (1997) and Yemen (2003).[82] The widely circulated claim that Mao's China doubling its life expectancies has now become seriously suspicious. The United Nations has re-numerated a 55% increase in life expectancy for Mao's China, cutting China's life expectancies under Mao by at least 10 years.[83]

Research into post-Mao reforms has mixed results. There can be little doubt that Deng Xiaoping's new policies successfully jump started China's stalled growth and development. So much so, the new growth after 1978 has comfortably redeemed Mao's wrongdoings. However, a range of issues has emerged regarding growth sustainability and social equality in several areas. First, China uses 15% of the world's energy, 30% of the world's steel and 54% of the world's concrete to produce only 5.5% of the world's GDP (2006).[84] To produce one unit of GDP China used 2.5 times more energy than India, four times more than the United States and seven times more than Japan (as at the end of the 1990s).[85] To demonstrate this problem, China is the largest steel producer in the world. But that has been achieved by a great many small producers: 3000 of them in total (as in 2000) whose efficiency has been suboptimal.[86] Secondly, China's distinctive input-driven growth model has made China a pollutant superpower in the world. Inevitably, China faces a huge bill to clean its air, water and soil, a bill which may significantly slow the country's growth and development in the near future. Thirdly, as China has become an open-and-large economy, its growth depends on other economies to provide China with raw materials, investment capital and advanced technology on the one hand and to absorb China's increasing outputs on the other. Here are the basic facts: China exports about 40% of its GDP and about 70% of the economy is linked to exports. However, as much as 90% of China's exports are manufactures which are price and income elastic, which means that China's export sales are not always guaranteed. Any slowing down in the world economy will put a brake on China's growth, apparent from the impact of the 1997 Asian Financial Crisis and 2008 World Financial Meltdown.

A way out seems either to speed up China's domestic consumption on the demand side or to slow down the current growth on the supply side; or a bit of both. But neither is easy. China's total wage bill (and hence its domestic market size) is less than 35% of its total GDP, which does not allow China's domestic consumption to effectively substitute China's exports. China's inventory will inevitably pile up; factories will close down. This is how the market always works. But, to slow down the current growth may be politically dangerous if the unemployment rate rises. In this context, the Chinese state has stepped in since 2009, pumping huge sums of money to fill in China's export-cum-demand gap. The government visible hand favours some 'key sectors' of the economy to establish monopoly, known as 'advancing state sector forcing the private sector to retreat' (*guojin mintui*).[87] But the side-effects are already too obvious in terms of causing market distortion and widespread official corruption.[88] It may lead to anything but sustainable growth. But at least, the economy has become more transparent.

3. Directions of Future Research

In the past two decades or so enormous research has been conducted with multiple lines of inquiries. One should feel confident that the momentum of scholarly pursuits will continue given China's increasingly importance in Asia and in the world.

In the field of China's pre-modern history, however, more detailed accounts for China's regional growth and development over the long run still deserve our attention. Comparisons between China's regions and with other countries have proved to be fruitful; more such comparison will still be needed.

Regarding China's economic history of modern time, that is, the post-1750 era, more research is needed in the areas of wars (Japanese invasions, Soviet invasion and civil wars) and political disasters (from mismanagements to purges and alright stupidity and self-destruction) because their impact has remained to a great extent unknown. Some have still been taboos.

Last but not the least, more efforts are needed to investigate the issues related to the state and state-building in China, an issue which was vital but has so far been overlooked.[89] Often resource allocation in China was done by the 'visible hand'. This was particularly relevant in the 20th century. We only have just started realising this research vacuum.

Notes

1. For example, Lewis (1946) and Hobson (2012).
2. For example, Weber (1963), Wittfogel (1957) and Pryor (1980).

3. For example, Fairbank (1978), Fairbank and Liu (1980) and Fairbank and Reischauer (1979).
4. For example, the Qing 'Westernisation Movement' and the 'Self-strengthening Movement' during the 1860s throughout the 90s, the bogus 'Christian' Taiping Movement in the 1850s and 60s, the Republican Movement and the Communist Movement since the 1900s and 1920s, respectively. Mao Zedong thus asserted that 'to copy from the Russians was our final conclusion' and 'only can [Russian] socialism save China'; Mao (1960, vol. 4, p. 1471) and Mao (1999, vol. 7, p. 214).
5. Pusey (1983), Dirlik (1989), Chow, Doak, and Fu (2001) and Wei and Liu (2002).
6. Lin (1995), Brook and Blue (1999), Wang (2001) and Wu (2001).
7. Needham (1954–1994), Elvin (1973) and Temple (1986).
8. Jones (1981 and 1990) and Mokyr (1990).
9. For example, Lin (1995).
10. For example, Wu (2001), Wang (2001), Wang and Liu (2001) and Liu (2001).
11. Anon (1969, pp. 69, 70 and 131).
12. For example, Fan (1964–1965) and Guo (1973).
13. Li (1981), Liu (2001), Wang (2001), Wang and Liu (2001) and Wu (2001).
14. See, for example, Wong (1997) and Pomeranz (2000).
15. Hobson (2012). For an earlier work, see Lewis (1946).
16. Brook and Blue (1999) and Hobson (2012).
17. Marx (1976, vol. 6, pp. 477–519) and Warren (1980). In late Qing China, the impact was obvious in the 'Westernisation Movement' side by side with unequal treaties; see Gilbert (1929), Yan (1955), Sun (1957), Wang (1963), Jia and Bao (1979), Xu (1986) and Xiong (1994).
18. For example, Davidson-Houston (1960), Heinzig (1971), Eunson (1973), MacFarquhar (1974, 1983 and 1997), Vladimirov (1975), Stephen (1977), Chinn (1979, pp. 375–394), Lin (1990), Becker (1996), Kung and Lin (2003, pp. 51–73), Zhang and Su (2000), Gao (2000), Chan (2001), Williams and Wu (2004), Chang and Haliiday (2005), Cao (2005), Li (2005), Chen (2005), Gao (2006), Song (2007), Yang (2008) and Dikotter (2011). See also, Rummel (1991).
19. For example, Wong (1997), Frank (1998), Pomeranz (2000) and Goldstone (2002, pp. 323–389).
20. For example, Jacques (2009), Zhang (2011) and Lee (2012).
21. The name 'California School' was coined by Jack Goldstone. It includes a group of *avant-garde* historians who all have their purses in California and view the world and world history from a non-Eurocentric (or non-Atlantic) way. They include A. G. Frank, R. B. Wong, Kenneth Pomeranz, and Jack A. Goldstone himself.
22. Pomeranz (2000).
23. For example, Vrise (2001, pp. 407–446), Huang (2002, pp. 149–176), Duchesne (2004, pp. 52–81). For a group debate, see 'Communications to the Editor' (2003, pp. 157–187).
24. Manning (2003), O'Brien (2006, pp. 3–41), Allen, Bassino, Moll-Murata and van Zanden (2011, pp. 8–38).
25. One only has to mention the recent events: the '20th World History Association Congress' was hosted by Beijing's Capital Normal University in July 2011; the 'Sino-West Economic Great Divergence Conference', by Tsinghua University in August 2012; and the 'World History Forum', by the Institute of World History of the Chinese Academy of Social Sciences in December 2012.

26. Allen (2001, pp. 411–447 and 2005, pp. 111–130).
27. Maddison (1998 and 2001). Noted, Maddison's methodology and source materials are open to debate.
28. The heroic counter-attack has been done by Rosenthal and Wong in their joined monograph (2011). See also, Li and van Zanden (2012, pp. 956–989).
29. Frank (1998), Flynn and Giraldez (1995, pp. 201–221 and 2002, pp. 391–427).
30. Deng (2008). See also, von Glahn (1996).
31. Elvin (1973) and Chao (1986).
32. Such re-calculation can be traced to Kennedy (1987). See also Landes (1999) and Li (1998 and 2000b).
33. Maddison (1998, 2001 and 2003).
34. Wu (1947), Ou (1947) and Liu and Yeh (1965).
35. For example, Liu (2010) and Guan (2012).
36. Pomeranz (2000).
37. See, for example, Gao (2000), Wagner (2001, pp. 175–197), Bao (2001), Zeng (2002, pp. 255–268), Hu (2004), Wang (2005), Liang (2006), Li (2007), Ma (2008, pp. 36–41), Cheng (2009), He (2010) and Yang (2012).
38. Berg (1998), Berg and Eger (2002) and Hobson (2004).
39. Gao (2005).
40. Li (1995, pp. 46 and 47), Li and Jiang (2005, pp. 440 and 441), also Zhou and Xie (1986, ch. 3). For a case study of Sichuan where the tenancy rate was one of the highest in the Empire, see Zelin (1986, pp. 517–518).
41. Gao (2005, pp. 213 and 214).
42. Li *et al.* (1983, p. 148).
43. Wei (1993, pp. 18–35) and Fang (2000, pp. 44–61).
44. Fei (2004, pp. 59, 177–179, 185–188).
45. Fei's estimate in prices was about three times in favour of the topsoil; see Fei (2004, p. 278).
46. Li (1995, pp. 36–46).
47. Lin (2008).
48. Feuerwerker (1984, pp. 297–326), Will (1990) and Deng (2011).
49. Wu (2000).
50. Lee and Wang (1999).
51. Li (2000a, pp. 337–344).
52. Li (2000b and 2003).
53. Grove (2006).
54. Liu and Wang (1996) and Liu, Wang and Zhao (1999).
55. Rawski (1989). Also see Chang (1969, pp. 1–60), Perkins (1969, pp. 266–289 and 1975, p. 117) and Bergere (1982).
56. For example, Yosuke (1938), Toa-Keizai (1931–1939), Anon. (1940) and Togo (1941). Also Myers and Peattie (1984) and Young (1997).
57. For the damning evidence, see Xie (1987) and Li, Gao and Quan (2009).
58. Zheng (2006, pp. 35, 46, 47, 187 and 464).
59. Bernstein (1984), Kung and Lin (2003), Cao (2005), Yang (2008), Fu, Hu, Feng and Dai (2008) and Dikotter (2010).
60. MacFaquhar (1983–1997), Yen (1988), Schoenhals (1996), Chang (1999), Zhang and Su (2000), Chong (2002), Walder, Esherick and Pichowicz (2006), Song (2007) and Yan and Wang (2009).

61. China's total factor productivity was negative under Mao's rule, see Liu and Liu (2008).
62. Deng (2011, chs. 7–9).
63. Ministry of Finance (1997, p. 479) and National Bureau of Statistics (2002b, p. 51).
64. Ministry of Finance (1997, p. 479).
65. National Bureau of Statistics (2004, p. 7).
66. National Bureau of Statistics (1991, p. 35).
67. National Bureau of Statistics (1986, p. 91 and 1998, p. 81); *Source*: National Bureau of Statistics (2004, p. 7).
68. Li (2000, p. 69).
69. Wen (2000, p. 177), Li (1993, pp. 302 and 303), Wang and Zhang (1993, pp. 75 and 76), Cui (1998, p. 144), Zhang, Zhou and Zhou (1993, p. 47).
70. Chen, Yang and Sun (2000, p. 92).
71. Based on Chen (2000, pp. 132 and 133).
72. National Bureau of Statistics (1986, p. 239).
73. Contemporary Agricultural History Study Group (1998, p. 251).
74. Chen, Yang and Sun (2000, p. 25).
75. National Bureau of Statistics (2003, pp. 186 and 461).
76. Hu (2008, pp. 1–6).
77. National Bureau of Statistics (2002a, p. 11 and 2003, p. 99).
78. Perkins (1988, pp. 638 and 640).
79. World Health Organization (2006, pp. 22–26).
80. Ibid. (p. 28).
81. Yu (1984, p. 740).
82. World Health Organization (2006, pp. 59–61).
83. United Nations' Population Division (2006). Available at http://esa.un.org/unpp/p2k0data.asp.
84. Liang and Wing (2008, p. 91).
85. Smil (1993, p. 73).
86. Sanders and Chen (2007, p. 195).
87. Du (2010, pp. 1–3).
88. The current social inequality has attracted much attention in Chinese academia, see, for example, Bramall and Jones (1993, pp. 41–70), Bian (1994), Li (2000), Personnel Department of the Party Central Committee (2001), Zhong (2002), Lu (2002), Sun (2004), Zhong (2004), Zheng and Li (2004), Li, Li and Sun (2004), Li (2005a), Li (2005b) and Kanbur and Zhang (2005, pp. 87–106). On corruption, see, for example, He (1998), Yang (2001), Hu (2001), He (2002), Li (2013) and Yang, 2013.
89. Deng (2011, ch. 1).

References

Allen, R. C. (2001) The great divergence: wages and prices from the Middle Ages to the First World War. *Explorations in Economic History* 38: 411–447.

Allen, R. C. (2005) Real wages in Europe and Asia: a first look at the long-term patterns. In R. C. Allen, T. Bengtsson and M. Dribe (eds.), *Living Standards in the Past: New Perspectives on Well-Being in Asia and Europe* (pp. 111–130). Oxford: Oxford University Press.

Anon. (1940) *The Japan-Manchoukuo Year Book, 1940*. Tokyo: The Japan-Manchoukuo Year Book Co.

Anon. (1969) *Mao Zedong Sixiang Wansui* (*Long Live Mao Zedong's Thought*). Beijing: Peking University, SOAS Library Copy.

Bao, W. (2001) *Songdai Difang Caizhengshi Yanjiu* (*A History of Local Finance during the Song Period*). Shanghai: Shanghai Classics Press.
Berg, M. (1998) Manufacturing the orient, Asian commodities and European industry, 1500–1800. In S. Cavaciocchi (ed.), *Prodotti e Tecniche d'Oltremare nelle Economie Europee* (pp. 394–396). Florence: Le Monnier.
Berg, M. and Eger, E. (eds.) (2002) *Luxury in the Eighteenth Century: Debates, Desires and Delectable Goods*. Basingstoke: Palgrave.
Bergere, M.-C. (1982) *The Golden Age of the Chinese Bourgeoisie*. Cambridge: Cambridge University Press.
Bernstein, T. P. (1984) Stalinism, famine and Chinese peasants. *Theory and Society* 13(3): 339–377.
Bian, Y. (1994) *Work and Inequality in Urban China*. Albany: Suny Press.
Bramall, C. and Jones, M. E. (1993) Rural income inequality in China since 1978. *Journal of Peasant Studies* 21(1): 41–70.
Brook, T. and Gregory, B. (eds.) (1999) *China and Historical Capitalism*. Cambridge: Cambridge University Press.
Cao, S. (2005) *Da Jihuang, 1959–1961 Niande Zhongguo Renkou* (*Great Famine and China's Population in 1959–1961*). Hong Kong: Times International.
Cao, S. (2007) Liangzhong tianmian tian yu zhejiangde erwu jiazhu (Two top soil rights and the 25 percent rent reduction in zhejiang). *Lishi Yanjiu* (*Study of History*) 2: 108–121.
Chang, J. K. (1969) *Industrial Development in Pre-Communist China*. Edinburg: University of Edinburg Press.
Chang, T. H. (ed.) (1999) *China during the Cultural Revolution*. Westport: Green Wood Press.
Chao, K. (1986) *Man and Land in Chinese History: An Economic Analysis*. Stanford: Stanford University Press.
Chen, Z., Yang, W. and Sun, M. (2000) *Zhongguo Guozi Liushi Zhuangkuang Diaocha* (*Investigation of Losses of State Assets in China*). Beijing: Law Press.
Chen, Z. (2000) *Shouru Chabie Pinkun Ji Shiye* (*Income Differentiation, Poverty and Unemployment*. Tianjin: Nankai University Press.
Cheng, M. (2009) *Songdai Wujia Yanjiu* (*Research into Song Commodity Prices*). Beijing: People's Press.
Chong, W.-L. (ed.) (2002) *China's Great Proletarian Cultural Revolution*. Lanham: Rowman & Littlefield.
Contemporary Agricultural History Study Group, Rural Economy Institute, Ministry of Agriculture (ed.) (1998) *Dangdai Zhongguo Nongye Biange Yu Fazhan Yanjiu* (*A Study of Agricultural Reforms and Development in Contemporary China*). Beijing: China's Agriculture Press.
Cui, X. (1988) Tongguo Tongxiao Yu Gongye Jilei (Government Monopsonic Procurement and Monopolistic Sale and Industrial Capital Accumulation). *Zhongguo Jingjishi Yanjiu* (*Research in Chinese Economic History*) 4: 134–144.
Deng, K. (2011) *China's Political Economy in Modern Times: Changes and Economic Consequences, 1800–2000*. London and New York: Routledge Press.
Deng, K. (2008) Miracle or mirage? Foreign silver China's economy and globalisation of the sixteenth to nineteenth centuries. *Pacific Economic Review* 13(3): 320–357.
Du, G. (2010) Guojin mintui de weihai he gengyuan (the negative impact and origin of the advancing state sector forcing the private sector to retreat). *Yanhuang Chunqiu* (*History of Chinese*) 3: 1–3.
Elvin, M. (1973) *The Pattern of the Chinese Past*. Stanford: Stanford University Press.
Fan, W. (1964–1965) *Zhongguo Tongshi Jian Bian* (*A Brief Panorama of Chinese History*). Beijing: People's Press.
Fang, X. (2000) Qingdai diannongde zhongnonghua (Tenants joining the middle-income group during the qing period). *Zhongguo Xueshu* (*Chinese Academics*) 2: 44–61.
Fei, X. (2004) *Xiangtu Zhongguo* (*Peasant Life in China*). Beijing: Beijing Press.
Feuerwerker, A. (1984) The state and the economy in late imperial China. *Theory and Society* 13(3): 297–326.
Flynn, D. O. and Giráldez, A. G. (2002) Cycles of silver: global economic unity through the mid-eighteenth century. *Journal of World History* 13(2): 391–427.

Flynn, D. O. and Giráldez, A. G. (1995) Born with a 'silver spoon': world trade's origins in 1571. *Journal of World History* 6(2): 201–221.
Frank, A. G. (1998) *ReOrient: Global Economy in the Asian Age*. Berkeley: University of California Press.
Frank, D. (2010) *Mao's Great Famine*. London: Bloomsbury.
Fu, S., Hu, G., Feng, D. and Dai, G. (2008) *Gaobie Ji-er 1978* (*No More Famine in China after 1978*). Beijing: People's Press.
Gao, C. (2000) *Songdai Huobi Yu Houbi Liutong Yanjiu* (*Currencies and Their Circulation in the Song Period*). Baoding: Hebei University Press.
Gao, W. (2005) *Zudian Guanxi Xinlun: Dizhu, Nongmin He Dizu* (*New Theory of Tenancy: Landlords, Tenants and Rents*). Shanghai: Shanghai Books.
Gilbert, R. (1929) *The Unequal Treaties, China and the Foreigner*. London: John Murray.
Grove, L. (2006) *A Chinese Economic Revolution*. Plymouth: Rowman & Littlefield.
Guan, Y. (2012) *Jindai Zhongguode Shouru Fenpei: Yige Dingliangde Yanjiu* (*Income Distribution in Early Modern China: A Quantitative Study*). Beijing: People's Press.
Guo, M. (1973) *Nuli Shidai* (*Slavery in Ancient China*). Beijing: People's Press.
He, H. (2010) *Songdai Xiaofei Shi* (*A History of Consumption during the Song Period*). Beijing: Zhonghua Books.
He, Q. (1998) *Xiandaihuade Xianjing* (*Trap of Modernisation*). Beijing: Today's China Press.
He, Z. (2002) *Fanfu Xinlu* (*New Path to Combat Corruption*). Beijing: Central Translation Services Press.
Hobson, J. M. (2004) *The Eastern Origins of Western Civilisation*. Cambridge: Cambridge University Press.
Hobson, J. M. (2012) *The Eurocentric Conception of World Politics: Western International Theory, 1760–2010*. Cambridge: Cambridge Press.
Hu, A. (2001) *Zhingguo Tiaozhan Fubai* (*China Facing the Challenge of Corruption*). Hangzhou: Zhejiang People's Press.
Hu, Q. (2008) Zhonggong zhongyang guanyu jiaoyu tizhi gaigede jueding chutai qianhou' (How was educational reform decided by the Chinese communist party central committee). *Yanhuang Chunqiu* (*History of Chinese*) 12: 1–6.
Hu, X. (2004) *Zhongguo Shougongye Jingji Tongshi, Song Yuan Juan* (*A General Economic History of Handicraft Industry in China, the Song and Yuan Periods*). Fuzhou: Fujian People's Press.
Jacques, M. (2009) *When China Rules the World*. London: Penguin Press.
Jia, Z. and Bao, Y. (eds.) (1880) *Chouban Yiwu Shimo, Xiaofeng Chao* (*A History of Qing Foreign Affairs: the Xianfeng Period*) Reprinted at Beijing: Zhonghua Books, 1979.
Jones, E. L. (1981) *The European Miracle*. Cambridge: Cambridge University Press.
Jones, E. L. (1990) The real question about China: why was the song economic achievement not repeated? *Australian Economic History Review* 30(2): 5–22.
Kanbur, R. and Xiaobo, Z. (2005) Fifty years of regional inequality in China. *Review of Development Economics* 9(1): 87–106.
Kennedy, P. (1987) *The Rise and Fall of the Great Powers*. New York: Ramdom House.
Kung, J. K.-S. and Lin, J. Y. (2003) The causes of China's great leap famine, 1959–1961. *Economic Development and Cultural Change* 51(2): 51–73.
Landes, D. (1999) *The Wealth and Poverty of Nations*. New York: W. W. Norton.
Lee, A. (2012) *What the U.S. Can Learn from China*. New York: Berrett-Koehler Publishers.
Lee, J. and Wang, F. (1999) *One Quarter of Humanity*. Cambridge: Harvard University Press.
Li, B., Gao, S. and Quan, F. (2009) *Riben Zai Dongbei Nuyi Laogong Diaocha Yanjiu* (*Survey of Slave Labourers under the Japanese Rule in Manchuria*). Beijing: Social Sciences Academic Press.
Li, B. (2003) *Duoshijiao Kan Jiangnan Jingjishi, 1250–1850* (*Multiple Dimensional View on Economic History of the Jiangnan Region, 1250–1850*). Beijing: Sanlian Books.
Li, B. (2000a) 'Duotai, Biyun Yu Jueyu: Song, Yuan, Ming, Qing Shiqi Jiangzhe Diqude Jieyu Fangfa Jiqi Yunyong Yu Chuanbo' (Abortion, contraception, and sterilisation: birth control methods and their spread in jiangsu and zhejiang during the Song, Yuan, Ming and Qing periods). *Zhongguo Xueshu* (*Academic Research in China*) 3: 337–344.

Li, B. (2000b) *Jiangnande Zaoqi Gongyehua, 1550–1850 (Proto-industrialisation in the Yangtze Delta, 1550–1850)*. Beijing: Chinese Social Science Academic Press.

Li, B. and van Zanden, J. L. (2012) Before the great divergence? Comparing the yangzi delta and the Netherlands at the beginning of the nineteenth century. *Journal of Economic History* 72(4): 956–989.

Li, J. (1997) Zhongguo jingji tizhi zhuanxing guochengzhongde hongguan tiaokong (macro control over the process of switching China's economic system). *Xinhua Wenzhai* (*Xinhua Compilation*) 4: 49–51.

Li, P. (2005a) *Shehui Chongtu Yu Jieji Yishi* (*Social Conflicts and Class Consciousness*). Beijing: Social Science Literature Press.

Li, P., Li, Q. and Sun, L. (2004) *Zhongguo Shehui Fenceng* (*Social Stratification in Contemporary China*). Beijing: Social Science Literature Press.

Li, Q. (2000) *Shehui Fenceng Yu Pinfu Chabie* (*Social Stratification and Income Inequality*). Xiamen: Lujiang Press.

Li, S. (1995) Lun Mingqing Nanfang Zudianzhide Teshuxing (On the Characteristics of the Ming-Qing Tenancy System in South China). *Zhongguo Nongshi*(*Agricultural History of China*) 2: 36–46.

Li, W. (1993) *Nongye Shengyu Yu Gongyehua Ziben Jilei* (*Agricultural Surpluses and Capital Accumulation for Industrialisation*). Kunming: Yunnan People's Press.

Li, W. (1981) Lun Zhongguo Dizhu Jingji Yu Nongye Ziben Zhuyi Mengya (On China's Landlord Economy and the Sprout of Capitalism in Agriculture). *Zhongguo Shehui Kexue* (*Social Sciences of China*), 1: 143–60.

Li, W. and Jiang, T. (2005) *Zhongguo Dizhuzhi Jingji Lun* (*The Landlord Economy in China*). Beijing: China's Social Sciences Press.

Li, W., Wei, J. and Jing, J. (1983) *Mingqing Shidaide Nongye Cibenzhuyi Mengya Wenti* (*Budding Capitalism in the Agricultural Sector during the Ming-Qing Period*). Beijing: China's Social Sciences Press.

Li, X. (2007) *Songchao Zhengfu Guomai Zhidu Yanjiu* (*Government Procurement System of the Song*). Shanghai: Shanghai People's Press.

Li, Y. (2005b) *The Structure and Evolution of Chinese Social Stratification*. Lanham: University Press of America.

Li, Z. (2013) *Shouru Fengpei Yu Shehui Fubai* (*Income Distribution and Society-wide Corruption*). Beijing: China's Long Peace Press.

Liang, G. (2006) *Nansongde Nongcun Jingji* (*The Rural Economy in the Southern Song Period*). Beijing: New Star Press.

Liang, S. and Wing, T. W. (eds.) (2008) *China's Dilemma*. Canberra: ANU, Brookings Institution, SSAP.

Lin, W. (2008) *Zhongguo Gudai Fumin Jiecen Yanjiu* (*The Making of the Well-to-do Stratum in Premodern China*). Kunming: Yunnan University Press.

Lin, J. Y. (1995) The needham puzzle: why the industrial revolution did not originate in China. *Economic Development and Cultural Change* 1: 269–292.

Liu, D. (2010) *Qianjindai Zhongguo Zongliang Jingji Yanjiu, 1600–1840* (*China's Total GDP, 1600–1840*). Shanghai: Century Press.

Liu, F. and Wang, Y. (1996) *Zhongguo Jindaide Shichang Fayu Yu Jingji Zengzhang* (*Market Development and Economic Growth in Early Modern China*). Beijing: Tertiary Education Press.

Liu, F., Wang, Y. and Zhao, J. (1999) *Zhongguo Jindai Jingji Fazhan Shi* (*A History of Economic Development in Early Modern China*). Beijing: Tertiary Education Press.

Liu, K. (2001) *Jianming Zhongguo Jingjishi* (*A Concise Economic History of China*). Beijing: Economic Science Press.

Liu, X. and Liu, G. (2008) *Zhongguo Jingjixue Sanshinian* (*Economics in China in the Past Thirty Years*). Beijing: Finance and Economy Press.

Liu, T.-C. and Yeh, K.-C. (1965) *The Economy of the Chinese Mainland: National Income and Economic Development, 1933–1959*. Princeton: Princeton University Press.

Lu, X. (2002) *Dangdai Zhongguo Shehui Jiecen Yanjiu Baogao* (*Survey of Social Strata in Contemporary China*). Beijing: Social Science Literature Press.

Ma, Y. (2008) Songdai jiating guimo zai tuisuan (re-estimation of the family size during the song period). *Zhongguo Shehui Jingjishi Yanjiu* (*Study of Chinese Social and Economic History*) 4: 36–41.

MacFarquhar, R. (1983–1997) *The Origins of the Cultural Revolution*. Oxford: Oxford University Press.
Maddison, A. (2001) *Chinese Economic Performance in the Long Run* (Paris: OECD, 1998); *The World Economy: A Millennial Perspective*. Paris: OECD.
Maddison, A. (2003) *The World Economy: Historical Statistics*. Paris: OECD.
Marx, K. and Engels, F. (1976) Manifesto of the communist party. In K. Marx and F. Engels (eds.) *Collected Works*, Vol. 6 (pp. 477–519). London: Lawrence and Wishart.
Maverick, L. A. (1946) *China: A Model for Europe*. San Antonio: Paul Anderson.
Ministry of Finance. (1997) *Zhongguo Caizheng Nianjian, 1997* (*China's Financial Year Book, 1997*). Beijing: Finaninal Magazine Press.
Mokyr, J. (1990) *The Lever of Riches*. New York and Oxford: Oxford University Press.
Myers, R. H. and Mark, R. P. (eds.) (1984) *The Japanese Colonial Empire, 1895–1945*. Princeton: Princeton University Press.
National Bureau of Statistics (1985) *Zhongguo Nianjian* (*China's Statistic Year Book, 1985*). Beijing: Economy Press, 1986.
National Bureau of Statistics (1991) *Zhongguo Tongji Nianjian, 1991* (*China's Statistical Year Book, 1991*). Beijing: China's Statistics Press.
National Bureau of Statistics (2002a) *Zhongguo Nongcun Zhuhu Diancha Nianjian, 2002* (*China's Rural Households Survey Year Books, 2002*). Beijing: China's Statistics Press.
National Bureau of Statistics (2002b) *Zhongguo Tongji Nianjian, 2002* (*China's Statistical Year Book, 2002*). Beijing: China's Statistical Press.
National Bureau of Statistics (2003) *Zhongguo Tongji Nianjian, 2003* (*China's Statistical Year Book, 2003*). Beijing: China's Statistics Press.
National Bureau of Statistics (2004) *Zhongguo Laodong Tongji Nianjian, 2004* (*China's Labour* Primary sector *Statistical Year Book, 2004*). Beijing: China's Statistics Press.
Needham, J. (1954–94) *Science and Civilisation in China*. Cambridge: Cambridge University Press.
Ou, P.-S. (1947) *National income of China, 1933, 1936 and 1946*. Nanking: Institute of social Sciences, Academia Sinica.
Perkins, D. H. (1969) *Agricultural Development in China, 1368–1968*. Edinburgh: Edinburgh University Press.
Perkins, D. H. (ed.) (1975) *China's Modern Economy in Historical Perspective*. Stanford: Stanford University Press.
Perkins, D. H. (1988) Reforming China's economic system. *Journal of Economic Literature* 26(2): 601–45.
Personnel Department of the Party Central Committee (2000–2001) *Zhongguo Diaocha Baogao: Xinxingshixiade Renmin Neibu Maoduo Yanjiu* (*2000–2001 Report of Survey of China's Internal Conflicts in the New Era*). Beijing: Central Translation Services Press.
Pomeranz, K. (2000) *The Great Divergence, Europe, China and the Making of the Modern World Economy*. Princeton: Princeton University Press.
Rawski, T. G. (1989) *Economic Growth in Prewar China*. Berkeley: University of California Press.
Rosenthal, J.-L. and Wong, R. B. (2011) *Before and Beyond Divergence, the Politics of Economic Change in China and Europe*. Cambridge: Harvard University Press.
Sanders, R. and Chen, Y. (2007) *China's post-Reform Economy*. London: Routledge.
Schoenhals, M. (ed.) (1996) *China's Cultural Revolution*. New York: M. E. Sharp.
Smil, V. (1993) *China's Environmental Crisis: An Inquiry into the Limits of National Development*. New York: M. E. Sharp.
Song, Y. (ed.) (2007) *Wenhua Dageming: Lishide Zhenxiang He Jiti Jiyi* (*The Cultural Revolution: Historical Truth and Collective Memories*). Hong Kong: Tianyuan.
Sun, L. (2004) *Shiheng: Duanlieshehuide Yunzuo Luoji* (*Disequilibrium: Mechanisms of Broken Society*). Beijing: Social Science Literature Press.
Sun, Y. (1957) *Zhongguo Jindai Gongyeshi Ziliao* (*Materials on Early Modern Industries in China*). Beijing: Science Press.
Temple, R. (1986) *The Genius of China: 3,000 Years of Science, Discovery and Invention*. New York: Simon and Schuster.
Toa-Keizai, C. (1931–1939) *The Manchuria Year Book, 1931–1939*. Tokyo: East-Asiatic Economic Investigation Bureau.
Togo, S. (1941) *The Manchoukuo Year Book, 1941*. Hsinking: The Asia Statistics Co.

United Nations' Population Division. (2007) World population prospects: the 2006 revision. Available at http://esa.un.org/unpp/p2k0data.asp
Von Glahn, R. (1996) *Fountain of Fortune*. Berkeley: University of California Press.
Wagner, D. B. (2001) The administration of the iron industry in eleventh-century China. *Journal of the Economic and Social History of the Orient* 44(2): 175–197.
Walder, A. G., Esherick, J. W. and Pickowicz, P. G. (eds.) (2006) *China's Cultural Revolution as History*. Stanford: Stanford University Press.
Wang, E. (1963) *Qingji Xinxing Binggongyede Xingqi* (*Rise of New Arms Industry during the Qing Period*). Taipei: Institute of Modern History, Academia Sinica.
Wang, G. and Zhang, X. (1993) *Woguo Nongye Xiandaihua Yu Jilei Wenti Yanjiu* (*Agricultural Modernisation and Capital Accumulation*). Taiyuan: Sshanxi Economy Press.
Wang, J. (2001) *Zhongguo Ziben Zhuyide Fazhan He Bufazhan* (*Development and Underdevelopment of Capitalism in China*). Beijing: China's Financial Economics Press.
Wang, L. (2005) *Songdai Kuangyeye Yanjiu* (*Mining and Metallurgy Sectors during the Song Period*). Shijiazhuang: Hebei University Press.
Wang, W. and Liu, T. (2001) *Zhongguo Jindaishi, 1840–1949* (*Modern History of China, 1840–1949*). Beijing: Tertiary Education Press.
Warren, B. (1980) *Imperialism: Pioneer of Capitalism*. London: Verso.
Wei, J. (1993) Qingdai Yazu Xintan (New Approach to Rent Deposits during the Qing). *Zhongguo Jingjishi Yanjiu* (*Research in Chinese Economic History*) 3: 18–35.
Wen, T. (2000) *Zhongguo Nongcun Jiben Jingji Zhidu Yanjiu* (*Basic Institutions in Rural China*). Beijing: China's Economy Press.
Will, P.-E. (1990) *Bureaucracy and Famine in Eighteenth-Century China*. Stanford: Stanford University Press.
Wong, R. B. (1997) *China Transformed*. Ithaca: Cornell University Press.
World Health Organization. (2006) *World Health Statistics 2006*. Geneva: WHO.
Wu, B. (1947) Zhongguo guomin suode (China's national income). *Shehui Kexue Zazhi* (*Social Sciences Magazine*) 9(2): 12–30.
Wu, C. (2001) *Zhongguode Xiandaihua, Shichang Yu Shehui* (*China's Modernity, the Market and Society*). Beijing: Sanlian.
Wu, S. (2000) *Zhongguo Renkoushi, Disan Juan, Liao, Song, Jin, Yuan Shiqi* (*Demographic History of China: the Liao, Song, Jin and Yuan Periods*). Shanghai: Fudan University Press.
Xie, X. (1987) *Mantie Shi Ziliao, Disi Juan, Diyi Fence* (*Materials for History of the South Manchuria Railway, Part 2*), Vol. 4. Beijing: Zhonghua Books.
Xiong, Y. (1994) *Xixue Dongjian Yu Wanqing Shehui* (*Western Knowledge Approaching China and Late Qing Society*). Shanghai: Shanghai People's Press.
Xu, T. (1986) *Yangwu Yundong Xinlu* (*Re-examination of the Westernisation Movement*). Changsha: Hunan People's Press.
Yan, C. and Wang, G. (2009) *Wenshi Qiuxin Ji* (*Truthful Accounts of the Cultural Revolution*). Beijing: Red Flag Press.
Yan, Z. (1955) *Zhongguo Jindai Jingjishi Tongji Ziliao Xuanji* (*Selected Statistical Data for China's Early Modern Economic History*). Beijing: Science Press.
Yang, J. (2008) *Mubei – Zhongguo Liushi Niandai Dajihuang Jishi* (*Gravestone for the Great Leap Famine Victims, Evidence from History*). Hong Kong: Tiandi Press.
Yang, L. (2012) *Songdai Chuban Wenhua* (*Printing Culture of the Song Period*). Beijing: Cultural Relics Press.
Yang, S. (2013) *Ba Quanli Guanjin Zhedude Longzili* (*Blocking Up Power in the Cage of Institutions*). Beijing: Fangzheng Press.
Yang, Y. (2010) *Shehui Zhuanqingqi Fa FubaiYanjiu* (*Counter-corruption during Social Transition*). Tianjin: Tianjin People's Press.
Yen, C.-C. (1988) *The Ten-Year History of the Chinese Cultural Revolution*. Taipei: Institute of Current China Studies.
Yosuke, M. (1938) *Building up Manchuria*. Tokyo: The Herald of Asia.
Young, L. (1997) *Japan's Total Empire, Manchuria and the Culture of Wartime Imperialism*. Berkeley: University of California Press.
Yu, G. (ed.) (1984) *China's Socialist Modernization*. Beijing: Foreign Language Press.

Zelin, M. (1986) The Rights of Tenants in Mid-Qing Sichuan: A Study of Land-Related Lawsuits in the Baxian Archives. *Journal of Asian Studies* 45(3): 517–518.
Zeng, X. (2002) Songdaide Shuangji Dao (Double-cropping of Rice in the Song Period). *Ziran Kexueshi Yanjiu* (*Study of History of Natural Sciences*) 3: 255–268.
Zhang, H. and Su, C. (eds.) (2000) *Huishou Wenge* (*Recollection of the Decade of Cultural Revolution*). Beijing: CCP History Press.
Zhang, W. (2011) *China Wave, Rise of a Civilizational State*. Shanghai: Shanghai People's Press.
Zhang, X., Zhou, W. and Zhou, W. (1993) *Zhongguo Nongye Jubian Yu Zhanlue Xuanze* (*Huge Changes in and Strategic Choices for China's Agriculture*). Beijing: China's Price Press.
Zheng, H. and Li, L. (eds.) (2004) *Dangdai Zhongguo Chengshi Shehui Jiegou: Xianzhuang Yu Qushi* (*Social Structure in Contemporary Urban China, Current Situation and Future Trend*). Beijing: People's University of China Press.
Zheng, Y. (ed.) (2006) *Jiang Jieshi Zenyang Shiqu Dalu* (*How Chiang Kai-shek Lost Mainland*). Hong Kong: Hong Kong Art and Literature Press.
Zhong, D. (2002) *Guomin Daiyu Bupingdeng Shenshi* (*Assessment of Unequal Entitlement amongst Citizens*). Beijing: China's Workers' Press.
Zhong, Z. (2004) *Dangdai Zhongguo Shehui Fenceng Zhuangkuangde Bianqian* (*Changes in Contemporary Social Stratification in China*). Shijiazhuang: University of Hebei Press.
Zhou, Y. and Xie, Z. (1986) *Qingdai Zudianzhi Yanjiu* (*Study of Tenancy in the Qing Period*). Shenyang: Liaoning People's Press.

3

DEMOGRAPHIC TRANSITION AND LABOUR MARKET CHANGES: IMPLICATIONS FOR ECONOMIC DEVELOPMENT IN CHINA

Yang Du*

Institute of Population and Labour Economics, the Chinese Academy of Social Sciences

Cuifen Yang

Beijing Information Science and Technology University

1. Introduction

Many countries have undergone demographic transitions.[1] However, the processes and impacts of demographic transition in China differ from those in other countries in a number of ways. Firstly, China may be the only country that has successfully implemented a population policy to affect its demographic processes. Secondly, significant changes in post-reform economic performance have occurred simultaneously with the demographic transition. In addition, the famine of 1959–1961 resulted in an estimated 30 million premature deaths and 33 million lost or postponed births (Kane, 1988). It was also followed by a sharp rebound in the birth rate that lasted for several years in the 1960s (Wang and Mason, 2005), which made the subsequent demographic transition process uneven.

The uniqueness of these events makes it difficult to understand China's demographic transition, which in turn influences policy making in China. Although China has already been faced with demographic challenges, the strict population policy is still ongoing. It is important to recognise those population policies that need to be adjusted now that the socioeconomic environment has changed. Therefore, this paper carefully reviews China's population policies and examines their role in economic development.

Demographic transition has impacted economic development in China. To a large extent, labour market changes, described as passing through the Lewis turning point (Cai, 2010), and

*Yang Du acknowledges financial support from the China National Science Foundation, project number 71173234.

China's Economy: A Collection of Surveys, First Edition. Edited by Iris Claus and Les Oxley. Published 2015 by John Wiley & Sons, Ltd.

evidenced by the shortage of unskilled workers and their rapidly rising wages, are driven by demographic variables. As a result of the labour market changes, labour costs are growing fast, which weakens China's competitiveness in labour-intensive industries and calls for the transformation of its economic growth pattern from one led by accumulation of production factors to one focused on productivity improvement. Due to the uneven process of demographic transition, however, labour market changes have exceeded policymakers' expectations.

The other great impact is China's rapidly ageing population. As a middle-income country, China has already been challenged by ageing. China has not yet constructed or financed a social protection system to support the elderly. Meanwhile, given the changing age structure, which is not favourable to continued economic growth, potential growth rates are decreasing, making it even more difficult to deal with the consequences of population ageing.

This paper examines the above issues and is organized as follows. The next section reviews demographic transition in China by addressing the country's population policy and its changing role, the problem of declining fertility, and the uniqueness of the transition. The Section 3 discusses the effect of demographic transition on recent changes in the labour market. Section 4 analyses the implications of demographic transition for economic development. Section 5 concludes the paper.

2. The Demographic Transition in China

China has witnessed a rapid demographic transition in recent decades. When discussing the drivers of the transition in China, the strict population policy is often addressed. China's population policy was rooted in the widespread belief, after World War II, that population growth restricted economic growth. Studies undertaken by the U.S. National Academy of Sciences and the United Nations predicted that the net effect of population growth would be negative (National Academy of Sciences, 1971; United Nations, 1973). The policy orientation was quite obvious at that time, so family planning was advocated in many countries, including China. According to Livi-Bacci (2012), in the 1980s there were 127 countries in the world supporting population control in a variety of ways.

2.1 *What are China's Population Policies?*

In the 1970s, China started to implement a strict population policy to contain the rapid growth of population. A so-called policy of 'later, longer, and fewer' (*Wan*, *Xi*, *Shao*) was introduced, which encouraged later marriage, extending the interval between births, and having fewer children. In 1980, the State Council declared the implementation of a stricter population policy, which required keeping the total population below 1.2 billion by the end of the century. Meanwhile, the Central Committee of China Communist Party issued its *Open Letter to All the Party Members and Youth League Members on Population Control*. The *Letter* called for all party members to respond to the State's policy and advocated one child per woman. More interestingly, the letter also commented: 'in thirty years, the very urgent problems of rapid population growth at present will have eased and an alternative population policy will be applied' which morally supports the argument made by those demographers who argue that current population policies should be adjusted (Zeng, 2006). In 1982, the population policy was designated as one of the *Fundamental State Strategies* in China, which made it more difficult to reform the policy if the population situation changed.

The population policy in China is usually described as the one-child policy. In fact, the current population policy could be categorised as consisting of four components applying to various groups of people. The first one is the well-known one-child policy, which covers all urban residents and the rural residents of Beijing, Tianjin, Shanghai, Jiangsu, Sichuan, and Chongqing. People covered by the one-child policy account for 35.9% of the total population in China. The second one is the so-called one and a half policy, which applies to rural couples who have already had a girl. Those couples are allowed to have a second child. The 19 provinces implementing the one and half policy include Hebei, Shanxi, Inner Mongolia, Liaoning, Jilin, Heilongjiang, Zhejiang, Anhui, Fujian, Jiangxi, Shangdong, Henan, Hubei, Hunan, Guangdong, Guangxi, Guizhou, Shannxi, and Gansu. This policy covers 52.9% of the total population in China, and represents the main component of China's population policy. The third component is the two-child policy, allowing rural residents to have two children without conditions. This policy covers the rural areas of Qinghai, Yunan, Hainan, Ningxia, and Xinjiang, totalling 9.6% of China's population. The fourth applies to some minorities, and allows a family to have three children. This policy covers 1.6% of the total population (CDRF, 2012).

The population policy has been fine-tuned in recent years. For instance, if spouses are both from a one-child family, they are allowed to have a second child. Seven provinces altered their policies prior to 2012 to allow rural families where one spouse is from a one-child family to have a second child. This became a nationwide policy in 2014. In general, the total fertility rate (hereafter TFR) is about 1.47 in China (CDRF, 2012). The total fertility rate is defined as the average number of children that would be born to a woman during her lifetime if (1) she were to experience the exact current age-specific fertility rates through her lifetime, and (2) she were to survive from birth to the end of her reproductive life. The TFR is obtained by summing the single-year age-specific birth rates at a given time.

It is believed that China is almost the only country to have effectively implemented a family planning policy. In contrast to other populous countries in Asia, Livi-Bacci (2012) attributes China's successful implementation of its population policy to the following reasons. First, China achieved success in public health, which significantly lowered the death rate. Second, China has efficient political administration systems, which improved the efficiency of policy implementation. In addition, some strict birth control measures were also used.

2.2 *Declining Fertility*

The strict population control policy did trigger a rapid decline in fertility rates, as shown in Figure 1. The crude birth rate, defined as the number of births in the total population, peaked at 43.4‰ in 1964 and has been declining since then. The following decade was the period with the fastest decreases in fertility rate. In 1975, the crude birth rate was 23.0‰. In the current century, the crude birth rate has been kept at a very low level and dropped to 11.9‰ in 2011. It is also worth noting that, as also indicated in Figure 1, the crude death rate has been at a low level for a long time in China. Improved health care and reductions in the infant mortality rate contributed most to the decline in the crude death rate. Although, it is easily ignored, keeping the death rate at a low level has contributed substantially to fertility declining in China (Zhao, 2004). Since 1965 China has successfully kept the crude death rate below 10‰. As a result, population growth rates have been going down over time. In 2012, the natural growth rate of population was 4.95‰.

To examine fertility levels more accurately, demographers tend to use TFR rather than the crude birth rates used in Figure 1. The greatest decline in Chinese birth rates took place before

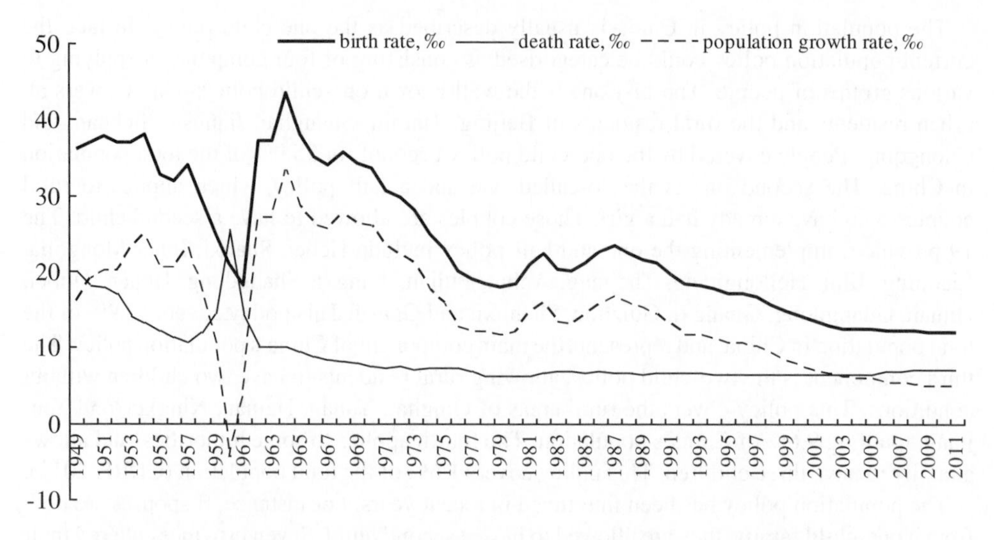

Figure 1. Crude Birth Rate, Crude Death Rates, and Population Growth Rates in China.
Source: National Bureau of Statistics (NBS), *China Statistical Yearbooks*, various issues.

1980, from TFR levels of approximately 6 in the 1960s to 2.75 in 1979 (Guo, 2008; Morgan et al., 2009). In the 1980s, the decline stopped and the TFR fluctuated around 2.5 (Guo, 2008). However, there appears to be no consensus amongst researchers and policymakers regarding the contemporary TFR. In its official documents, the former National Committee of Population and Family Planning[2] (2009) insisted that the TFR in China has been maintained at 1.8 since the mid 1990s, which is significantly higher than the results from other surveys and studies (Guo, 2010). After reviewing the results based on various fertility surveys, Guo (2012) believes that the current TFR is around 1.5, and his argument is supported by a simulation based on the sixth census data from 2010. Using two rounds of census data, a simulation by Yin et al. (2013) indicated a TFR in 2010 as low as 1.43, which is close to the stated policy fertility rate of 1.42. More detailed results of this study are displayed in Figure 2.

Guo (2012) rightly points out the possible risks in decision-making if misleading fertility rates are used by policymakers. A decision based on 1.8, which implies that a universal two-child policy has been implemented, may incorrectly influence the demographic trend in China. According to Guo (2012), from 1994 to 2005, the total number of new additions reported by the National Bureau of Statistics (NBS) was about 221 million, but the actual number is only 190 million according to the sixth census. During this period, there were 31 million people over-reported in official statistics. One of the consequences of using an upwardly biased fertility rate is to misunderstand demographic and economic dynamics. For example, the increasing labour shortage that has taken place since 2003 is beyond policymakers' expectations. The speed of ageing was also unexpected due to misunderstanding regarding fertility rates in earlier years. More importantly, if we keep using the biased TFR to project future population trends, it will definitely provide wrong messages. For example, the total population will peak in 2029 if the TFR level is assumed to be 1.8 while the peak will be 5 years earlier if a TFR of 1.4 is assumed.

Even without agreement on what the exact TFR currently is in China, there is consensus that the fertility rate is below replacement levels (requiring a TFR of 2.1). There has been a very obviously declining fertility rate over the past three decades. Strict and well-implemented

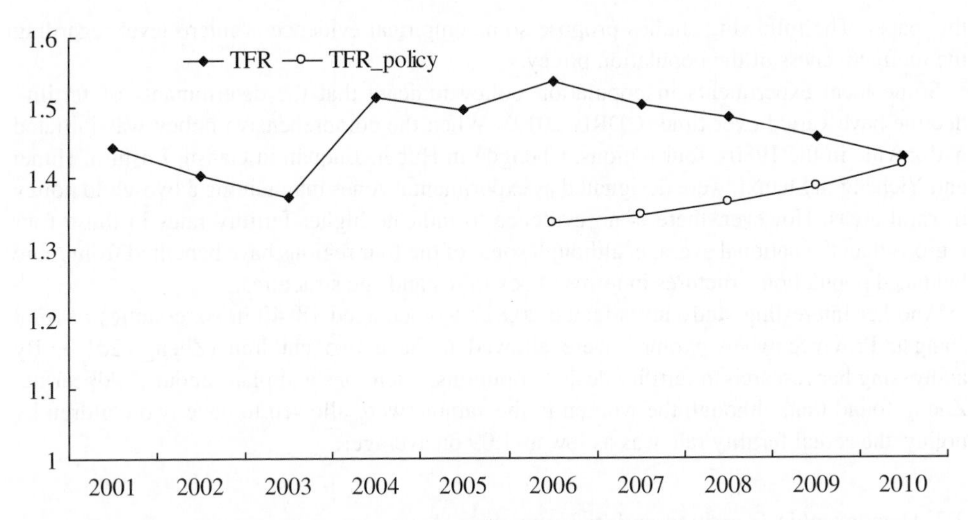

Figure 2. The Policy and Actual TFR in since 2001.
Source: Adapted from Yin et al. (2013)

population control policy complicates the determinants of fertility decline, but the process of fertility decline in China does follow the general pattern that has been observed in many other countries. As we have already noted, the visible decline in TFR occurred before this century. Considering the simultaneity of economic growth and fertility decline, Du (2005) analysed the determination of fertility decline through per capita GDP growth, development in education, and enforcement of population policy, using the panel data from provinces between 1978 and 1998. The empirical results indicate that the implementation of the population policy only had an effect on TFR decline between 1978 and 1989 and was statistically insignificant between 1990 and 1998, while per capita GDP and educational attainment dominated the decline over the whole period.

The effect of economic development on fertility decline has been demonstrated in many developed countries where population control policies do not exist. Even before the strict policy was initiated in the 1970s, some scholars (Lavely and Freedman, 1990) pointed out that education and urbanisation had been negatively correlated with fertility in both urban and rural China prior to the initiation of the substantial family planning programmes. Recent studies also observe that the determination of fertility has been taken over by economic development rather than the population policy *per se* (Yin et al., 2013).

It is of great policy relevance to clarify the determinants of fertility decline and their roles at different stages of demographic transition. First, as in the implementation of any policy, the enforcement of population policy has administrative costs. When the population polices were designated as Fundamental State Strategy, both central and local governments made great efforts to enforce the policy (Yang & McElroy, 2000; Yuan, 2000). However, if the population policy no longer determines the dynamics of demography, it does not make sense to keep the policy and provide it with resources. Second, we believe the current population structure is not desirable for economic development. However, the ineffectiveness of population policy on demography implies that using population policy to change population trends is not a solution. In other words, policymakers will have to live with the demographic facts in China and sustain economic growth by reforming the economic system, which is discussed later in this paper. The following studies propose some empirical evidence at micro level regarding the ineffectiveness of the population policy.

Some local experiments in population policy indicate that the determinants of fertility decline have varied over time (CDRF, 2012). When the comprehensive policy was initiated nationwide in the 1980s, four regions, Chengde in Hubei, Jiuquan in Gansu, Enshi in Hubei and Yicheng in Shanxi, were designated as experimental zones maintaining a two-child policy in rural areas. However, there is no evidence to indicate higher fertility rates in those four regions than the national average, although some of the four regions have benefited from more balanced population structures in terms of sex ratios and age structures.

Another interesting study investigated 20,827 women aged 18–40 in six counties of rural Jiangsu Province where women were allowed to have two children (Zheng, 2013). By addressing her research to fertility desires, opinions, intentions and plans about childbearing, Zheng found that, although the women in the sample were allowed to have two children by policy, the actual fertility rate was as low as 1.09 on average.

2.3 *Demographic Transition and Its Uniqueness*

As noted earlier, both the strict population control policy and socioeconomic development have played active roles in the decline in fertility in China, which means that China has spent less time than many other countries in completing the process of demographic transition (Heuveline, 1999). It has taken China about 30 years to complete the process of demographic transition that has taken more than a hundred years in most industrialized countries. Hussain (2002) notes various outcomes of demographic transition in China. He points out that the Chinese demographic transition in the last century was not only to slow down the rapid growth in total population, but reflected the impacts of changing population structures on socioeconomic developments, such as dependency ratios and the composition of dependents, the structure of the working age population, and the size and composition of families.

Figure 3 presents the changing population structure based on all the six rounds of population census conducted in China. It is obvious that the age structure in China has changed from a typical triangle in the 1950s and 1960s to a pyramid with a shank base in 2010. The figure also indicates that the speed of age structure alteration has accelerated in the new century. For example, the proportion of people older than 65 in the total population increased 0.7 percentage points from 1982 to 1990, 1.4 percentage points from 1990 to 2010, and 1.9 percentage points from 2000 to 2010.

As Wang and Mason (2005) point out, China's population age profile contains some unique characteristics. The drastic fertility decline occurred within a relatively short time period, rarely seen elsewhere in the world. It is this uniqueness that has brought about some dramatic changes in the labour market. It also brings China an ageing society at the stage of middle income for the country as a whole.

3. The Effects on China's Labour Market

The Chinese labour market has witnessed a great change since 2003. The most prominent feature of this change is the growing labour scarcity, as evidenced by the shortage of unskilled workers and their rapidly increasing wages. According to a rural household survey conducted by the NBS, the average real wages for rural migrant workers have grown 6.7% per annum from 2001 to 2006, and 12.4% per annum from 2006 to 2011. As Table 1 shows, the numbers

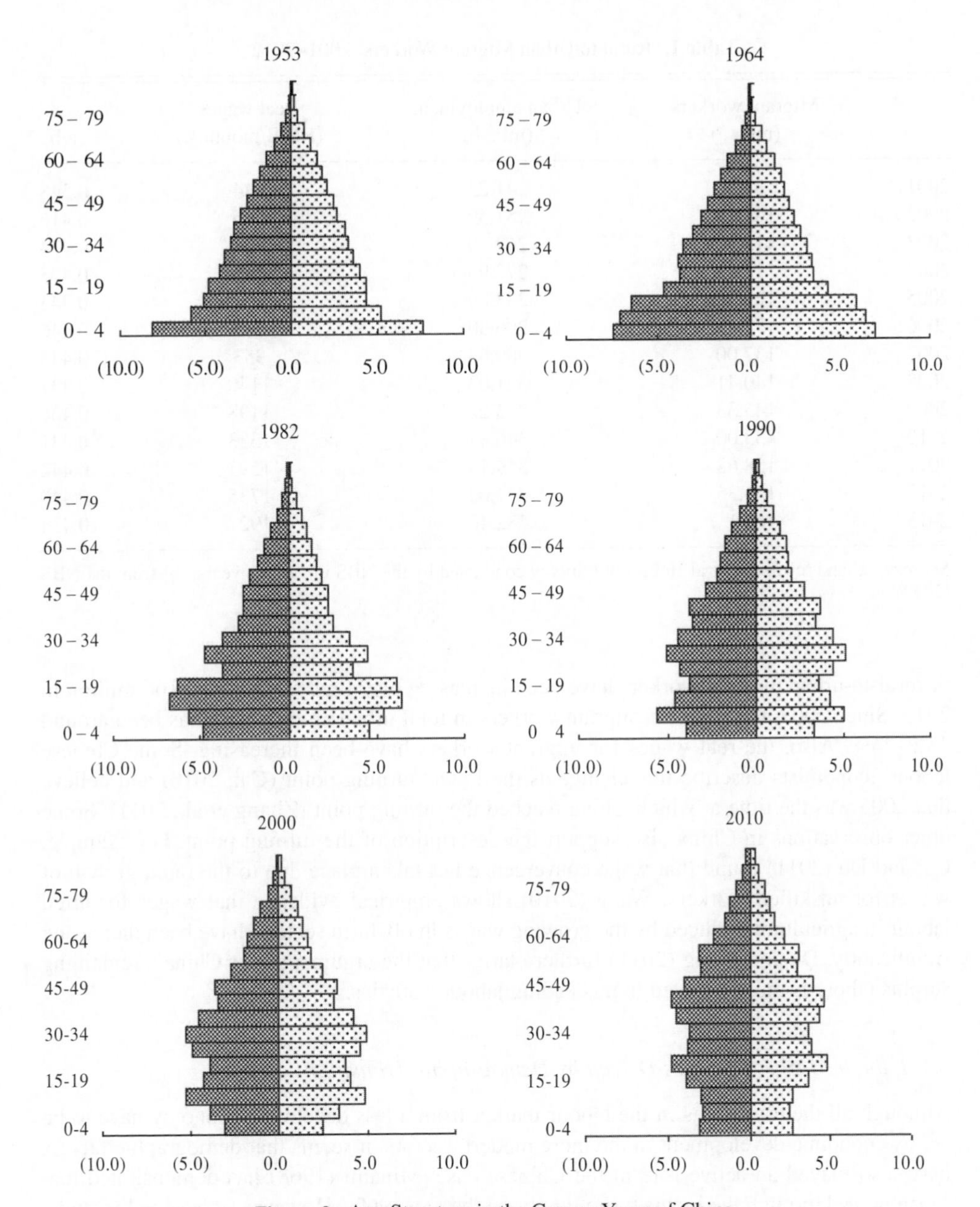

Figure 3. Age Structure in the Census Years of China.

Note: The horizontal axis is the percentage of the total population, and the vertical axis is the age structure of the population.

Sources: The various rounds of population census in China.

Table 1. Rural to Urban Migrant Workers: 2001–2012

	Migrant workers (mln, a)	Urban employment (mln, b)	Real wages (RMB/month, c)	a/b
2001	84.00	241.23	644	0.348
2002	104.70	251.59	666	0.416
2003	113.90	262.30	703	0.434
2004	118.23	272.93	756	0.433
2005	125.78	283.89	821	0.443
2006	132.12	296.30	889	0.446
2007	137.00	309.53	953	0.443
2008	140.41	321.03	1140	0.437
2009	145.33	333.22	1198	0.436
2010	153.00	346.87	1383	0.441
2011	158.63	359.14	1593	0.442
2012	163.36	371.02	1735	0.440
2013	166.1	382.40	1927	0.434

Sources: 'a' and 'c' from Rural Household Survey conducted by the NBS in various years, 'b' from the NBS (2012).

of rural-to-urban migrant workers have been increasing over time and totalled 166 million in 2013. Since 2003, the share of migrant workers in total urban employment has been around 43%–44%. Also, the real wages for migrant workers have been increasing. Some Chinese labour economists describe this change as the Lewis turning point (Cai, 2010) and believe that 2003 was the time at which China reached the turning point (Zhang et al., 2011). Some other observations in China also support the description of the turning point. For example, Cai and Du (2011) found that wage convergence has taken place due to the rapid growth of wages for unskilled workers. Wang (2010) shows empirical evidence that wages for hired labour in agriculture, induced by the growing wages in off-farm sectors, have been increasing significantly. Du and Wang (2011) further clarify that the argument over China's remaining surplus labour is mostly rooted in misleading labour statistics.

3.1 *Labour Market Changes Driven by Demographic Transitions*

Although all the transitions in the labour market from a less developed economy have to be led by economic development in the more modern sectors, it seems that demographic factors have also played an active role in the Chinese case. Minami (1968) has demonstrated that Japan passed through the Lewis turning point in the late 1960s. However, at least in his study, Minami did not address the importance of demographics in the Japanese transition. We do not deny the importance of demand-side factors in driving the labour market changes in China, but the demographics do determine why the changes have taken place at certain points in time.

Thanks to steady and rapid economic growth in recent decades, the Chinese economy has ranked at the very top level globally, which has created a very large demand for labour. Current economic theory implies that 1 percentage point of economic growth will create new jobs, if employment elasticity remains constant. Using two rounds of Economic Census data, which were taken to be the most reliable statistics available to measure economic activities

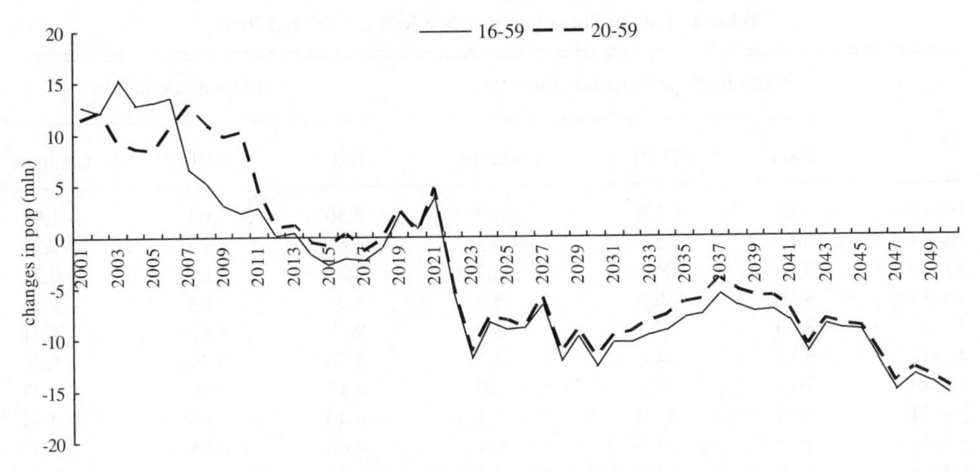

Figure 4. Annual Changes in Population: 2001–2050.
Source: Authors' projection.

in China, Du and Wang (2011) estimated that the average rates of employment growth per annum from 2004 to 2008 were 5.68% for the secondary sector and 8.69% for the tertiary sector. Employment elasticity with respect to value added was 0.468 for the secondary sector and 0.758 for the tertiary sector. Based on those parameters, Du (2013a) estimates that, even growing at its current potential growth rate, the economy will create more than 10 million job vacancies every year between 2016 and 2020.

In this context, the demographic changes may explain why China has met the Lewis turning point in recent years. According to the Chinese Labour Law, people are allowed to work once they have reached the age of 16. In practice, however, most people between 16 and 20 are still in school, since China started to expand its higher education significantly in the early 2000s. Figure 4 plots the changes in population aged 16–59 and 20–59 to reflect the impacts of demographic transition on labour supply. As Figure 4 shows, the marginal supply of labour in China has already been constrained by the rapid demographic transition. For example, in 2007 the net increase in the working age population, that is, people aged 16–59, dramatically dropped to 6.5 million from 13.4 million in the previous year. Both lines indicate that total labour availability starts to decrease around 2013.[3]

Once new entrants to the labour market are fewer than the jobs available, the labour market will adjust spontaneously by raising the wage rates: this may encourage the participation of those who had previously left the labour market. In this case, however, the economy would bear more costs in using labour, which weakens its competitiveness in labour-intensive sectors. This new trend calls for China to transform its growth pattern from one driven by accumulation of production factors to one driven by improvement in productivity. The labour force participation rates over time are provided in Table 2 by age groups.

With population ageing, the proportion of available labour in the total population shows more rapid changes than the total number in the workforce. Population projection assuming a TFR level of 1.4 indicates that the percentage of the population of working age (age 16–64) peaked in 2013 at 71.9% and will be 70.2% in 2020, 67.5% in 2030, and only 58.3% in 2050. Looking forward, the total labour force will be decreasing very soon. In Figure 5, both the available workforce age definitions of 16–59 and 16–64 are plotted. If the working age

Table 2. Labour Force Participation Rates: 2005 and 2010

	Labour force participation rates (%)			% of total population		
	2005	2010	Changes	2005	2010	Changes
16–19	26.0	21.8	−4.2	7.56	5.63	−1.93
20–24	69.1	62.8	−6.3	7.86	9.25	1.39
25–29	81.6	84.3	2.7	7.26	7.61	0.35
30–34	82.6	86.0	3.4	8.97	7.03	−1.94
35–39	82.5	85.5	3.0	9.68	8.67	−1.01
40–44	80.7	84.4	3.7	8.28	9.34	1.06
45–49	70.6	78.5	7.9	6.13	7.96	1.83
50–54	49.9	57.0	7.1	6.40	5.86	−0.54
55–59	29.5	37.6	8.1	4.68	6.05	1.37
60–64	11.5	13.8	2.3	3.35	4.34	0.99
65+	2.5	2.7	0.2	7.85	8.65	0.8

Source: Adapted from Du and Lu (2013).

population is defined as ages 16–59, the total size of the labour force peaked at 907 million in 2013 and will decrease rapidly after 2021. Under the other definition, the total available workforce will peak at 981 million in 2016 and will decrease somewhat more slowly after that. This trend predicts that demographic factors, which have been believed steady in the short run, will dominate the labour market situation in the future.

China's unique demographic transition and its association with labour market trends are essential to understanding recently emerging employment phenomena. The supply-side

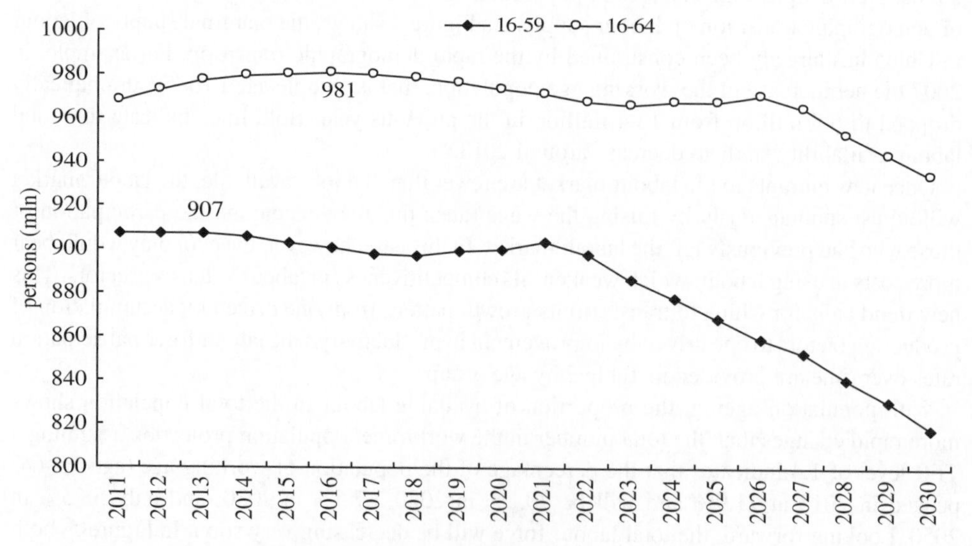

Figure 5. The Total Available Workforce in China.
Source: Authors' projection.

factors explain the puzzle of why China can keep employment stable when the aggregated demand has been depressed since the global financial crisis of 2008. From a policy perspective it is also important to distinguish whether the labour market trend is driven by supply- or demand-side factors.

In some developed countries, the demand side has taken a leading role in labour market changes. For example, skill-biased technological changes (SBTC) in the United States have been raising the wages of workers with college educations and increasing income inequality between educated and less-educated workers (Acemoglu, 2002). Unlike the labour market changes driven by SBTC, when labour transitions are mostly driven by demographic factors, as evidenced by the current circumstances in China, the most prominent features are the shortage of unskilled labour and rapidly growing wages for unskilled workers. The policy implications of these two types of labour market changes differ from each other.

First, the labour shortage triggered by demographic changes is helpful in reducing income inequality, since previously low-income groups have faster wage growth under such conditions. In a country like China, where growing income inequality is a major concern, this has a positive effect on socioeconomic development.

Second, although SBTC widens the income gaps, it encourages both the private and the social sectors to invest in education, since the returns on education are seen to be increasing. In contrast, labour market changes driven by demographics simply increase the opportunity costs of education, which in turn increases the school dropout rate. In particular, in poor areas where families tend to have high discount rates (i.e., they are less willing to forego some current income for higher income in the future), the growing wages for unskilled workers mean a more expensive compulsory education (Du, 2013b). In this case, the government has to propose policies to intervene in the negative externalities of the labour market change.

In addition, the implications for economic development could be different between the two types of labour market change. SBTC promotes technological changes, innovations, and productivity improvement, which sustain economic development. In contrast, labour market changes driven by demographic transition simply increase the labour costs and weaken competitiveness in labour-intensive sectors, but do not necessarily encourage human capital investment and innovation.

3.2 *Older Workers*

The challenge to the labour market caused by demographic factors is not only reflected in the decreasing size of the labour force due to reduced birth rates. Ageing of the existing workforce also impacts on effective labour supply. The mandatory retirement ages are 60 for males and 55 for females. In some occupations, the mandatory retirement ages are younger than those specified in the general regulations. Figure 6 displays the projected changes in age structure within working age groups.

First, changes in the youngest subgroup and the oldest subgroup are antagonistic. In 2011, the subgroup of people between 16 and 30 accounted for one third of the working age population, and that share will decrease to 31.2% in 2016 and 27.6% in 2020. By 2030, the youngest group of workers will only be one fourth of the total. Accordingly, the oldest group will make up a greater share of the working age population. In 2011, persons aged between 51 and 64 accounted for 21.3% of the working age population, but the share will go up to 24.0% in 2016, 27.9% in 2020, and 32.2% in 2030. In 2050, when China becomes a very aged country, the proportion of the workforce aged below 30 years will only be 22.3%, and those older than 50 years will make up 37.2% of the total.

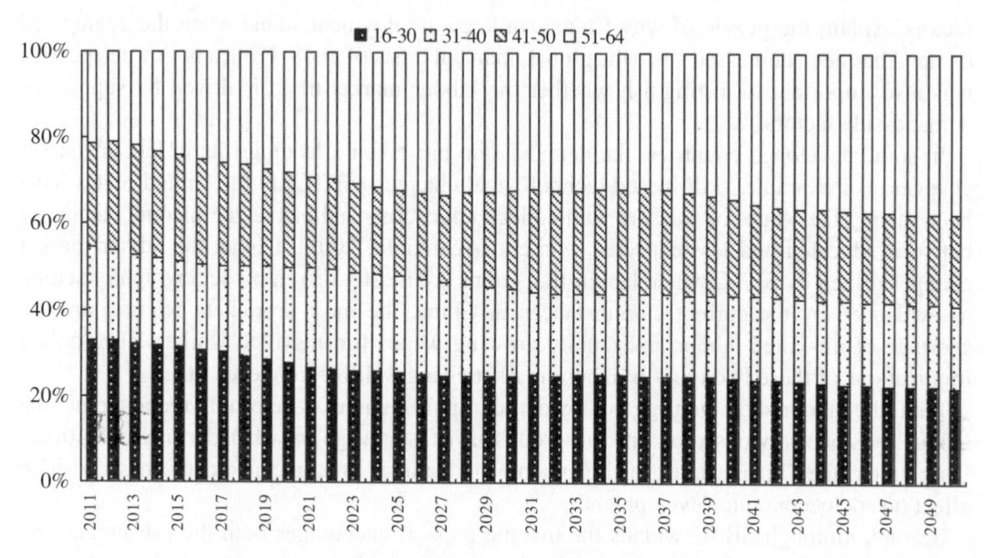

Figure 6. Age Composition of Working Age Population.
Source: Authors' projection.

In contrast, the middle age groups will remain stable over the next two decades. When demographic ageing is becoming increasingly serious, it is fortunate to have a relatively stable number of workers between the ages of 31 and 50. This group has high participation rates and high productivity. In 2011, the share of people between 31 and 50 was 45.6% of the working age population. It will be 44.5% in 2020 and 43.0% in 2030. So from 2011 to 2030, people aged between 31 and 50 steadily account for 42–46% of the working age population.

Even without the decreasing size of the working age population, the older worker effect *per se* will shrink the size of the effective labour supply because older people have lower participation rates in the labour market. Table 3 presents the labour participation rates by age group, based on the 1% population sampling survey in 2005 and the sixth census in 2010. The participation rate over the lifecycle shows an inverted-U shape. Both sets of data indicate that the participation rates for males sharply decline after 50, and for females after 45 (Du and Lu, 2013).

Assuming a similar pattern of participation over the lifespan in the future, it is easy to imagine that the effective labour supply will be shrinking due to the older worker effect. Based on the labour force participation rates by age in 2010 from Du and Lu (2013), Figure 7 presents the predicted effective labour supply, taking account of the differences in participation among different age groups. Demographers predict that the population of working age will decrease by 3.4%, from 968 million in 2011 to 935 million in 2030. Combining this with the older worker effect, the effective labour supply will decrease by 6.9%, from 752 million in 2011 to 700 million in 2030. In addition, as indicated in Figure 7, the total population between 16 and 64 will peak in 2016. When considering the heterogeneity of labour force participation among different age groups, the effective labour supply will peak 2 years ahead of this.

There are undoubtedly other factors also affecting labour force participation. For instance, further expansion of higher education may increase the years of schooling of the young cohort and reduce their labour market participation. Improved social protection, which is believed to

Table 3. Cohort Effects of Education: 2010 and 2020

	No schooling	Primary	Junior high school	Senior high school	Vocational education	College	(%) Graduates and above
2010							
16–19	0.8	10.1	73.9	14.1	1.0	0.1	0.0
20–24	0.8	8.0	62.9	19.2	6.4	2.7	0.1
25–29	0.9	9.4	57.1	17.3	8.8	5.9	0.5
30–34	1.3	14.6	56.4	15.4	7.5	4.3	0.5
35–39	1.6	20.0	56.3	12.8	5.7	3.2	0.3
40–44	2.2	25.0	54.6	11.1	4.3	2.5	0.2
45–49	3.1	25.6	48.0	16.8	4.1	2.1	0.3
50–54	6.6	39.0	37.2	12.5	3.3	1.2	0.1
55–59	10.7	51.7	28.9	5.8	2.0	0.8	0.1
60–64	16.3	60.5	20.3	2.2	0.4	0.3	0.1
2020							
16–19	0.8	10.1	73.9	14.1	1.0	0.1	0.0
20–24	0.8	8.0	62.9	19.2	6.4	2.7	0.1
25–29	0.8	10.1	73.9	14.1	1.0	0.1	0.1
30–34	0.8	8.0	62.9	19.2	6.4	2.7	0.1
35–39	0.9	9.4	57.1	17.3	8.8	5.9	0.5
40–44	1.3	14.6	56.4	15.4	7.5	4.3	0.5
45–49	1.6	20.0	56.3	12.8	5.7	3.2	0.3
50–54	2.2	25.0	54.6	11.1	4.3	2.5	0.2
55–59	3.1	25.6	48	16.8	4.1	2.1	0.3
60–64	6.6	39.0	37.2	12.5	3.3	1.2	0.1

Source: Authors' calculation based on the sixth census data.

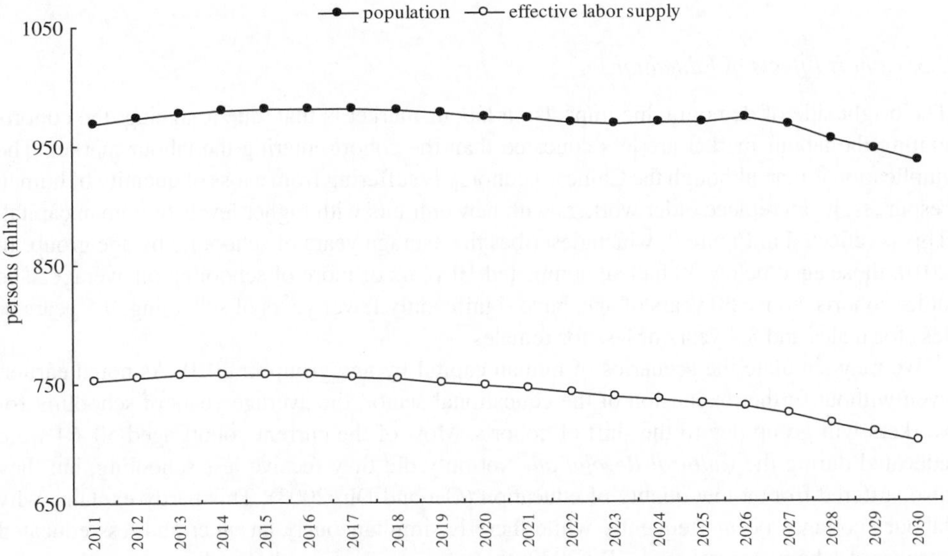

Figure 7. Effective Labour Supply: 2011–2030.
Source: Authors' projection.

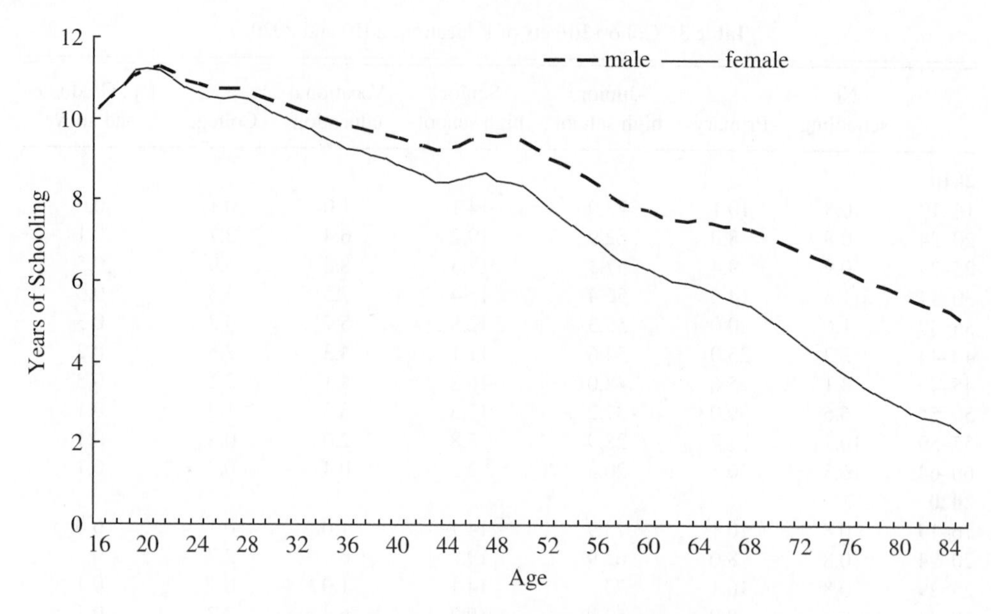

Figure 8. Years of Schooling by Age in 2010.
Source: Authors' calculation based on the sixth Census.

have happened in China, might negatively affect the labour supply. Extending the retirement age may increase the participation of older workers. *Ceteris paribus*, increasing wages promote labour participation. However, all those conditions rely on further reforms of current labour market institutions while demographic analysis gives us the potential for future labour supply.

3.3 *Cohort Effects of Education*

The bright side of demographic impacts on labour market is that, due to ageing, the cohorts exiting the labour market are less educated than the cohort entering the labour market. The implication is that, although the Chinese economy is suffering from a loss of quantity of human resources, it can replace older workers with new entrants with higher levels of human capital. This is reflected in Figure 8, which describes the average years of schooling by age group. In 2010, those aged below 30 had all completed 10 years or more of schooling on average. The older cohorts, above 50 years of age, have significantly fewer years of schooling, 9.5 years or less for males and 8.4 years or less for females.

We may simulate the scenarios of human capital by age group in 2020. As noted earlier, even without further expansion of the educational sector, the average years of schooling for workers will go up due to the shift of cohorts. Most of the current cohort aged 50–64 were educated during the *Cultural Revolution*. Not only did they receive less schooling, but they also suffered from a low quality of education (Cai and Du, 2003). This partly explains why labour shortages occur frequently while there is simultaneously an older and less educated surplus of labour in rural areas. By 2020, the present group aged 50–64 is expected to have left the labour market. As we can see in the upper panel of Table 3, the present cohort aged 40–54, the substitute group, has significantly higher levels of education.

Table 4. Ageing and GDP per Head in Selected Countries

	Years required or expected for population aged 65+ to increase from 7% to 14% (a)	Year in which 14% of the population is aged 65+ (b)	GDP per head in the year in which 14% of the population is aged 65+
France	115	1980	20,289
Sweden	85	1975	19,330
Australia	73	2011	37,257
Canada	65	2009	34,527
Poland	45	2011	17,968
United Kingdom	45	1975	16,000
Spain	45	1992	20,299
Japan	26	1996	28,661
Hungary	53	1994	11,595
South Korea	18	2011	27,554
United States	69	2013	45,283 (c)
China	26	2026	68,04 (d)

Note: GDP per head, US$, constant prices, constant PPPs, reference year 2005. 'c' data in 2012, 'd' data in 2010.

Sources: Column 'a' and 'b' are from Kinsella and Gist (1995). The GDP per head is from OECD statistics, http://stats.oecd.org/

Ignoring the subtle differences in mortality rates among adjacent age groups, we shift from the young cohorts to the next oldest cohorts to look at the human capital composition in 2020. For the youngest cohort, we conservatively assume there will be no education expansion and that new entrants will have the same level of education as the groups they substitute. The lower panel of Table 4 presents education by age groups in 2020 under those assumptions.

Based on the results in Table 3, weighted by the size of the population in each age group, it is estimated that the average years of schooling were 8.86 in 2010 and will be 9.30 in 2020. In other words, without additional investments in education, the cohort effect will improve the stock of human capital by about 5%. There is no doubt that the cohort effect in education is helpful for China to deal with the ongoing challenges of an ageing population. However, this beneficial cohort effect merely implies that China will have the potential to improve productivity by making use of better quality human resources. Turning the potential into real productivity requires a competitive and flexible market and effective exploitation of the available human resources.

4. The Implications of Demographic Transition for Economic Development

The implications of demographic transition for economic development in China are important and inspiring. In the past few decades, when China had rapid demographic transition and rapid growth simultaneously, it is widely accepted that China reaped its first demographic dividend to promote economic growth. With this great achievement, China successfully escaped general poverty and has been growing as a middle income country. However, China's economic development is already facing demographic challenges, including ageing, a shrinking workforce and growing labour costs, which will slow economic growth.

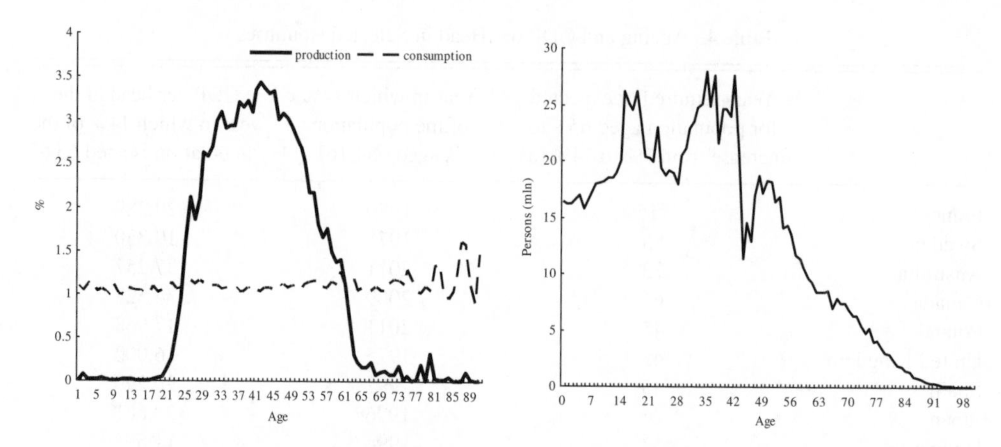

Figure 9. Age Profile Production and Consumption in 2005.
Source: The left panel is from authors' calculation based on urban household survey data. The right panel is based on the *Yearbook of Population and Labour Statistics* in *2006*, China Statistical Press.

4.1 *Demographic Dividend and Potential Growth*

According to Wang and Mason (2005), the first population dividend is defined as increases in the growth rate of income per capita that come about when the productive population grows at a faster rate than the total population. A second demographic dividend may arise because changes in age structure can influence the processes that lead to the creation of wealth. Population ageing will lead to rapid accumulation of capital. When this occurs, the capital-intensity of the economy will raise labour productivity (output per worker). From 1982 to 2000, the support ratio[4] increased by 28%, an average annual rate of 1.3%, and accounted for 15% of China's economic growth between 1982 and 2000 (Wang and Mason, 2005). Using the methodology of growth accounting by considering the impact of the dependency ratio[5] on economic growth, Wang et al. (2004) also explored the contribution of the demographic dividend to economic growth in China. They found that, from 1982 to 2000, the total dependency ratio decreased 20.1%, which brought about 2.3 percentage points of economic growth per annum. In other words, the population dividend accounted for 25% of GDP growth during the period.

The reason that certain age structures in a population are favourable to economic growth is rooted in lifecycle production and consumption patterns. Using national representative urban household survey data, we find a steady age profile pattern of production and consumption over time. Figure 9 presents an example for 2005. As indicated in the left panel of Figure 9, people aged between 24 and 60 are more productive in comparison to their consumption level. By contrast, the groups aged below 24 and above 60 tend to consume more and produce less. Through private and public transfers, society has to allocate resources to support the younger and older groups. Although the production and consumption pattern over the lifecycle might be stable over time in a country, the age structures determined by the demographic transitions are dynamic. The right panel in Figure 9 displays the age structure of the population in 2005. At that time, it can be seen that the age structure was favourable to economic growth because the productive group accounted for a large proportion of the total population, meaning that such a society can achieve high saving rates to support investments.

In addition, the consumption structure *per se* is correlated with the age structures. Du and Wang (2011) found that the elderly tend to reduce their work-related expenditures but significantly increase spending on medical care: the latter is not favourable to economic growth.

As a result of demographic transition, the period with the first demographic window must eventually come to an end. The total dependency ratio in China further declined from 42.6% in 2000 to 34.2% in 2010, but it has been increasing since then. Demographic variables determine declining potential growth rates in the future. According to Cai and Lu (2013), the average annual potential economic growth rate drops to 7.2% between 2011 and 2015, and 6.1% between 2016 and 2020. The declining potential growth rate implies that additional economic stimulus plans to pursue high growth rates would be more costly than before at the macro level.

4.2 *Ageing and Economic Development*

In 2011, more than 185 million persons were 60 years or older, which accounted for 13.7% of the total population in China: those who were 65 or over accounted for 9.1% of the total population (NBS, 2012). It is estimated that there will be 234 million people aged 60 or above, accounting for 16% of the total population, by 2020: those who are 65 or above will account for 11.2% of the total population in 2020.

As a middle income country, the challenges arising from ageing are obvious. One of them is that China may not have enough economic resources to support the growing number of the elderly. Table 4 lists the years required or expected for the percentage of the population aged 65 or above to increase from 7% to 14% in some developed countries and the GDP per head in the year each country reaches 14% of its population aged 65 or above. On average, the selected developed countries took 58 years to complete the transition from 7% to 14% of the population aged 65 or above. Not surprisingly, China requires much less time. The average per capita GDP in the year all countries reach 14% is USD 21,225 at the constant value for year 2005 and measured in PPPs. Using comparable prices, the per capita GDP of China was USD 6,804 in 2010. Interestingly, if China maintains 7% annual growth, its GDP per head will reach USD 20,087 when its elderly population is 14%. In other words, if China can make its growth sustainable in the coming decade, the ageing issue will not be so unaffordable.

5. Policy Implications and Future Research

5.1 *Policy Implications*

This paper reviews China's unique demographic transition, its determinants, and its impacts on the labour market and economic development. Although China has implemented a strict population control policy for more than three decades, a host of empirical studies have indicated that the policy's role in fertility determination has been replaced by economic development. In other words, the great efforts the Chinese government has made to enforce its population policy seem unnecessary. It's time for Chinese policymakers to accept the fact that fertility is already very low and that the trend may not be reversible.

More seriously, economic development in China has already been challenged by demographic structures rather than by the total size of the population. Demographic factors are one of the fundamental forces driving the Chinese labour market to pass through the Lewis turning point. As noted earlier in this paper, the changes driven by the labour supply side make the Chinese case different from the transitions in developed economies motivated by technological changes. In particular, some impacts of the changes, for example, the negative externality effect on schooling, need to be addressed by policy changes.

In the long run, the demographic variables interact with economic variables. However, in contrast to the economic dynamics, demographic variables are more stable. Considering that fertility is mostly determined by development, China has to live with the demographic facts although the age structures may not be favourable to continued economic growth. Accordingly, the key strategy for development is to adapt China's new endowment structure and to promote relevant technological changes, innovations and productivity improvements, which will rely on comprehensive reforms in both economic and social systems.

5.2 *Future Research*

As discussed in this paper, the unique process of demographic transition in China and its impacts on the labour market and economic development raises important and interesting areas for future research.

First of all, it is of great policy relevance to look at the impacts of labour market changes driven by demographic factors. It is easy to predict the forthcoming shortage of labour and rising wages, altering the relative price of production factors and challenging the growth pattern. But more importantly, how should policymakers respond when the changing labour market outcomes are mostly driven by demographic factors rather than technological changes?

Second, it is important to further examine how each element of demographic change affects future economic development in China. As noted in this paper, the shrinking labour supply and the positive cohort effects of education take place simultaneously. To sustain economic development, policymakers must find a way to make use of the latter to offset the negative impacts of labour shortage.

Third, dealing with ageing at a country's middle-income stage challenges both academia and decision makers. Given the uniquely ageing workforce in China, the policy response could also be different from existing experiences elsewhere.

Notes

1. Demographic transition is a transitioning process from high fertility rate, high death rate and high natural growth rate of population to low fertility rate, low death rate and low natural growth rate of population.
2. The Committee was merged with the Ministry of Health in 2012.
3. Defining available labour as the population aged 15–59, the National Bureau of Statistics stated that the total labour force started decreasing in 2012 (NBS, 2012).
4. The support ratio is the ratio of the effective number of producers to the effective number of consumers; see Wang and Mason (2005).
5. The dependency ratio is the number of dependents to the working age population, that is, the number of people aged below 16 and above 64 in relation to the number of people aged between 15 and 64.

References

Acemoglu, D. (2002) Technical change, inequality, and the labour market. *Journal of Economic Literature* 40(1): 7–72.

Cai, F. (2010) Demographic transitions, demographic dividend, and Lewis turning point in China. *China Economic Journal* 3(2): 107–119.

Cai, F. and Du, Y. (2003) Destructive effect of cultural revolution on physical and human capital. *China Economic Quarterly* 2(4): 795–806.

Cai, F. and Du, Y. (2011) Wage increases, wage convergence, and the Lewis turning point in China. *China Economic Review* 22(4): 601–610.

Cai, F. and Lu, Y. (2013) Population change and resulting slowdown in potential GDP growth in China. *China & World Economy* 21(2): 1–14.

China Development Research Foundation (2012) *China Development Report: Changes in Population Trend and Adjustment in Population Policies*. Beijing: China Development Press.

Du, Y. (2005) The formation of low fertility in China and its impacts on long run growth. *World Economy* 28(12): 14–23.

Du, Y. (2013a) "Recent employment situations and policy recommendations", unpublished memo.

Du, Y. (2013b) Do the recent labor market changes negatively affect schooling? *China & World Economy* 21(2): 38–55.

Du, Y. and Lu, Y. (2013). Labour Supply situations and policy at China's new stage of economic development. In F. Cai (ed), *China Population and Labour Report, No. 14*. Beijing: Social Sciences Academic Press.

Du, Y. and Wang, M. (2011) Population ageing, domestic consumption and future economic growth in China. In J. Golley and L. Song (eds.), *Rising China: Global Challenges and Opportunities* (pp. 301–314). Canberra, ACT: Australia National University Press.

Guo, Z. (2008) China's low fertility and its determinants. *Population Research* 28(4): 16–24.

Guo, Z. (2010) The low fertility rate in China and the demographic risk of ignoring it. *International Economic Review* 90(6): 112–126. (In Chinese)

Guo, Z. (2012) Rethinking the population trend in China. *International Economic Review* 92(1): 96–111. (In Chinese)

Heuveline, P. (1999) The global and regional impact of mortality and fertility transitions, 1950–2000. *Population and Development Review* 25(4): 681–702.

Hussain, A. (2002) Demographic transition in China and its implications. *World Development* 30(10): 1823–1834.

Kane, P. (1988) *Famine in China, 1959–61: Demographic and Social Implications*. New York: St. Martin's Press.

Kinsella, K. and Gist, Y. (1995) *Older Workers, Retirement, and Pensions. A Comparative International Chartbook*. U.S. Census Bureau IPC/95–2RP. Washington, DC: US Government Printing Office.

Lavely, W. and Freedman, R. (1990) The origins of the Chinese fertility decline. *Demography* 27(3): 357–367.

Livi-Bacci, M. (2012) *A Concise History of World Population*, 5th edition. Hoboken, NJ: Wiley-Blackwell.

Minami, R. (1968) The turning point in the Japanese economy. *Quarterly Journal of Economics* 82(3): 380–402.

Morgan, P., Guo, Z. and Hayford, S.R. (2009) China's below-replacement fertility: recent trends and future prospects. *Population and Development Review* 35(3): 605–629.

National Academy of Sciences (1971) *Rapid Population Growth: Consequences and Policy Implications*, Vol. 2, Baltimore, MD: Johns Hopkins Press for the National Academy of Sciences.

National Bureau of Statistics (2012) *China Statistics Yearbook in 2012*. Beijing: China Statistical Press.

National Bureau of Statistics (2013) The China Statistical Communiqué in 2012. Retrieved from http://www.stats.gov.cn/english/StatisticalCommuniqu/

National Committee of Population and Family Planning (2009) *Handbook of Data on Population and Family Planning in Common Use*. Beijing: China Population Press.

United Nations. (1973) *The Determinants and Consequences of Population Trends*. Department of Economic and Social Affairs, Population Studies No. 50, Vol. 2, New York: United Nations.

Wang, D., Cai, F. and Zhang, X. (2004) Saving and growth effects of demographic transition: the population factor in the sustainability of China's economic growth. *Population Research* 28(5): 2–11.

Wang, F. and Mason, A. (2005) Demographic dividend and prospects for economic development in China. *United Nations Expert Group Meeting on Social and Economic Implications of Changing Population Age Structures*, 31 August-2 September, Mexico City, Mexico.

Wang, M. (2010) The rise of labour cost and the fall of labour input: has China reached Lewis turning point? *China Economic Journal* 3(2): 137–153.

Yang, D.T. and McElroy, M. (2000) The effect of population policy on fertility in China. *Chinese Journal of Population Science* 3: 18–22.

Yin, W., Yao, Y. and Li, F. (2013) Evaluation on Fertility levels and adjustments in population policy: analysis on provincial fertility levels. *Social Sciences in China* 6: 109–128.

Yuan, X. (2000) Demographic transition and future population trends of China. *Chinese Journal of Population Science* 1: 40–45.

Zeng, Y. (2006) A soft landing with the two-children-late-birth policy: need and feasibility. *Social Sciences in China* 58(2): 93–109.

Zhang, X., Yang, J. and Wang, S. (2011) China has reached the Lewis turning point. *China Economic Review* 22(4): 542–554.

Zhao, J. (2004) An empirical analysis of demographic transition and economic growth in China. *China Economic Quarterly* 3: 819–837.

Zheng, Z. (2013) The choice of having a second child and its implication for future family structure in China. In A. Buchanan and A. Rotkirch (eds.), *Fertility Rates and Population Decline: No Time for Children?* (pp. 157–165). Basingstoke, UK: Palgrave MacMillan.

4

PENSION REFORM IN CHINA: CHALLENGES AND OPPORTUNITIES

Yong Cai
University of North Carolina

Yuan Cheng
Fudan University

1. Introduction

China is in the process of establishing a nationwide social insurance system that will cover the whole population for basic pension and medical insurance by 2020. The policy goal is to 'provide basic insurance, promote social equality and ensure sustainability'. If it succeeds, the new system will be a great improvement on China's old social insurance system which has been criticized as segmented, regionally imbalanced, fiscally inefficient and socially and economically unsustainable.

China's old social insurance system is a result of a three-decade patchwork based on an old socialist model, a process constrained by economic and political circumstances, swayed by interest-group infighting and suffering from by lack of long-term objectives. For example, on top of a basic old-age pension for rural residents and non-salaried urban residents, China runs two more tiers of employment-based public pension: pension plans for non-governmental workers funded by contributions from employees and employers, and pension plans for government employees (including public institutions) funded entirely from the government budget. According to the 2010 census, less than one third of those aged 60 and above relied on social insurances as their main source of income. There is also a prominent urban–rural divide: while 70% of the urban elderly relied on public programmes as their main source of income, only 10% of rural elderly were in this situation. The new reform merges two old non-employment-based schemes that covered rural residents and non-salaried urban residents in China. The new reform will also push to integrate these with employment-based pension systems.

China's Economy: A Collection of Surveys, First Edition. Edited by Iris Claus and Les Oxley. Published 2015 by John Wiley & Sons, Ltd.

Behind this new round of reform, pressure is building up in China on many different fronts: demographic pressure from an ageing population; social pressure from changed family structures; political pressure from rising inequality; and economic pressure from sustainability issues. In combination, they make pension reform an urgent and critical matter that is likely to determine the country's future. On top of this is the development of state capacity that is now ready to take up a fundamental challenge like this.

China is facing a demographic tsunami of population ageing. The process is already underway, and is expected to hit the country economically and financially in the next few decades. China's ageing tsunami is a result of the combination of two demographic transitions: rapid decline in fertility and rapid increase in life expectancy. As a demographic over-achiever (Wang and Deborah, 2009), fertility and mortality transitions that happen typically on a century-scale in other countries are squeezed into a decade-scale in China. China's fertility was halved in less than a decade in the 1970s. It dropped from a pre-transitional level of six children per women to below replacement in just two decades. At the same time, China doubled its life expectancy at birth from around 35 years in pre-PRC times to over 70 years by the end of the 20th century. With people living longer, but having fewer children, the population is ageing both in absolute terms as measured by the total number of elderly and in relative terms as measured by the proportion of elderly in the whole population (Du and Yang, 2014).

Moreover, the demographic pressure caused by ageing in China will stay high for the foreseeable future. It is expected that fertility and mortality in China will continue their current trends for some time to come. China's fertility has stayed below replacement for more than two decades and is now among the lowest in the world (Cai, 2013). Experience in China's more developed neighbours like Japan, South Korea, Taiwan and Singapore suggests that raising fertility is an even more challenging task than lowering it. While conventional wisdom attributes much of China's low fertility to its infamous one-child policy, research suggests that it was driven more by socioeconomic development (Cai, 2010). Even with the newly announced relaxation of the one-child policy and possibly more drastic changes down the road, China's fertility is expected to stay low and possibly drop further. At the same time, increased living standards and access to health care will continue to push life expectancy in China to new higher levels. For example, China's life expectancy at birth jumped another 3–4 years between 2000 and 2010, much faster than the world average. This rapid population ageing makes it especially urgent to establish a sustainable pension system.

The rapid increase in social and economic inequality has led to political pressure for pension reform in China. China's rapid economic growth in the last several decades has been accompanied by an equally rapid increase in the level of inequality (Wang and Deborah, 2009). China's Gini coefficient has been inching close to 0.5 over the last decade, and is now one of the highest in the world. Such income inequality means that the enormous wealth accumulation that has occurred in China is concentrated in the hands of a small segment of society. For example, asset-based wealth accumulation like that from skyrocketing real estate prices favours urban families more than rural families. While many welfare programmes and public transfers are intended to counter the rises in inequality and living costs, empirical research suggests they often have negative effects on social equality in China because they are locked into to the old socialist hierarchies: they favour those inside the government more than those outside the government, and urban residents rather than rural. Political pressure is building up in China to establish a new social insurance and welfare system not only to provide basic security for the old and the poor, but also to promote social fairness and address the problem of social inequality (Wang *et al.*, 2014).

China's economic boom over the past few decades has laid the necessary economic foundation to address the problems in its social insurance system. China had one of the longest and fastest periods of economic growth in the world over the past three decades. The economic boom was achieved via a drastic increase in labour productivity and fundamental changes in economic structure. It was also accompanied by the establishment of financial markets and the expansion of state capacity. China is in an age of abundance: China's foreign exchange reserve has exceeded 4 trillion dollars; total government revenue has reached RMB 13 trillion; and the total reserve of China's Social Insurance Fund has reached over RMB 4 trillion. These provide the necessary resources to address the problem of population ageing. While China is often labelled as 'getting old before getting rich', at least China is no longer a poverty-ridden country.

Even with its newly found wealth, the window of opportunity for a comprehensive pension reform in China is not as wide as many would hope for. Double digit hypereconomic growth will not continue as China faces more and more structural pressure from its economic model, from the environment and from its ageing population. In 2012, China registered its first annual economic growth rate that was substantially below past levels in a decade. Though its almost 8% annual growth rate is still among the world's fastest, it is a third below the average for the preceding decade. Such a sudden and substantial drop can be traced to many factors, but it may not be a coincidence that it occurred when China registered a decline in its labour force population, the first in a long while.

The substantial drop in economic growth may well mark the beginning of the end of China's hypergrowth era. In a way, China's economic boom over the past three decades was achieved on borrowed time from its emerging ageing challenge. Rapid fertility and mortality transitions provided China with a generational opportunity, with a huge demographic dividend from a relatively young, productive and healthy population. By some calculations, 10%–20% of China's economic growth over the past three decades can be attributed to this demographic dividend, which has now been exhausted (Wang and Mason, 2008). The demography of China is increasingly becoming a burden on China's economic growth. Not only does it directly change the ratio of workers to dependents, but it also affects China's macro-economic performance. On top of demography, rising labour costs, mounting environmental pressure and intensifying global competition make it increasingly difficult for China to continue its hypereconomic growth. Without a structural transformation of its economy, China could fall in to the so-called middle-income trap.

Chinese leadership has focused on urbanization as a main strategy to avoid the middle-income trap, but its prosperity hinges on the success of reform in the social safety net. The hope for urbanization is that it will stimulate the growth of the service industry and private consumption. However, without equal treatment and sufficient protection from the government and social safety nets, most of the rural migrants, who have been and will continue to be the main sources of labour for urbanization, will not be able to sustainably integrate into urban existence, making the labour market unequal and inefficient. A fair and adequate social insurance system is one of the most important pillars needed for this urbanization strategy.

In sum, reform of China's pension system is demographically urgent, economically necessary and socially and politically essential. The rising of a modern state that encroaches into traditional family functions and responsibilities not only provides a natural vehicle for a social welfare programme, but also can help provide economic efficiency, political stability and social suitability. China is no exception to this global trend. Its socialist history and strong state tradition makes a state-backed pension system the most viable option facing such a demographic and social reality.

In the following sections, we first lay out the demographic background for China's pension reform. We then review the history of China's pension system and proposed reform options. We conclude with discussion on the opportunities and challenges faced by the reform.

2. Demography

China's population ageing is unfolding at a previously underappreciated pace. China's elderly population (aged 65+) is now more than the entire population of Japan. China's 2010 census revealed one surprising result: China's ageing was occurring at a faster rate than previously projected. The census showed China's population aged 60 and above had reached a total of 178 million, accounting for 13.26% of the total population, up by 2.93% in just one decade. Those aged 65 and over reached over 120 million, accounting for 8.87% of the total population, up by 1.91% as compared with the 2000 census; both numbers are higher than the official Chinese government projections and the United Nations' predictions. China's 11th 5-year plan projected that those aged 60 and over would reach 174 million or 12.78% of the total population by 2010, while the World Population Prospects 2010 estimated that this number would be 169.4 million or 12.6% of the total population (United Nations, 2011). Two main factors explain the underestimates: the underappreciation of increase in life expectancy and the overadjustment of China's fertility level.

Reduction in mortality in China is happening at a faster rate than previously anticipated. Both the Chinese government and the UN have been making their population projections on the assumption of life expectancy (at birth) improving at about 2 years per decade. However, China's 2000 and 2010 censuses suggest that the improvement could be as high as 3–4 years in the decade in between the two measurements. Such a speedy decline of mortality is in line with China's rapid economic growth and improvement in health care access, and fits with similar experience in other countries (Cai, 2013).

Even with this rapid improvement, mortality's direct contribution to ageing is still relatively small in comparison to the more dramatic change embedded in China's age structure – the historical and continuing decline in fertility. While ample evidence has shown that fertility has been around 1.5 children per woman in China for at least a decade, the Chinese government was slow to officially acknowledge its severity by insisting that China's fertility was 1.8 children per woman. China's fertility level now is among the lowest in the world, below the average of the more developed world (1.7).

Projecting into the future, the basic demographic trends that drive China's population ageing process will continue. China's economic growth has certainly provided the material foundation for further reduction in mortality. The UN projects that life expectancy at birth in China will continue to increase at about 1–1.5 years per decade for some decades to come. If history is a guide, these estimates are likely to be too conservative. The end of epidemiological transition also means that China will not only have to take care of more elderly, but also treat them for more expensive diseases, like diabetes, cardiovascular diseases and cancers.

The UN (2010) estimated China's life expectancies at 69.6 for males and 72.9 for females in 2000, and 71.6 for males and 75.0 for females in 2010. The UN estimates for 2010 are substantially lower than what was observed in the Chinese census. The UN's projection is about 10–15 years behind the progress in China (Cai, 2013). Nevertheless, the projections show that China has entered an accelerated ageing period. The UN's medium fertility variant projects that the total population aged 60 and above will increase to 340 million by 2030, accounting for 24% of the total population, and to 440 million by 2050, accounting for 34% of the total population. Even its high fertility variant still sends the proportion of the population aged 60 and above to over 30% before levelling off.

Sustained low fertility means that the size of the young labour force will decline more rapidly than previously projected. In 2010, the size of the young workforce aged 20–24 was about 116 million. By 2020, it will be reduced to 94 million, an almost 20% drop in 10 years. The net impact of declining numbers of workers in this age range on the labour market is actually greater, as a result of recent expansion in higher education enrolments. In the 10 years from 2000, China's college education annual enrolment tripled, from 2.2 million to 6.6 million. The number of students currently in college (mostly aged 18–21) rose drastically, from 5.6 million in 2000 to 22.3 million in 2010. Expansion of higher education means an even more drastic decline in the availability of young labour than is suggested by fertility decline alone. This is why the shortage of young unskilled labour has been felt more acutely in recent years. Sustained low fertility, moreover, means that the decline in labour supply will continue beyond 2020. The size of the young population aged 20–24 by 2030 will only be 67 million; more than 40% smaller than it was in 2010.

In general, Eastern China and the urban areas are the forerunner of China's demographic transition, while the vast western provinces are lagging behind the national trend. One of the consequences of demographic transition in China is the shortage of young workers in developed regions, including the big cities and coastal areas. On the whole, China's urban employment has grown faster than rural employment since 1978 and this trend will remain in the near future. Selective migration is viewed as one of the most efficient measures to cope with the structural shortage of labour and the worsening ageing process (United Nations, 2000). Based on the case of Shanghai, Peng and Cheng (2005) found that cities benefited from the demographic dividend because younger people migrated to the city. This internal migration helped alleviate pressures on the pension system but pressures will start emerging because of population ageing. Encouraging internal migration could prolong the time span for applying the demographic bonus in the urban areas while providing opportunities for poor rural areas, thus resulting in a win/win situation. Even though the rural areas are exporting and losing their young and able population, they have benefited significantly from migration in terms of remittances and lower unemployment.

Reform of China's pension system is both demographically urgent and socially essential. While people in China have traditionally relied on family to provide care for the elderly, moving away from the traditional family model towards a state solution is both a trend of modern society, and a natural result of social transformation. Whereas family support provides a kind of insurance, it is informal and limited to the family. In contrast, a pension system provides a far broader base, depending on the design. Obviously declining fertility and increased migration have overthrown the traditional family institution, so that many can no longer rely on their own children for either financial support or physical help. Partly due to the one-child policy, about one third of all Chinese families have only one child, and the share is much higher among younger couples. The decline in fertility and increase in migration have cut the average family size in China from 4.4 in 1982 to 3.1 in 2010. The fragility and fluidity of the family make it increasingly risky as the foundation for old-age support. More fundamentally, the market-based economy mandates a social solution to counter the inherent risk embedded in the market. With most economic activities happening outside of the family arena, and society being organized more around individuals than families, the rise of public institutions like social pensions is unavoidable, as has been observed all around the world (Peng and Guo, 2000).

3. China's Pension System Reform: Challenges and Issues

A pension, put simply, is a form of transfer of payments to the elderly through a collective entity, often a government. The economic life cycle and a mismatch between material needs and the ability to satisfy those needs through one's own labour, determine that intergenerational transfer is necessary to raise the young and to take care of the old. In traditional agricultural societies, the need for transfer was realized mostly within the family, which served as a basic unit for reproduction and economic production. Families were responsible for raising their own children and taking care of the sick and the old. At the time, the transfer was mostly downwards in the form of childcare, not only because human vulnerability during infancy and childhood means total dependence on parents for a child's survival, but also because high mortality required high fertility, thus placing a heightened burden on parents. In comparison, care for the elderly was limited because of short life expectancies and because the majority of older people worked until they were very close to death.

Pensions become necessary with increased longevity and the demise of the traditional family, and have become viable with the rise of the modern state and the market economy. Four interconnected changes in modern society have contributed to the rise of pensions: a demographic transition featuring a decline in fertility and an increase in life expectancy; a social reformation highlighting the rise of individualism and the demise of the traditional family; a political transformation with an enhanced role of government in daily life; and an economic revolution enabling long-term monetary planning.

Although pension systems vary in design, in general, they can be divided into two categories: one is the defined-contribution pension system and the other is the defined-benefit pension system. In a defined-contribution system, employers and employees make regular contributions to the pension account. Usually the contributions are a certain percentage of salary and are often income tax deductible. The pension benefit therefore depends on the accumulated contributions and the total return on the assets in the account and is not defined when the contributions are made. In a defined-benefit pension system, the benefit rather than the contribution is defined according to years of service and, in most cases, the salary level of the employees.

By definition, the defined-contribution pension system is fully funded. The defined-benefit pension system can be further divided into unfunded and funded pension plans. The unfunded defined-benefit pension plan is commonly called Pay-as-You-Go (PAYG). For PAYG, the pension distribution is paid directly by the pension sponsors, which comes from an enterprise's revenue, or from the current employees as social security contributions, or from the government. In a funded defined-benefit pension plan, all the contributions are invested in a fund, which is invested in a way which will meet the future benefit payment needs.

To fulfil different purposes, some innovative hybrid types of pension plan have been developed. We introduce two such plans, which are closely related to the following discussions. One is called the conditional defined benefit system, in which individuals have defined-contribution individual accounts but also a guaranteed minimum amount of benefit. The government pays any short-fall between the promised benefit and the annuity provided by the defined-contribution account (Feldstein, 1999). Such a design provides a safety net for low-income employees.

The other is called the notional unfunded defined-contribution pension system, which is a hybrid of the PAYG and the defined-contribution pension plan. Like the PAYG, the benefit paid to current retirees is financed by social security contributions. However, unlike PAYG, an individual account is set up. Employees are credited for contributions to their accounts without any assets actually being deposited (Williamson and Shen, 2004), which is supposed to provide incentives for employees to remain in the workforce longer.

3.1 *China's Pre-Reform Pension System*

The very first pension scheme in China was regulated under the National Labor Insurance Regulation in 1951. The pension benefit (replacement rate) was 50%–70% of employees' salaries. To fund the pension distribution, enterprises paid 3% of their total salary bills, of which 70% was paid directly to retirees and 30% contributed to a national master pool as a form of pre-funding. However, during the Cultural Revolution (1966–1976), with the disbanding of trade unions and the Ministry of Labor, which was responsible for administrating the pension scheme, the national pool was terminated (Holzmann *et al.*, 2000).

Until the late 1980s, as summarized by Trinh (2006), China's pension system was an urban- and enterprise-based, PAYG system and financed by enterprises' revenue. It was part of a cradle-to-grave security system provided by state-owned enterprises (SOEs) to their employees. This was closely connected to the central-planned economy, which featured public ownership, life-long employment, restricted labour mobility and non-existent unemployment. The pension benefits were solely financed from the work unit's operational expenses rather than by employees' contributions. The state as the owner of SOEs was ultimately responsible for funding retirees' pension claims.

The early stage of pension reform during the 1980s and 1990s transformed the old unfunded PAYG system provided mainly by SOEs and government institutions to a funded contribution-based social security pension. As Zhao and Xu (2002) described, the reform of China's pension system went hand-in-hand with the reform of SOEs. Before the 1990s pension reform, changing employment in China meant the change of industry and pension pools, and leaving the pool meant losing all previously accumulated pension benefits. Lack of portability of pension benefits became a major stumbling block to the restructuring of SOEs since any kind of lay-off would induce heavy resistance and reforming the pension system was a pre-requisite for China's labour market reform. Throughout this stage, the government implemented a series of pension scheme reforming pilot initiatives in an effort to (1) replace enterprise insurance with social insurance by setting up social pooling systems for industries in urban areas; (2) require individual contributors to shoulder the burden of pension costs; (3) establish voluntary pension schemes and individual savings plan to supplement pensions (Holzmann *et al.*, 2000).

3.2 *Three-Part Urban Pension System*

The State Council Document No. 26 in 1997 laid out the so-called three-part pension system, in which SOEs were no longer directly involved with pension and other social welfare payments to retired people. The retirement ages for a normal pension are 60 for men, 50 for blue-collar women and 55 for white-collar women (Dunaway and Arora, 2007; Piggott and Lu, 2007; Oksanen, 2010).

The first part of the three-part pension system, also called the basic pension plan, states that retirees in the future will receive a defined benefit financed by a PAYG system. Enterprises contribute 22% of total employees' wages to a Basic Pension Fund managed by municipal or provincial authorities. Only employees who have contributed for 15 years are scheduled to receive a basic pension plan, which equals 20% of the regional average wage. Those with shorter contribution histories are not eligible for the basic pension plan.

The second part, which started in 1997, is a defined-contribution funded system and involves compulsory contributions for future benefit claim eligibility. Employees and their enterprises originally contributed 11% of workers' wages to individual accounts managed by municipal or provincial authorities. Of the 11%, the minimum portion for the individual to contribute was 4%, which could increase to an upper limit of 8%. The difference between the individual contribution and 11% came from the contributions made by the enterprises. Since 2006, enterprises no longer contribute to individual accounts and employees contribute 8% of their wages to individual accounts.

The third part is voluntary pensions including enterprise annuity schemes, individual retirement plans and other pension schemes organized by industries or localities.

The basic pension plays a key role in providing retirement benefits to low-income earners, and is important for reducing income inequality and providing insurance. The basic pension redistributes income across generations from younger workers to older people, who tend to have lower incomes because they are no longer in paid employment. The basic pension system is also redistributive because higher income earners contribute a larger proportion to the basic pension as they earn higher incomes and tend to have longer contribution terms, but all retirees receive a universal basic pension of 20% of the average regional wage.

The defined-contribution funded system, like the basic pension, also provides longevity insurance by paying benefits on an annuity basis. Moreover, by linking earnings to retirement savings through individual accounts, higher income earners can rely on the pension system to secure higher pension benefits in retirement. This feature of the pension system becomes increasingly important as earnings are rising rapidly in China, especially those of higher income earners.

Voluntary pensions can accommodate the wide differences that exist in a country as large and diverse as China. As an important element of China's three-part pension system, the enterprise annuity scheme has received surprisingly little attention in the literature and policy reviews. The enterprise annuity scheme was first introduced in 1991, but is underdeveloped in terms of participation rates and asset accumulation. The provisional regulations on enterprise annuity schemes were released in 2004, and were replaced by the revised enterprise annuity scheme management regulations in 2011 (Hu, 2005). According to the 2004 scheme (Ministry of Labor and Social Security Statement No. 20), the maximum enterprise annuity contributions made by businesses cannot exceed 1/12 of the total salary payment to employees. The sum of business contributions and individual contributions cannot exceed 1/6 of the total salary payment. All contributions go to individual enterprise annuity accounts.

Nationwide, the State Council is the entity that creates pension-related policy. All urban workers are eligible to participate in the pension system. Contributions made by employees are withheld from their salary by their employers and transferred to the municipal government and into the individual accounts. Self-employed individuals are eligible to participate in the pension system, and are entitled to the same PAYG part as employees of businesses.

By 2011, total contributions to occupational pension funds in China were 41 billion RMB, and total investment assets amounted to 132 billion RMB. Although the enterprise annuity scheme is regarded as an important second pillar of the pension system, it is mainly only implemented by big SOEs or monopolistic companies (such as railway, electricity and communication industries), as a form of benefit to employees. Taxation incentives only pertain to the basic pension and the defined-contribution funded system and there are currently no tax incentives to participate in voluntary pension schemes.

3.2.1 *Fragmentation*

The system under the 1997 regulations is divided along rural–urban lines and regionally fragmented with decentralized financial and administrative management (Peng, 2011).

Although designed as a national pension system, the three-part pension system has been from its beginning, and will be into the near future, fragmented and it remains largely municipality based at an operational level. In some areas in fact, pensions are still enterprise based and there are huge differences in rules and contribution rates across provinces. Also the benefit level varies across regions, and between urban and rural sectors, which causes long-term inequality (West, 1999; Salditt *et al.*, 2007).

Employer compliance with social security obligations cannot be assumed in transitional economies such as China, where monitoring and enforcement is weak (Nielsen and Smyth, 2008). Nyland *et al.* (2006) reported that in 2001 in Shanghai, the city with the highest governance capability in China, 71% of employers paid less than their mandated social insurance contributions. Compliance problems keep current social security contribution rates unnecessarily high. To improve social security contribution compliance, it would be desirable to have a single set of regulations for mandatory pensions, preferably in the form of legislation that is enforceable, although it may be necessary to allow for regional variation in basic benefit levels due to different living costs across the regions (Chen, 2004).

There should be a single national pension administration,[1] which receives all pension revenues and delivers pensions, to make income redistribution and risk sharing more effective. Social security contributions should be collected by the tax authority, with the revenue delivered promptly to the pension administration (Hu and Stewart, 2009).

The contribution base should be changed to match the definition of earnings used in determining income tax liability (say including housing benefits), with the contribution rate adjusted so that total contributions are broadly unaffected by the change (Barr and Diamond, 2008[2]).

Salditt *et al.* (2007) assessed the process of establishing a national old-age insurance system from the re-design of the pension system in 1997 to the end of 2006. They noted that in spite of significant institutional reforms, such as altering the replacement rate[3] to reward additional contributions (State Council Statement 38) and introducing the enterprise annuity scheme (State Council Statement 42), the scope of the system is still limited, with a coverage rate among urban employees below 50%, and the rural population remaining outside the national pension system. They also emphasized that extending coverage via improved compliance by employees and businesses, and a continued financial commitment by central government to the National Social Security Fund (NSSF) are crucial to cushion the coming increase in old-age pension recipients.

Beland and Yu (2004) adopted a broad institutionalist[4] framework to analyse pension policies through the interplay of four factors: decentralization and limited administrative capacity; feedback effects from previously enacted pension schemes; liberalization and economic reforms; and dominance of the neo-liberal financial paradigm commonly associated with the World Bank. Feedback effects mean that policymakers must take into account vested interests attached to established public policies. The concept of policy feedback is also linked with the idea of social learning. Beland and Yu (2004) found that administrative problems and feedback effects from economic reforms have exacerbated the fragmentation of the Chinese pension system rather than unifying it and warned of potential social discontent if the government fails to effectively guarantee the economic security of urban workers and retirees while implementing pension reforms.

In the long term, there is little doubt that China would be better off with a single and unified pension system covering the whole country, just as most other countries have. In the short term, however, it may only be feasible for China to establish a province-based pension system, which is more unified than the enterprise- and county-based alternatives, but nevertheless retains a degree of fragmentation. If pension reform is seen as a process of redistributing costs and benefits, then reform inevitably imposes costs on some groups and brings benefits to others. For obvious reasons, those whose interests are damaged in the process resist changes, while those whose interests are advanced support change. Conflicts between losers and winners affect the outcome of reform.

3.2.2 *System Deficit and Limited Coverage*

Even though the Chinese pension system reform has made tremendous progress, it is facing enormous challenges in dealing with a population that is ageing faster than was previously anticipated. The current pension schemes do not ensure the necessary funding for the expanding elderly population. Pensions in most areas run a deficit, as a result of pension spending exceeding the ability to collect contributions. It is estimated that pension deficits could be as large as 10% of GDP by 2050.[5]

Although the current pension policy was created to develop a multi-pillar pension scheme, corporate pensions have very limited coverage, and private financial pension insurance is next to non-existent. Contributions from employers and workers outside the SOE sector also remain limited, due to the lack of incentives for participation, because the required social security contributions are high, the system is redistributive, and individual accounts earn low returns. The lack of incentives is also due to the deeply rooted concern over empty individual accounts: local governments often use the contributions of workers to their individual accounts to finance the pensions of the current retired generation on a PAYG basis. Participation is low also because of low enforcement rates and low penalties for non-compliance.

The priority for the future must be to extend coverage first to currently non-covered urban workers and eventually to the rural population. The income support element in the pension system should be widened and deepened. Enhancing old-age security in rural areas should be a high priority.

There was an extreme perspective which argued that under the current system, assuming a replacement rate of 25%, an annual deficit in the urban basic pension system would emerge as early as 2015. Combined with a lack of policy reform regarding the one-child policy and the PAYG system, the total deficit would be equivalent to 95% of the total annual GDP by 2050 (Gao and Wang, 2011).

As early as 1996, employing an integrated simulation model, which incorporated a representative pension fund, demographic trends, development of the economy and the labour market, and government behaviour under different pension arrangements, McCarthy and Zheng (1996) estimated the scope and speed of population ageing among the elderly, the cost of supporting the old and the impact of different reform options and pension arrangements. In addition to scenario analysis on the commonly recommended reform options, such as, delaying retirement age, altering GDP growth rates, changing the contribution and replacement rates and establishing fully funded individual accounts, they proposed that China should move towards a transparent and decentralized system with a fully funded, portable defined-benefit pension plan instead of the current PAYG system.

Wang *et al.* (2004) attempted to quantitatively assess the sustainability of the defined benefit PAYG system and the effects of combined reform measures with a recursive dynamic computable general equilibrium model, using 22 age and gender labour groups, 7 production sectors and 2 representative households. They set up three sets of simulation, including limited changes within the PAYG system, transition scenarios akin to programmes that the government was implementing, and a new multi-pillar option proposal that would finance the transition cost from shifting between pension systems with tax revenues. Wang *et al.* (2004) found that the PAYG system was not financially sustainable: the implicit pension debt was estimated at 46%–64% of GDP in 2000. Expanding coverage under the existing system would improve the financial situation in the short run but weaken it in the long run because of population ageing, as suggested by Peng and Cheng (2005). The third scenario, which uses tax revenue to finance transition cost, leads to a pension system that is financially sustainable and generates a significant accumulation of reserves, suggesting that China still has a good chance to make the three-part pension system financially sustainable.

3.2.3 *Investment-Based Accounts*

Investment-based accounts, which constitute the second part of China's pension system, may help build workers' confidence in the pension system and develop the financial system. But perhaps more importantly investment-based accounts allow keeping the long-run tax rate much lower than under a PAYG system. Using a numerical example assuming 7% growth in real wages and a marginal product of capital of 12%, Feldstein (1999) demonstrated the advantage of investment-based accounts. He showed that in order to finance a defined benefit target of 25% of the average regional wage for those who have worked for 40 years, by switching from PAYG financing to a funded plan,[6] social security contributions could be reduced from 9% of wages to 3% or less. Alternatively, if the overall pension were a conditional defined benefit only filling the gap between the defined-contribution annuity and a minimum acceptable retirement income, the financing cost would be cut by more than 50%. Contributions to the basic pension investment-based accounts could be financed with a broad-based tax such as a value-added tax as suggested by Wang *et al.* (2004).

In China, financial markets are still at an early stage of development. In the short run, investment-based accounts are likely to result in low returns or high risks. Feldstein (1999) pointed out that without the support of financial market reform, investment-based accounts would benefit a future generation at a higher cost to today's workers in China. In particular, China needs more reform to stop the practice of heavily subsidizing inefficient SOEs at the cost of devaluing social pension funds. According to Feldstein's estimation, the implicit taxation imposed on social pension funds was as high as 100%, driving the real return on pension funds to zero.

Williamson and Shen (2004) argued that the introduction of a notional defined-contribution (NDC) system could be an important part of the solution to the social security problems China is facing. NDC offers consumption smoothing to today's contributors in a similar way to funded DC schemes. Under NDC, because no fund is actually built up, it does not require today's (poorer) workers to make larger contributions so that future (richer) generations of workers can make smaller contributions. NDC also does not require the considerable private-sector financial capacity of funded schemes. Therefore it is less risky for workers, since the rate of return avoids the short-run volatility of asset returns in capital markets. NDC could be the basis for future moves to full or partial funding. However, under NDC, the accounts are permanently empty and workers and firms may not have confidence that the government will actually pay the benefits. Many may therefore continue to be reluctant to pay social security contributions. Also Feldstein (1999) suggests that because an NDC system is PAYG, the tax rate in the long run still will have to be high.

The advantage (lower cost) of a fully funded plan compared to PAYG depends on the allowable set of investment options. Since 2001, the state has allowed pension funds to extend their investment options from banking deposits and government bonds to include equity. However, China's banking system and its stock and bond markets are not mature enough to offer an efficient capital market for operating a fully funded pension system (Beland and Yu, 2004).

Another determining factor in realizing the advantages of a fully funded plan is sound administration and management. For example, Huang (2003) pointed out that the three-part pension system initiated in 1997 failed to stipulate penalties for non-compliance. Beland and Yu (2004) argued that under the three-part pension system, most of the money paid to individual accounts, which was supposed to be invested in an independently managed investment fund, was used to meet the pooled fund's deficit. Inefficient, costly and sometimes corrupt management is perceived as a source of pressure on the pension system (Selden and You, 1997).

3.2.4 *Effects on Savings*

Whereas high private savings may provide supplemental means of living in old age, the welfare gains from insurance are lost. Individuals must save a lot as a precaution against loss of income and to avoid outliving their resources. Transferring resources from private savings into an insurance-based system will therefore give large welfare gains. On the other hand, private savings are flexible, both in the sense that means can be invested, thereby giving an additional benefit, and that over time, savings can be higher in periods when income is relatively high or needs are relatively low. Mandatory pensions do not have these advantages, but give the substantial benefit of insurance. Therefore, there is a trade-off between private savings and mandatory pensions as a means of living in old age. Voluntary pension programmes present a third way, but may present moral hazard problems. People may not plan as carefully for their retirement and save as much as they would otherwise do when they know that they will receive a public pension (Wang, 1995).

A particular challenge for China is the potential gains from the transition of some of the high private precautionary savings for old age into pension contributions. The household savings rate has increased substantially in recent decades (see e.g. Chamon and Prasad, 2008; Shimek and Wen, 2008; Ma and Wang, 2010), reaching 25% in 2005. One explanation is the precautionary motive against future expenditures on housing, education, health care and old age, reflecting the perception of an insufficient social safety net. Even with the introduction of new national health care and pension systems in the late 1990s and 2000s, household private savings remain high and any offsetting effect by the provision of social security is not easy to uncover in aggregated time series data.

To encourage individuals to voluntarily contribute to the third part of the pension system (individual accounts), although in principle the contributions are subject to individual income tax as regulated in 1999,[7] the updated decree in 2013[8] allows deferral of income tax on the business contribution and on part of the individual contribution (up to 4% of individuals' taxable salary) until the pension benefit is distributed. The income tax (but not the capital gains tax) on the investment return accumulated in the individual account can also be deferred until distribution.

However, in the current context, there are several obstacles to the effective functioning of tax incentives for voluntary pension contributions (private pension savings), including the fact that for low-income employees, the 2013 decree generates negative incentives. For example, assuming in 2014 an employee whose total salary is below the tax threshold chooses not to contribute to an individual account, she/he does not pay any income tax in 2014. However, if she/he decides to contribute, the contribution and the induced investment return will be subject to income tax without any entitlement to threshold deduction when it is claimed in 2040. Contributions and earned income from low-income employees are taxed at a higher rate than if they had been taxed at the time the contributions were made and the income was earned. For high-income employees, assuming no income tax policy changes are expected between the commencement of contributions and the time of pension claim, two things are required for them to contribute willingly: one is that the pension funds are invested so as to generate higher returns (or less risks) than other investments; the other is that the income tax rate is much lower than the capital gain tax rate because the investment returns to the pension fund are treated as income, whereas investment returns to private investment/savings are subjected to a capital gains tax. In the current context, neither condition is clearly fulfilled.

3.2.5 *The Transition Path*

The pensions of workers who retired before 1998, and the accrued pension entitlement of current workers for employment prior to 1998, represent China's legacy obligation, or implicit pension debt. The legacy obligation of providing pensions to these people should be separated from the new social security pension system. They should be treated as an inherited national debt (Barr and Diamond, 2008). Dunaway and Arora (2007) suggested one way to accelerate further reform is to separate the legacy obligation associated with the reforms initiated in 1997 from the costs of setting up a new pension system that covers both urban and rural workers.

Since the benefits of transiting between pension systems will be shared by many future generations, it is appropriate to share the costs over generations as well. As a result, the government decided in 2003 to transfer some of its shares in SOEs, particularly those that were being listed on stock markets, to the NSSF.[9] An additional advantage of the transfer of shares is that the NSSF as a long-term strategic shareholder can oversee the performance of these companies and improve corporate governance.

The World Bank (McCarthy and Zheng, 1996) and other international think tanks have proposed a comprehensive reform package for China's pension system such as increasing the retirement age and adjusting the replacement/contribution rates. However, there has been almost no progress with these suggested reforms. In China, the pension system operates at a provincial rather than a national level in the sense that every province has its own independent pension account. Ideally under the PAYG framework, every province would have its own retirement age and replacement/contribution rates because of differences in life expectancy and the cost of living across provinces. But with free movement of labour and capital, this would lead to a problem of 'free ride'. Provinces would have an incentive to lower the contribution rate and retirement age and increase the replacement rate because provincial social security accounts are guaranteed by the central government. Thus the only available option is to have uniform regulations across the country and any changes in contribution/replacement rates and the retirement age would need to be supplemented with side payments between provinces to account for the different cost of living and life expectancy across regions. Implementing such interprovincial payments probably is not feasible under China's current fragmented pension system. To implement further pension reform it may be inevitable but to move to a centralized pension system.

3.3 *The Rural Pension System*

According to law, all rural households have a claim to a parcel of collectively owned land, providing a base level for household income. However, the cultivable land per rural household is a mere 0.07 ha per person and keeps falling due to industrialization, construction of residential buildings and land degradation (Peng, 2011).

In rural areas, only local government employees, including state teachers and employees of state farms, are eligible for the basic pension. For rural areas, the central government has designed and is promoting a special pension insurance programme: voluntary savings plans (defined contribution and fully funded) targeted at individuals with rural household registration (farmers, employees of rural enterprises and the rural self-employed) between 20 and 60 years of age. Pension payments begin at age 60 based on contributions and accrued interest. Social security provisions rest on the assumption that the rural population is self-employed, despite increasing non-agricultural employment in rural areas and rising migration to cities as a result of easing internal migration restrictions (Hussain, 1994).

In the 1990s, the central government carried out an experimental social pension scheme for rural residents. In 1997, more than 80 million (about 10% of the rural population) were included in the trial scheme but the experiment ended in total failure partly due to poor management and partly due to the 1997 Asian financial crisis when China was on the brink of banking disaster. Bad management was understandable since the spirit of the experimental rural pension scheme was simply a duplication of the pre-reform urban pension system. In order to avoid bankruptcy, in 1998 the central government ruthlessly terminated this experiment to the detriment of peasants' benefits.[10] Although there has been no scientific study on this shock's long-term effects on Chinese people's confidence of government-backed social security systems, the fact is that China, since that time, has had a very long vacuum in pension reform initiatives targeting people in rural areas.

In 2009, the New Rural Pension Plan,[11] a national framework for rural pensions initiated at the county level indicated that China's pension system had made its first step to benefit the broader rural areas (Dorfman *et al.*, 2013). In February 2014, it was announced at an executive meeting of the State Council[12] presided over by Premier Li Keqiang, that China will integrate basic old-age insurance systems for rural and urban residents to allow people to have equal access to the pension system.

4. Recent Initiatives

China's Social Insurance Law was released in 2010 and took effect on July 1, 2011, marking a milestone in Chinese social security development. In 2011, the State Council introduced a social insurance for urban residents pilot scheme, which covers all urban non-employed residents, and which was aimed to achieve country-level coverage by the end of 2012.

Regarding pension reform, policy changes have mainly been proposed and implemented in Shanghai to help ease the fiscal burden of pension payments and to meet increasing demand for private voluntary pension schemes. On October 1, 2010, Shanghai's Human Resources and Social Security Bureau launched a trial programme that entitled workers to defer retirement beyond the mandatory retirement ages until age 65 for both genders without deferral adjustment. Outside the trial programme, people have the option of continuing to work without pension reduction, but often in a different job, at a lower wage and without further pension accrual.

Shanghai is also due to carry out the first trial in China on tax-deferred pension insurance schemes.[13] The pilot trial is regarded as an important step in exploring the expansion of pension insurance on an individual basis. The proposed tax-deferred retirement savings accounts are similar to the US 401(k) plans and individual retirement accounts (IRAs). Under the 401(k) plan, retirement savings contributions are provided (and sometimes proportionately matched) by an employer, deducted from the employee's paycheck before taxation (therefore tax-deferred until withdrawn during retirement), and limited to a maximum pre-tax annual contribution of $17,500 (as of 2013).[14] An IRA is a form of 'individual retirement plan', provided by financial institutions, that provides tax advantages for retirement savings in the United States.[15]

The rationale behind the proposed tax-deferred retirement saving accounts in China is based on the belief that they may help develop financial markets including pension insurance. This is because as an increase in the after-tax rate of return is likely to lead people to shift at least part of their savings into these tax-preferred vehicles. However, if the policy objective is capital market development, a cheaper and perhaps less risky strategy may be financial deregulation, including allowing the entry of foreign financial institutions.

5. Future Research Directions

China's rapid economic growth has led to profound changes in family structure and old-age support. With reduced family structure, traditional family care for the elderly has gradually been replaced by social security. Thus new forms of old-age support need to be studied. In addition, uncertainties in population forecasting, massive urbanization and migration of rural workers to urban areas pose challenges to pension reform. Due to the variations in economic development in China, inequalities, both in terms of pension provision and pension wealth across regions require the attention of policymakers. Rather than dealing with these issues separately, they need to be incorporated into the main analysis to develop a broader perspective.

Given the size of the country, the diversity of economic structure and the extent of institutional variation, the lack of high-quality data has always been a major challenge in pension research. The Chinese government has been very conservative in providing pension-related data. As a result, Chinese universities have invested heavily in constructing survey systems in recent years. Among these are the Chinese Family Panel Studies[16] (CFPS), the China Health and Retirement Longitudinal Study (CHARLS), the General Social Survey (CGSS[17]) and the Fudan Yangtze River Delta Social Transition Survey (FYRST).

The CFPS were initiated with the aim of providing high-quality household data about Chinese society by surveying the general adult population through rigorous sampling, carefully designed questionnaires and the most advanced face-to-face CAPI system.[18] CHARLS is a biennial survey conducted by the National School of Development (China Center for Economic Research) at Peking University. It consists of several modules such as demographic information, family organization and financial transfer, health, work, retirement and pension, income and expenditure. FYRST is managed by Fudan University and is a long-term longitudinal survey involving about 9,000 households, focused on the Yangtze delta area.

With more and more high-quality micro data sets becoming available from the CFPS, CHARLS, FYRST and other surveys, it is possible to analyse and quantify the effects of pension provision (including the impact of factors such as formal and effective retirement ages, wage and pension coverage) on labour market participation, savings and other economic decisions. From a policy perspective, carrying out empirical estimations and simulations is important because the results and findings can help design, evaluate and enhance pension policies.

For example, a well-designed life-cycle model with dynamic optimization of pension portfolios would allow assessing the effects of tax-deferred pension accounts on intertemporal pension wealth accumulation for working-age individuals and the cost to the government of providing such schemes. Since the tax-deferred pension has not yet been implemented, an economic experiment could be conducted on a random sample of the working-age population, by presenting participants with a series of pension savings alternatives, including tax-deferred pension accounts, to simulate a variety of pension wealth accumulation paths. Through this experimental study we would be able to derive important parameters of the demand side, and predict the possible effects of tax-deferred pensions on life-cycle pension wealth accumulation, including, for example, the analysis of the impact of institutional settings (contribution rates, employer matching requirements and vesting alternatives), demand elasticities, income/substitution effects, distributional effects and fiscal costs.

For China, it would also be interesting to investigate the impact of economic incentives on the provision of occupational pensions by businesses, wage-moderation effects, the participation of individuals and their risk assessment of defined benefit and defined-contribution schemes.

Acknowledgements

This research was supported by funding from the Key Construction Program of the National '985' Project (Grant no. 2011SHKXZD010) and Shanghai Pujiang Program (14PJC004) and Natural Science Foundation of China (Grant no.71273059). We also would like to thank Iris Claus and the anonymous referees for their comments.

Notes

1. http://economics.mit.edu/files/691
2. http://economics.mit.edu/files/6310
3. The replacement rate is a measure of how effectively a pension system provides income during retirement to replace earnings, which were the main source of income prior to retirement.
4. Theories of social policy development can be grouped into two categories: societal accounts and institutional accounts. The first underline autonomous factors, while the latter directly call attention to the characteristics of political institutions.
5. http://www.china.org.cn/business/2012-06/15/content_25654231.htm
6. Investment in existing government bonds or non-government corporate securities.
7. Letter No. 694 [2009] of the State Administration of Taxation.
8. Statement No. 103 [2013], Ministry of Finance of the People's Republic of China.
9. http://www.actuaries.org/PBSS/Colloquia/Tokyo/LECKIE_StuartP.pdf
10. http://www.ce-china.cn/article/1031.html
11. State Council Document (GuoFa) 2009 No. 32.
12. http://www.chinadaily.com.cn/china/2014-02/07/content_17271377.htm
13. http://www.chinadaily.com.cn/china/2008-10/01/content_7071828.htm

14. http://en.wikipedia.org/wiki/401(k)
15. http://en.wikipedia.org/wiki/Individual_retirement_account
16. http://www.psc.isr.umich.edu/research/project-detail/34795
17. http://www.cssod.org/
18. Computer-assisted personal interviewing (CAPI) is an interviewing technique in which the respondent or interviewer uses a computer to answer the questions. http://en.wikipedia.org/wiki/Computer-assisted_personal_interviewing

References

Barr, N. and Diamond, P. (2008) *Reforming Pensions: Principles and Policy Choices*. Oxford: Oxford University Press.

Beland, D. and Yu, K.M. (2004) A long financial march: pension reform in China. *Journal of Social Policy* 33(2): 267–288.

Cai, Y. (2010) Social forces behind China's below replacement fertility: government policy or socioeconomic development. *Population and Development Review* 36(3): 419–440.

Cai, Y. (2013) China's new demographic reality: learning from the 2010 census. *Population Development Review* 39(3): 371–396.

Chamon, M. and Eswar, P. (2008) *Why are saving rates of urban-households in China rising*? Working Paper, International Monetary Fund, WP/08/145.

Chen, Y. (2004) *A macro analysis of China pension pooling system: incentive issues and financial problem. International Conference on Pensions in Asia: Incentives, Compliance and Their Role in Retirement.* Tokyo: Hitotsubashi Collaboration Center, February 23–24.

Dorfman, M.C., Holzmann, R., O'Keefe, P., Wang, D., Sin, Y. and Hinz, R. (2013) *China's Pension System: A Vision*. Available at: http://elibrary.worldbank.org/doi/book/10.1596/978-0-8213-9540-0 Accessed March 13, 2014.

Du, Y. and Yang, C. (2014) Demographic transition and labour market changes: implications for economic development in China. *Journal of Economic Surveys* 28(4): 617–635.

Dunaway, S. and Arora, V. (2007) Pension reform in China: the need for a new approach. Working Paper, IMF, WP/07/109.

Feldstein, M. (1999) Social security pension reform in China. *China Economic Review* 10(2): 99–107.

Gao, P. and Wang, D. (2011) Current balance and reform options for China's pension system. *Comparative Studies (in Chinese)* 53: 24.

Holzmann, R., Mac Arthur, I.W. and Sin, Y. (2000) Pension systems in East Asia and the Pacific: challenges and opportunities. World Bank Social Protection Discussion Paper No. 0014. Country Profile for China.

Hu, Y. (2005) Private (occupational) pensions in China: a note on recent developments. Working Papers id: 234. eSocialSciences. Available at http://econpapers.repec.org/paper/esswpaper/id_3a234.htm Accessed March 31, 2014.

Hu, Y. and Stewart, F. (2009) Licensing regulation and the supervisory structure of private pensions: international experience and implications for China. OECD Working Papers on Insurance and Private Pensions, No. 33. OECD Publishing, Paris.

Huang, J. (2003) Economic restructuring, social safety net, and old-age pension reform in China. *American Asian Review* 21(2): 171–198.

Hussain, A. (1994) Social security in present-day China and its reform. *American Economic Review* 84(2): 276–280.

Ma, G. and Wang, Y. (2010) China's high saving rate: myth and reality. BIS Working Papers No. 312. Bank For International Settlements, Basel.

McCarthy, F.D. and Zheng, K. (1996) Population aging and pension systems: reform options for China. World Bank Policy Research Working Paper 1607. World Bank, Washington, DC.

Nielsen, I. and Smyth, R. (2008) Who bears the burden of employer compliance with social security contributions? Evidence from Chinese firm level data. *China Economic Review* 19(2): 230–244.

Nyland, C., Smyth, R. and Zhu, C.J. (2006) What determines the extent to which employers will comply with their social security obligations? Evidence from Chinese firm level data. *Social Policy and Administration* 40(2): 196–214.
Oksanen, H. (2010) The Chinese pension system: first results on assessing the reform options. European Economy: Economic Papers 412. European Commission, Brussels.
Peng, X. (2011) China's demographic history and future challenges. *Science* 333(6042): 581–587.
Peng, X. and Cheng, Y. (2005) Harvesting the demographic bonus. *Asian Population Studies* 1(2): 189–205.
Peng, X. and Guo, Z. (2000) *The Changing Population of China*. Oxford, UK: Blackwell.
Piggott, J. and Lu B. (2007) Pension reform and the development of pension systems: an evaluation of World Bank assistance. Background Paper, China Country Study. World Bank, Washington, DC.
Salditt, F., Whiteford, P. and Adema, W. (2007) Pension reform in China: progress and prospects. OECD Social, Employment and Migration Working Papers, No. 53. OECD Publishing, Paris.
Selden, M. and You, L. (1997) The reform of social welfare in China. *World Development* 25(10): 1657–1668.
Shimek, L. and Wen, Y. (2008) *Why Do Chinese Households Save So Much? International Economic Trends,* August. St. Louis, MO: Federal Reserve Bank of St. Louis.
Trinh, T. (2006) *China's Pension System*. Deutsche Bank Research Current Issues, February 17.
United Nations. (2000) *Replacement Migrations: Is it a Solution to Declining and Ageing Populations*? New York, NY: United Nations Population Division, United Nations.
United Nations. (2011) *World Population Prospects. The 2010 Revision*. New York, NY: United Nations.
Wang, F. and Deborah, D. (2009) Poverty and wealth in post-socialist China: an overview. In D. Davis and W. Feng (eds), *Creating Wealth and Poverty in Post-Socialist China* (pp. 3–19). Stanford, CA: Stanford University Press.
Wang, F. and Mason, A. (2008) The demographic factor in China's transitions. In L. Brant and T. Rawski (eds), *China's Great Economic Transformations* (pp. 136–166). Cambridge, UK: Cambridge University Press.
Wang, C., Wan, G. and Yang, D. (2014) Income inequality in China: trends, determinants and proposed remedies. *Journal of Economic Surveys* 28(4): 686–708.
Wang, S. (1995) China: pension provision and pension administration. Background paper for World Bank project. World Bank, New York, NY.
Wang, Y., Xu, D., Wang, Z. and Zhai, F. (2004) Options and impact of China's pension reform: a computable general equilibrium analysis. *Journal of Comparative Economics* 32: 105–127.
West, L.A. (1999) Pension reform in China: preparing for the future. *The Journal of Development Studies* 35(3): 153–183.
Williamson, J. and Shen, C. (2004) Do notional defined contribution accounts make sense as part of the old-age security mix for China? *Journal of Aging & Social Policy* 16(4): 39–57.
Zhao, Y. and Xu, J. (2002) China's urban pension system: reforms and problems. *Cato Journal* 21(3): 395–415.

5

THE EVOLUTION OF THE HOUSING MARKET AND ITS SOCIOECONOMIC IMPACTS IN THE POST-REFORM PEOPLE'S REPUBLIC OF CHINA: A SURVEY OF THE LITERATURE

Jie Chen
Shanghai University of Finance and Economics

Xuehui Han
Asian Development Bank

1. Introduction

With an annual production of 10 million new housing units and a market value as high as US$1 trillion, the People's Republic of China now represents the world's largest housing market. However, the Chinese housing sector has evolved from a welfare-based system to a fully commercialized market within a remarkably short period. As early as the late 1980s, Lim and Lee (1990) considered this transition to be one of largest social experiments in the history of housing development and predicted that it would have far-reaching ramifications in the Chinese economy and in society. Since the beginning of this century, the Chinese housing market has experienced sustained dramatic growth. As claimed by Wang and Wang (2012), no other large region in the modern era has exhibited a similar high property appreciation rate over such a long period. Wang and Wang (2012) believe that, in combination with the uniqueness of the People's Republic of China's political system, institutional environment, culture background, and unprecedented economic growth, the fast-growing housing market in the People's Republic of China provides an ideal laboratory to study some of the fundamental issues of real estate.

Nonetheless, despite the rapidly growing literature on the Chinese housing market in recent years, no work has offered a comprehensive summary of these studies. This paper endeavors to provide a systematic overview of the key literature in the field to assist both scholars and

China's Economy: A Collection of Surveys, First Edition. Edited by Iris Claus and Les Oxley. Published 2015 by John Wiley & Sons, Ltd.

general readers to gain a quick grasp of current knowledge and insights into the Chinese housing market. We also wish to note the research gaps in the area and suggest directions for future research. Limited by scope and space, we have reviewed only the literature that directly relates to the housing market in the urban People's Republic of China and regretfully excluded papers that address the land market and urban management. In addition, we have focused only on studies that are related to the mainland and have excluded the literature on Hong Kong, China; Macau, China; and Taipei,China. The remaining sections of this paper are organized as follows: section 2 reviews the literature that studies the transformation of the housing sector from a welfare housing system to a liberated housing market in the mainland of the People's Republic of China; section 3 reviews the literature that examines the performance of the Chinese housing market in the postreform period since 1998; section 4 provides the key findings of this paper, identifies research gaps and suggests potential research topics for future studies.

2. Development of the Housing Market

The housing sector in the urban People's Republic of China has experienced several fundamental restructurings since the communists came to power in 1949. In general, we can categorize the development of the Chinese housing sector into three distinctive phases: the prereform welfare housing period (between 1949 and 1978), the dual-track reform period (from 1978 to 1998), and the postreform market-dominated period (since 1998).

2.1 *The Prereform Welfare Housing Sector (1949–1978)*

After gaining political power, the Chinese communist government started to eradicate the private ownership of land and housing in urban areas by nationalization. Public rental housing became the predominant form of housing provision in the urban People's Republic of China. Lim and Lee (1990) argued that the state provision of public welfare housing was proclaimed to be an essential symbol of the superiority of socialism over capitalism. Chen and Gao (1993) suggested that the socialist model of housing provision is based on an egalitarian political and economic ideology, in which the state is obligated to provide guaranteed, standardized, subsidized, equal access to housing. Zhang (1997) examined the evolution of the Chinese housing policy between 1949 and 1978 and argues that the Maoist housing policy was mainly shaped by ideological and political considerations. Zhao and Bourassa (2003) suggested that prereform, the work unit (employer)-dominated welfare housing system involved a mixture of socialist ideology, welfare philosophy, and clan tradition (members of the same organization work and live together and then build close interpersonal relationships).

An extensive literature has also explored the social and economic reasons that underpinned the predominance of public rental housing. For example, Lim and Lee (1990) linked the state provision of housing to the low building capacity of the construction sector, the importance of ensuring the health and productivity of State-Owned Enterprises (SOE) workers and the urgent need to accommodate growing numbers of urban residents at low cost. Zhang (1997) interpreted the Maoist housing policy as being a part of an integrated national economic and political policy designed to serve the whole national development strategy. Wu (1996) also noted that the work unit-based public housing provision comprised an essential component of social organization and labor production under the Chinese planned economy. Zhang (2000a) suggested that the integration of work and living under the work unit-based quasi-clan system was supposed to produce loyalty and social stability.

2.2 *Dual-Track Housing Reform (1978–1998)*

Against the backdrop of general economic reform, the Chinese government launched housing reform in 1978. There are three basic policy components of the Chinese housing reform: rent reform; the privatization of public housing; and the build-up of a housing market. Wang and Murie (1996) showed that a series of small-scale pilot institutional reforms helped to invigorate the maturation of the Chinese housing market. Shaw (1997) broke down the process of the Chinese housing reform into four phases: the subsidized housing sale phase (1978–1985), the rent increases with subsidies phase (1986–1988), the preferential housing sale phase (1989–1990), and the full-scale reform phase (1990–1998).

2.2.1 *Driving Forces of Reform*

The literature has sought to explain why the housing reform was initiated. Lim and Lee (1990) suggested that the changes to Chinese housing policies were steered by the new political ideology of private ownership and price mechanisms. Lim and Lee (1993) argued that changing the concept of housing from 'welfare goods' (socialist welfare rights) to 'market goods' (commodity) constituted the essential spirit of the housing reform.

However, most other studies believe that the launch of the housing reform was mainly due to economic reasons. The World Bank (1992) argued that the People's Republic of China's housing reforms were initially aimed at alleviating the extreme housing shortage by decentralizing housing investment decisions and investments; a major goal was to reduce the soaring fiscal burden of urban housing subsidies.[1] Wang and Murie (1996) suggested that the incompatibility of the welfare housing system with the People's Republic of China's general economic transition became the dominant force for reforming the urban housing sector. Chen (1996) explained why the welfare housing system constituted a major obstacle to economic liberalization: it distorted the real cost of housing. Employees have to give the housing allocated to them back to the work unit if they leave, which contributed to the immobility of the labor force by tying employees to work units, and hampered the competiveness of SOEs by imposing onerous social responsibility. Fleisher *et al.* (1997) noted that liberalizing the housing market was a critical step in promoting labor mobility. They provided evidence that interprovincial migration was affected by the quantity of available housing but not the cost of housing. Lai (1998) concluded that over time, economic development gained priority on the agenda of the People's Republic of China's housing reform.

2.2.2 *Institutional Forces*

The housing reform should be understood along with various aspects of the gradual transformation of socialist financial operation, land management, and urban governance. Lai (1998) argued that housing reform in the 1990s benefited greatly from the emergence of a liberalized economy in general and that the liberalization of financial capital was a particular catalyst. Zhang (2000b) examined the restructuring of the Chinese housing finance system and showed that most funding was directed to housing production rather than housing consumption. Hui (2001) reviewed the key features of the Housing Allowance Scheme in Guangzhou and discussed how it had been used to enhance homeownership among middle-income households. Wu (2001) provided a review of the emerging land market in Chinese cities and concluded that the increasing market-based allocation of land greatly propelled housing marketization. Fu and Somerville (2001) found that the government's density constraints on redevelopment sites in Shanghai had been increasingly affected by economic factors. Ding (2003) reviewed the evolution of land policy since the 1980s and found that land marketization helped to promote the efficiency of land use and then increased the rationalization of housing allocation.

2.2.3 *Micro Forces*

Many studies show that the market-oriented housing reform fuelled Chinese households' demand for quality housing. Zhou and Logan (1996) discussed new forms of housing inequalities that were linked to new class divisions rather than simply to income inequality. Using data from a household survey in 1993 in Shanghai and Tianjin, Logan *et al.* (1999) found empirical evidence that the housing allocation system favored people with political connections and higher socioeconomic backgrounds and that the inequalities rooted in socialism were strengthened by the institutional reforms. Using large-scale survey data that were collected in 1997 in nine major cities, Fu *et al.* (2000) showed that Chinese urban workers' intention to buy commodity housing was affected not only by housing mismatch, liquidity constraints, risk attitudes, and affordability but also by differentials in access to publicly subsidized housing and commodity housing prices. Huang and Clark (2002) used national household survey data collected in 1996 to analyze how housing tenure choices in a transitional housing system were mediated by both economic factors and institutional constraints, that is, the *hukou*[2] system.

The economic inefficiencies of state regulation of the housing sector were also explored in the literature. Wang (2011) built a theoretical framework to show that the direction and magnitude of the price impacts of privatizing state-owned housing on the equilibrium of housing prices in the private market depend on the degree of misallocation of state housing before privatization. Using panel data from the Chinese Health and Nutrition Survey (CHNS), Wang (2011) suggests that the mismatch led to tenants of public housing in the prereform People's Republic of China consuming 15% less housing services than they would have in the private market and privatization resulted in a 7% increase in equilibrium housing prices in the private market.

2.2.4 *Macro Factors*

There have been numerous discussions of the significance of housing liberation in the People's Republic of China's socioeconomic transition. The World Bank (1992) considered encouraging private ownership of housing to be a major component of the transition from a socialist regime to a market economy. Lai (1998) suggested that the emergence of a liberalized housing market and the related liberalization of financial capital and land management were instrumental in promoting a market-driven economy and enabling 'growth-first' urban governance. Wang and Murie (1999) explored how the Chinese government had used the development of a commercialized housing sector as an engine to drive future urban economic development and reforms.

In July 1998, in an unexpectedly radical manner, the State Council ordered the in-kind distribution of welfare housing to be rapidly terminated. Most literature considers the complete abandonment of the People's Republic of China's employer-based welfare housing program to be a key component of the Chinese government's stimulus package to counteract the negative shocks of the 1997 Asian financial crisis (Man, 2011; Wang, Shao *et al.*, 2012). An overwhelming majority of the public housing stock was privatized within a few years. Adams (2009) estimated the size of the privatized public housing stock at the end of the 20th century to be 2.5 million square meters and associated with an implicit market value of approximately RMB Yuan 2.5 trillion or roughly 32% of the People's Republic of China's GDP in 1998. However, several studies, including those of He and Wu (2009) and Lee and Zhu (2006), interpreted the massive housing privatization as an outcome of market-driven urban planning ideology and showed that housing inequality, social polarization, and spatial segregation increased following the increasing predominance of the market in housing provision.

2.3 *Postreform Institutional Development (Since 1998)*

Contrary to the voluminous literature on the People's Republic of China's housing reform, relatively few studies have aimed to understand the postreform institutional development of the Chinese housing sector. Ye and Wu (2008) reviewed how the Chinese government took macro measures, including the control of interest rates, banking credit, and land supply, to regulate the urban housing market from 1998 to 2007. Stephens (2010) argued that the Chinese postreform housing regime does not present a distinctive model but fits well in the enabling market-housing model (making the market effective while leveraging limited public resources to the greatest use) that was advocated by the World Bank (1992) in the early 1990s. Deng, Shen *et al.* (2011) provided a thorough introduction to recent developments in housing policy in the People's Republic of China, including increasing real money supply (M2), enlarging loan balances, and expanding government expenditures simultaneously. Wang and Murie (2011) reviewed the development of new types of public housing programs in the postreform People's Republic of China. Wang, Shao *et al.* (2012) attempted to link the Chinese experience of the housing system between 1998 and 2010 with theoretical debates about neoliberal housing regimes, which involve reduced state intervention and the assertion of the superiority of market processes in the housing sector. Zhu (2013) employed the theory of policy networks to explain how the old policy network hindered the shift of the housing policy paradigm even after the hierarchy of housing policy goals had been altered.[3] Chen *et al.* (2014) argued that the recent massive construction of public housing in the People's Republic of China is widely believed to be an economic vehicle to counteract the shocks of the global economic downturn and a regulation tool to cool down the overheating residential property markets. They further show that the recent changes in public housing policy can be seen as a strong signal of a shift of ideology from 'productivist welfare' to 'developmental welfare'.

A central theme in recent literature is an analysis of the relationship between the market and the state in the Chinese postreform housing regime. Zhang (2006) argued that the introduction of a market system is a 'political' process and showed that the state continued to be the builder of the market in the Chinese housing sector after the 1998 reform. Meanwhile, Zhang (2006) also noted that the growth of market forces diluted and eroded the power of the state and the housing market then became increasingly dependent on the governance of market institutions. While earlier literature has alleged that the presence of 'authoritarian centralized control' in the Chinese postreform economy is a reaction to marketization rather than a socialist legacy. He and Wu (2009) argued that the mixture of market logic and state authority logic in the People's Republic of China's urban governance is an effective management system to cope with the problems of neoliberalism. Wang, Shao *et al.* (2012), however, interpreted the swift responses of the housing policy to internal and external economic shocks as evidence that the People's Republic of China's urban neoliberalism is a contingent type rather than the ideal type of neoliberalism.[4] Wang, Shao *et al.* (2012) also noted that housing policy development in the postreform People's Republic of China is determined by a balance of several overriding policy objectives, which include the promotion of economic growth through efficient allocation of housing-related resources and ensuring political consolidation and social stability by maintaining the affordability of housing for mainstream society.

The role of intermediary organizations in the maturation of the Chinese housing market has also attracted attention in the literature. Using a case study in Guangzhou, Tang *et al.* (2006) analyzed how property agents have helped to facilitate the housing transaction process and how their operations and performances are shaped by the urban housing regulatory framework in the People's Republic of China.

The rapid upsurge of housing prices in most major Chinese cities since 2003 has caused housing affordability issues to become one of the People's Republic of China's top social concerns. In tandem with this trend, a great deal of literature has focused on discussing the affordability crisis and the government's response to this challenge. Chen *et al.* (2010) assessed the trend of housing affordability in Shanghai from 1995 to 2008 and found that, while there was a decline in the affordability for each cohort of market entrants, housing affordability improved considerably with increasing age. Deng, Shen *et al.* (2011) showed that housing affordability has become a central concern in the Chinese housing policy since 2007, and providing affordable housing through public provision is the state's major response to address this challenge. Stephens (2010) suggested that the Chinese government's greater commitment to supply-side subsidies is partly due to specific demographic and rapid urbanization pressures in the People's Republic of China. 'The recent emphasis on public housing for the poor is a good example of how government resources can be used to address a pressing social need' (World Bank, 1992). Nevertheless, Wang and Murie (2011) argued that '(in the People's Republic of China) state housing provision is seen as an important economic driver rather than socially necessary'. Similarly, Huang (2013) alleged that the Chinese central government juggles the provision of low-income housing toward conflicting economic and social-political goals and therefore causes constant changes in its low-income housing policy. Huang (2013) cited this as the major reason for the failure to provide adequate housing for the poor in the early postreform era and expressed doubt about the likely success of the recent massive expansion of public housing construction in the People's Republic of China, that is, the plan to construct 36 million units of public housing from 2011 to 2015. Zhu (2013) offered a perspective based on the policy network theory to account for the inertia of the housing policy paradigm shift.

Government intervention may prove to be a solution to immediate social needs while supporting the long-term trend of central state-owned developers becoming more active 'national-level' developers. For example, Wu *et al.* (2012) showed that the role of SOEs in land transactions has increased dramatically in recent years. However, this shift could create a moral hazard, arising from central SOEs believing that they are too important to fail because of guarantees from the central government. Combined with their access to low-cost capital from state-owned banks, this also helps to explain SOEs' behavior in bidding up land prices. Providing restructuring incentives also opens the door for immoral activity by some SOEs attempting to acquire cheap land in the quest to be recognized as future 'national-level' developers.

3. The Functioning of the Housing Market in the Postreform People's Republic of China

Among the various aspects of the housing market, we discuss the dynamics of price, housing demand and supply, the housing finance system, growing housing inequality, housing market socioeconomic impacts, and the implications of the housing market for other markets. We find that the depth and breadth of studies on the various aspects vary greatly.

3.1 *The Dynamics of Price*

Since 1998, the booming housing market has been widely considered to be a key engine for sustained economic growth in the People's Republic of China (Chen, Guo and Zhu, 2011). The rapid soaring of housing prices in major Chinese cities has attracted substantial attention in the literature.

There is a huge body of literature devoted to identifying whether there is a bubble in the Chinese urban housing market. When the bubble issues are analyzed for the People's Republic of China, there are two general categories: country-aggregated level and city-/province-specific studies. The general trend is that before 2005, because of data limitations, city-specific studies usually focused on a few major cities such as Beijing and Shanghai, for examples, see Hui and Yue (2006) and Shen *et al.* (2005). From 2005 onward, time series data from more cities became available and made city-specific analysis more viable for providing a country-wide analysis.

3.1.1 *Disputes on Bubbles*

In the postreform era, the first round of 'bubble' claims goes back to 2003. Rapid growth in the real estate price index is often used as an indicator to show accumulating bubbles, as Shen *et al.* (2005) demonstrated in their analysis of Beijing and Shanghai. Using the monthly housing price index for new dwellings in Beijing and Shanghai, they applied cointegration and generalized impulse-response analyses to argue that the housing price in Beijing was more integrated/less responsive to fundamental variables and that Shanghai was less integrated but more responsive to fundamental variables. With a reduced form function for considering both demand and supply sides, they concluded that there was a bubble in 2003 that accounted for 22% of the housing price in Shanghai but that there was no significant evidence of a bubble in Beijing in the same year.

Around the same time, Hu *et al.* (2006) analyzed whether the rises in housing prices (bubbles) were driven by fundamental elements at an aggregated country level, by using quarterly data from 1990 to 2005. They decomposed house prices into fundamental and nonfundamental components. The fundamental component is driven by income and interest rates, and the nonfundamental component is driven by house price inflation in past quarters. By employing both parametric and semiparametric regressions, they noted that the housing price was mainly driven by fundamental components. Speculation (represented by past house price inflation) was significant but contributed little to the housing price variations.

Although a threat of bubbles is a common impression of the Chinese housing market, research findings that reject the existence of bubbles are surprisingly strong compared with those claiming bubbles are occurring. The typical bubble-opponent group includes Ren *et al.*

(2012) and Chen and Funke (2013). Ren *et al.* (2012) introduced the hazard rate modeling framework into real estate market analysis in the People's Republic of China. Using annual data from 1990 to 2009 for 35 cities, they constructed a baseline fixed effect model to estimate unexpected returns on real estate assets. They further applied a hazard rate analysis (the probability of having a negative abnormal return in period $t + 1$ after having positive abnormal returns in the previous continuous period t) to the unexpected returns estimated from the baseline model to test whether the hazard rate increases along with the length of previous positive abnormal returns in period t. A bubble could exist when the hazard rate does not increase with t.[5] However, Ren *et al.* (2012) did not find significant evidence for a bubble in the People's Republic of China.

Chen and Funke (2013) adopted the recursive unit root test to spot the beginning and the end of potential speculative bubbles in the Chinese housing price cycle. Between 2009 and 2010, there was a significant sign of "explosive" price, but this diminished after 2010. Therefore, they concluded that the evidence for speculative house price bubbles in the People's Republic of China is weak in general. Using quarterly data from 2004 to 2010 for 35 Chinese cities, Ahuja *et al.* (2010) argued that the current levels of house prices as a whole do not seem significantly higher than the levels that would be justified by underlying fundamentals, except for the potential overvaluation in some cities and luxury segments.

Dreger and Zhang (2013) conducted one of the few studies that documents strong evidence of bubbles. Using annual data from 1998 to 2009 for 35 cities in the People's Republic of China, they applied a panel cointegration model to draw an inference on the size of the bubbles. They identified a fundamental-driven bubble with a size of 25% of the equilibrium value at the end of 2009. The bubble was particularly large in cities in the southeast coastal areas and special economic zones. Another strong indication of a bubble comes from Wu *et al.* (2012). They provided stylized facts for Beijing and the other seven cities in the urban People's Republic of China. They found that the price-to-rent ratio[6] showed growth rates of 30–70% for the eight cities from 2007 to 2009. For the first quarter of 2010, the price-to-rent ratio reached 45.9 for Beijing, 65.5 for Hangzhou, and 45.5 for Shanghai, which implies a low user cost level of approximately 2–3% of house value. To justify such low user cost, housing price appreciation rates of 4.5–6.6% are needed. Therefore, a modest decline in the expected appreciation of the housing market will induce a 40% reduction in housing prices. The major increases are in land prices. The real constant quality land price has increased 800% from 2003 to 2009. Half of the increase occurred between 2007 and 2009.

One interesting phenomenon in the analysis of real estate market bubbles is the opposing findings among researchers. Shen *et al.* (2005) and Dreger and Zhang (2013) both identified real estate bubbles. The former identified a bubble in Shanghai in 2003 and the latter identified a 25% of equilibrium value equivalent bubble across 35 cities in 2009; both of the studies applied a cointegration type of modeling framework. On the other hand, no bubble was identified using other methodologies such as the hazard rate analysis of Ren *et al.* (2012) or the recursive unit root analysis of Chen and Funke (2013). The implied difference between the bubble-supporting group and bubble-opponent group is how they define the bubbles. The bubble-supporting group identifies the 'equilibrium' value of the underlying real estate using fundamental variables. Any deviation from the equilibrium value is identified as a bubble. In contrast, while the bubble opponents incorporate the fundamental variables into the model, they raise the bar for recognizing a bubble. For a deviation to become an indicator of a bubble, it has to show 'persistency', in the form of either a significant increase over time as in hazard rate analysis or an 'explosive' nature as in recursive unit root analysis.

3.1.2 *What Role Does Policy Play in Generating Bubbles?*

To investigate how monetary stimuli and liquidity drive real estate prices and generate bubbles, Deng, Morck *et al.* (2011) considered the period from the fourth quarter of 2008 to the first quarter of 2010. They showed that the stimulus package had established a boom in the real estate market via the SOEs. Because the government has direct control over SOE banks and large nonfinancial enterprises, SOEs have to respond quickly to government stimulus announcements. In order to maximize firm value, the SOEs are reluctant to make irreversible investments in property, plant, or equipment. As a reversible investment alternative, the real estate market becomes the most popular form of corporate investment. Deng, Morck *et al.* (2011) employed a hedonic regression of land parcel prices to identify the contribution of the buyer's characteristics (central government SOE, local SOE, or listed company) to the constant quality land price.[7] A dramatic increase in constant quality land price (almost a doubling) was found in 2009, especially for central government SOEs.

Another interesting line of research is to identify the effect of the constraint of fundamentals on housing prices and bubbles. For example, Zhang *et al.* (2013) developed a three-sector model (agriculture, manufacture, and housing) to analyze how much housing price distortion is caused by the central government policy of having a minimum of 180 million hectares of land reserved for agriculture in the People's Republic of China. By calibrating the parameters in the model with real economic values, Zhang *et al.* estimated the ratio of the housing price under land control to the housing price without land control for the years from 1998 to 2009. The ratios are all higher than one. In 2009, the ratio was 1.36. This means that the land control policy alone can explain 36% of the deviation of housing prices from their intrinsic value.

3.2 *The Demand Side*

The explosion in housing demand over the last decade has been widely attributed to the People's Republic of China's rapid demographic transition. Chen, Guo and Wu (2011) reviewed the dynamics of the Chinese housing market up to 2005 and found that the migration of population from rural to urban areas has generated more pressure on housing prices in the coastal provinces than in the inland provinces. They also found that the level of urbanization in different regions affects house sale prices. In addition, Wang *et al.* (2011) investigated the association between growing globalization and housing demand in the urban People's Republic of China. From a different perspective, Wei *et al.* (2012) suspected that the People's Republic of China's widening gender imbalance fuels Chinese men's motivation to buy a larger home in order to enhance their competiveness in the marriage market: this could be a driving force behind the recent run-up in housing prices.

Fawley and Wen (2013) explored the store-of-wealth function of housing. They argued that because of its speculative nature, the bubble generated by store-of-wealth demand might burst, especially when income growth rates and savings rates start to decline.

Along with the expanding freedom of Chinese households' housing choices, a large number of studies have sought to unravel Chinese individuals' housing preferences and housing decisions in a market context. Using data from a stated preference experiment in Beijing in 2001, Wang and Li (2004) found that households in Beijing attach greater importance to neighborhood- and location-related attributes than to dwelling-related characteristics when considering home purchase decisions. Similar findings were offered by Wang and Li (2006) in the case of Guangzhou in 2001. Using household survey data collected in five cities in

2003, Zheng *et al.* (2006) showed that inadequate property rights for privatized previously state-provided homes, inadequate access to housing finance and spatial mismatches between job-market and housing-market opportunities hinder households' housing choices and result in a Pareto-inefficient spatial structure in Chinese cities.

Examining the housing market in Shanghai, Han (2010) analyzed the demand for housing types (location, unit price, and size) based on household demographic characteristics. The price to income ratios, age composition, and size of the household are all important determinants of demand. Using stated preference panel data, Cheng *et al.* (2014) employed a mixed logit modeling framework to analyze housing preference/demand in Shanghai. They found that the 30/90 policy (limiting the proportion of housing with sizes greater than 90 m^2 to a maximum of 30% of the total newly constructed residential housing issued by the GOSCPRC[8] in 2006) induces a shortage in larger apartment supply and an overabundance of smaller apartments. The implied movers' subsidy increases along with income and transaction taxation shifts the demand from larger apartments to smaller ones.

To investigate the demographic determinants of real estate ownership and geographic ownership dispersion, Coulson and Tang (2013) conducted a survey of 5160 homeowners or potential homeowners in 10 Chinese cities. They found that employees of SOEs are more likely to invest in real estate than employees of domestic private companies. Less wealthy individuals tend to invest outside of big cities because of the high city prices and *hukou* holders tend to invest locally.

Zhou (2011) examined the effect of uncertainty on individuals' housing choices and found that uncertainty of income, employment, and expenditure significantly and negatively affects urban residents' housing choices.

3.3 *The Supply Side*

Significant attention has been given to inspection of the Chinese government's failure to control spiraling prices after several rounds of regulation. In addition to movements in the demand fundamentals, Wang and Wang (2012) believe that the unique land auction and presale systems used in the Chinese property market produce significant supply rigidity and help to fuel sustained price inflation. Zhang *et al.* (2013) developed a theoretic model to argue that the stringent policy of land use control accelerates the appreciation of housing prices, which is supported by the results of the calibration.

However, relatively little literature has been devoted to empirical analysis of the supply side of the Chinese housing market. The Chinese government's monopoly on land supply is distinct from any other major advanced economies. This is a key to understanding the dynamics of the housing supply in the People's Republic of China and therefore has attracted extensive attention in the literature (Deng *et al.*, 2008; Ding and Lichtenberg, 2011; Fu and Somerville, 2001; Wu, 2001). Exploring 531 land lease transactions in Beijing from 2003 to 2010, Qu and Liu (2012) found that both the selling mechanism and bidder characteristics affect the price outcome of land auctions. Apparently, the land auction system has direct impacts on developers' construction decisions and feeds into housing prices. Wu *et al.* (2012) studied the property market in Beijing and seven other cities and found that much of the increase in housing prices can be attributed to land price increases. They also found that SOEs that were controlled by the central government paid 27% more than other bidders for an otherwise equivalent land parcel.

Given the huge geographic scale and the significant variations in Chinese regional markets, most attention in the supply-side literature is focused on understanding the differentials of supply dynamics across regions. Mak *et al.* (2012) studied real estate investment in a panel data set of 22 provinces from 2001 to 2006 and found that demographic, economic, and planning factors are the major determinants of variations in real estate investment across regions. Using a panel data set consisting of 35 Chinese cities from 1998 to 2009, Wang, Chan *et al.* (2012) estimated the implied national price elasticity of housing supply to be in the range of 2.8–5.6, which is moderate. Nonetheless, Wang, Chan *et al.* (2012) found a much wider variation in city-level price elasticity of the housing supply (ranging from −7.70 to 37.05 with a mean of 7.23). They attributed the variations in regional supply elasticity to differences in not only economic and regulator factors but also in geographical constraints.

Microlevel analysis of supply dynamics is rare. Barros *et al.* (2013) are perhaps the only investigators so far to examine Chinese developers' supply decisions. They applied a survival model with heterogeneity on the sale of 728 projects in Beijing from 2001 to 2009 and found that more expensive, higher-quality and more centrally located projects have shorter delays in sales.

Studies on the performance of real estate companies are also very limited. Huang *et al.* (2011) used the listed real estate companies from 2004 to 2009 to investigate ownership structure's impact on firm performance. They found that concentrated ownership and state ownership have positive and significant effects on a firm's performance, as measured by Tobin's Q (which is defined as the sum of the market value of equity and the debt of the company divided by the total assets' book value excluding intangible assets). Borrowing the idea of entropy from thermodynamics, Wei and Shao (2013) developed an index system to evaluate the financial competiveness of listed real estate companies. They included four aspects to represent financial competiveness, including profitability, solvency, sustainable development, and operational capacity. For each aspect, three to five indicators are chosen. The entropy for each indicator is calculated and these values are used to synchronize all indicators into one index. The companies were ranked according to their index scores. For listed real estate companies in the People's Republic of China, after investigating the linkage between their index ranks and their disaggregated aspects, profitability, operational capability, and sustainable development are strongly signaled by the index, but solvency is not.

3.4 *The People's Republic of China's Housing Finance System*

In the prereform era, housing was solely financed by the government. With the housing market reform, financing through the banking sector was introduced, but it was limited to housing development (Zhang, 2000b). Mortgage loans were introduced to home buyers in 1994 but grew at a very slow pace. In 1998, only 13% of the RMB Yuan 264 billion (about US$32 billion in 1998) housing loans by Chinese banks were home owner mortgages (Han, 1999). The housing mortgage loan became more attractive driven by an interest rate that was 10 basis points lower than commercial mortgages set by the People's Bank of China. The default rate on home buyer mortgages has declined compared to the default rate on project loans to SOEs. With these structural changes, the real booming of mortgage loans to home buyers came in the postreform period (Deng and Fei, 2008). By 2005, the People's Republic of China had become the largest residential mortgage market in Asia, with an outstanding balance of more than RMB Yuan 2 trillion (Deng and Liu, 2009).

The Chinese housing mortgage loan market has developed rapidly since 1999, which has attracted studies of its diversified risk and default rate. Based on a unique micro data set of mortgage loan history collected from a major Chinese residential mortgage lender between March 1998 and October 2002, Deng *et al.* (2005) found that, in addition to borrower's characteristics, macroeconomic factors and risk-sharing mechanisms also play major roles in determining prepayment and default risks.

Enriching the data set used by Deng *et al.* (2005) by including property information and developers' characters with each loan, Deng and Liu (2009) found that collateral information is also important in determining mortgage termination risk. They also argued that the potential difference in risk premiums between the forward and spot housing markets in the People's Republic of China can be as high as 250 basis points. Cheng and Han (2013) employed a one-period life cycle model in which the utility function consists of three components: the utility of consumption of housing and nonhousing goods; the utility of owning a house on mortgage; and the utility of bequest expectations. The put option value associated with mortgage loans provided by the bank enters into the utility of owning a house on mortgage. Using Chinese data, Cheng and Han (2013) showed that there is a huge uncertainty associated with the future population of the People's Republic of China, which generates high values for put options.

3.5 *Growing Housing Inequality*

As in other transitional economies that have privatized their housing sectors, the booming housing market in the People's Republic of China is swiftly producing polarizing property wealth gaps. However, several studies have noted that marketization alone cannot explain the significant inequalities of the urban property regime. For example, Lee and Zhu (2006) argued that housing privatization under housing reform laid the foundation for growing housing inequality in the postreform People's Republic of China.

Sato (2006) examined housing inequality in the urban People's Republic of China in 1999 and showed that for employees working in the public sector, communist party membership status and working in central-/provincial-level state-owned work units[9] generated significant positive premiums in the imputed rent[10] for the housing they owned,[11] but for those working in the business sector, communist party membership status and state-owned work unit status did not generate such significant premiums in imputed rents.

Through comparative analysis of the data from the 2000 national census and the 1995 national 1% "by-census,"[12] Yu (2006) found evidence that the housing gap was widened after the massive housing privatization of the late 1990s. He argued that the increasing distributional inequality of housing consumption was deliberately produced by the Chinese government with the aim of inducing market-based disciplines.

While recent studies have found that inequality of housing consumption has not continued to significantly increase among permanent residents in the urban People's Republic of China with the deepening of marketization (Huang and Jiang, 2009; Li, 2012; Logan *et al.*, 2009, 2010), there is strong evidence that migrants, especially rural-to-urban migrants, are becoming more disadvantaged in the Chinese urban housing market (Zheng *et al.*, 2009). Using three waves of census data, Zhang and Chen (2014) traced the development of housing conditions in Shanghai in 2000–2010 and found that there are substantial disparities in housing overcrowding prevalence across residents with different *hukou* status. In particular, the incidence of overcrowding among rural migrants remained at a very high level over this period.

3.6 *Socioeconomic Impacts*

A large body of literature has been devoted to studying the interaction between housing market development and the aggregate economy. The revenue from land sales and the tax income from housing transactions has become a growing part of government income in the People's Republic of China (Man and Hong, 2011). Employing Vector Error Correction Model and Granger-causality techniques on a panel data set of provincial-level data from 1999 to 2007, Chen, Guo and Zhu (2011) showed that housing investment appears to act as both a driver and follower in the People's Republic of China's economic fluctuations, but its role in economic growth varies greatly across regions. Furthermore, several studies found that housing privatization and housing price appreciation significantly affected the consumption behavior of Chinese urban residents (Gan *et al.*, 2010; Peng *et al.*, 2008).

The development of the real estate market in the urban People's Republic of China is closely connected with urban regeneration. Dowall (1994) provided an evaluation of urban redevelopment policies and practices in the transitional People's Republic of China. Dowall (1994) suggested that Chinese municipal governments should encourage more real estate developers to take up these projects to enhance the financial feasibility and transparency of urban redevelopment projects. Based on a survey in Shanghai in 2001, Wu (2004) found that the majority of relocation in Shanghai was driven by involuntary displacement (forced resettlement due to urban renewal, infrastructure development, or workplace-housing allocation) rather than voluntary moves (i.e., commodity housing purchase or work-related). Meanwhile, Wu (2004) also found that urban redevelopment generated the lowest return of space improvement for relocated households across the various modes of relocation.

He and Wu (2005) showed that, since the early 1990s, privately funded and property-led redevelopment has replaced government-backed urban redevelopment in Shanghai and other major Chinese cities. Using a case study of the Xintiandi project in Shanghai, He and Wu (2005) revealed how progrowth coalitions between the local government and developers were formed under the entrepreneurial capability of the local government. Recent analyses of urban regeneration in the People's Republic of China looked into the impacts of real estate redevelopment on urban growth (Hao *et al.*, 2012; Yang and Chang, 2007; Ye, 2011) and the affected households' welfare gains and losses (Shin, 2009; Song *et al.*, 2012; Wang *et al.*, 2009). Cheng (2012) noted the changing pattern of urban renewal in the People's Republic of China.

The emergence of a private-ownership-based housing market also greatly transformed social structures in the urban People's Republic of China. The formation of homeowner associations (HOA) and their rising "grassroots-democracy" role in neighborhood governance and citizen participation exemplifies this impact and thus has attracted significant attention from academia. Drawing upon the theory of social movements and organizations and using survey data in Beijing, Wang, Yin *et al.* (2012) found that both community features and HOA leaders' characteristics have significant impacts on HOA's adoption of governance structures. Another issue related to the impacts of the private housing market on social structure in the People's Republic of China is the emergence and implications of 'gated' communities[13] (Douglass *et al.*, 2012; Song and Wu, 2010; Wu, 2005). For example, Douglass *et al.* (2012) found that 'gated' communities exclude underprivileged groups from basic services as well as limiting social contact between socioeconomic groups.

3.7 *Interactions with Urbanization*

Clearly, rapid urbanization is one of the fundamental driving forces behind the recent development of the urban housing market in the People's Republic of China (World Bank and DRC, 2013). On the other hand, the booming urban housing market has contributed greatly to reshaping the economic connections between rural and urban areas (Man, 2011).

However, there is very limited literature that analyses the urban and rural housing market in the People's Republic of China in a synchronized framework. Hu *et al.* (2010) employed a dynamic material flow analysis model[14] for the period 1990–2010. In their study, they recognized two changes in resource management caused by massive rural-urban migration: an increase in urban housing stock acting as a sink of raw materials and a decrease in rural housing stock potentially becoming a source for secondary materials. By assuming various scenarios for key parameters such as population, per capita floor area, and dwelling lifetime, they predicted declining construction activity for the coming decade in the urban housing system and noted that levels of future construction activity will depend on the pace of urbanization.

Despite rapid urbanization, rural-urban migration in the People's Republic of China is still subject to many institutional restraints. The *hukou* system (urban registration system) has been constantly noted as a major constraint on the housing-related choices of rural-urban migrants. Whalley and Zhang (2007) argued that the *hukou* system limits the purchase of urban housing by rural residents and generates inequality in household wealth. They used a numerical simulation method to show that higher urban house prices retard rural labor movement into urban areas. Using housing surveys and interviews conducted in Beijing and Shanghai, Wu (2004) documented that the general disadvantage experienced by migrants has its roots in the institutional restrictions associated with the *hukou* system that outweigh the combined effects of socioeconomic factors. Based on a survey carried out in Shenzhen and a multinomial logit model, Song *et al.* (2012) found that when the respondent holds a local *hukou*, the probability of renting a unit in an urbanizing village is much lower than for those who do not hold a local *hukou*. Urbanizing villages are presumably low-cost and aimed at rural-urban migrants, and therefore favored by non-*hukou* holders. The authors' study provides an explanation of the failure of the redevelopment programs launched by the urban authorities, which are targeted at demolishing the substandard housing units self-built by native farmers, in order to bring in new commercialized development constructed by real estate developers.

4. Summary and Future Research Directions

The transition from a welfare housing sector to a liberalized housing market is one of the most important reforms in the People's Republic of China. In the past three decades, market-oriented housing reform has helped to transform the nature of labor mobility, employment connections, family relationships, lifestyle, social values, urban governance, and other issues in a much broader social sphere in the People's Republic of China. In terms of construction output, investment and the mean-level improvement of housing conditions, the Chinese housing market has seen great achievements. However, it has also resulted in several major problems including rapid price inflation, chaos and instability, excessive speculation, increasing unaffordability, and an unbalanced investment structure. Meanwhile, rapid changes in the housing market exemplify the dynamics and complexity of the People's Republic of China's socioeconomic transformations (Yu, 2006). The dramatically growing Chinese housing market provides great opportunities to test some existing fundamental economic theories and to initiate new thoughts on urban and housing issues (Wang and Wang, 2012).

4.1 *Contributions to the General Literature*

Most of the studies we surveyed in this paper are applications of the existing real estate analysis framework to the Chinese housing market. There are few studies that contribute to the general analytic framework. For example, Chen *et al.* (2010) contributed to the general literature on housing affordability by showing that affordability should not be analyzed in a static manner. They instead proposed a dynamic perspective of affordability measurement that accounts for the interaction of income growth potential and housing finance utilization. Chen *et al.* (2013) demonstrated the similarities and dissimilarities of the People's Republic of China's public housing policies compared to those of advanced economies.

Wang and Li (2004) pioneered the stated preference experiment to compare household preferences. Similarly, Zheng *et al.* (2006) chose a contingent-value approach to reveal the constraints on households in choosing dwellings. Cheng *et al.* (2014) utilized stated preference panel data with a mixed logit model to reveal choice preferences by allowing for individual heterogeneity. The stated preference data approach is useful for policy makers because it can help predict the demand response toward a certain type of housing even if this type of housing does not yet exist in the market. Another advantage is that by constructing panel-type stated preference data, the model can incorporate the heterogeneity of individual behaviors, which significantly improves predictability.

4.2 *Research Gaps and Future Research Directions*

Based on the discussion in section 3, the term 'bubble' lacks a consistent definition. Whether any deviation from the equilibrium price should be used to quantify a bubble or whether the deviation must be persistent to justify the existence of a bubble deserves careful investigation.

Many studies on real estate pricing rely on the effect of macroeconomic policies such as GDP and interest rates, but only a few have looked at the impact of housing market-related policies on prices. Moreover, macroeconomic policy also adds to the ambiguity of whether a policy-induced price increase should be recognized as a 'bubble'. Further investigation is needed to redefine the term 'bubble' from the policy perspective.

Generally, supply-side analyses are still scarce, and the following topics are largely untouched: (1) the presale system and its impact on housing supply;[15] (2) the relationship between land supply and housing supply; and (3) real estate agents and their roles in property transactions.

As noted in the survey, microlevel analyses of supply dynamics and real estate companies' performance and behavior are rare and deserve more research.

Another obvious gap lies in the role played by financial intermediaries. With the maturation of the market economy and financial system reform, financial intermediaries are becoming increasingly important in driving both households' and developers' behavior. Future studies on the role played by financial intermediaries would be helpful.

Acknowledgments

The views expressed in this publication are those of the authors and do not necessarily reflect the views and policies of the Asian Development Bank (ADB) or its Board of Governors or the governments they represent. ADB does not guarantee the accuracy of the data included in this publication and accepts no responsibility for any consequence of their use. By making any designation of or reference to a particular territory or geographic area, or by using the term 'country' in this document, ADB does not intend to make any judgments as to the legal or other status of any territory or area.[16] We also would like to thank Orlee P. Velarde and anonymous referees for their comments. The research is supported by funding from the National Science Foundation of China (71173045), Key Social-Science Research

Project of the Ministry of Education of the People's Republic of China (13JZD009), and the "Shu Guang" Project (13SG35) supported by Shanghai Municipal Education Commission and Shanghai Education Development Foundation.

Notes

1. According to a national survey conducted in 1985, only 10% of the surveyed households were satisfied with their housing: 35.6% of Chinese urban residents were living in overcrowded housing (per capita housing space less than 4 square meters); less than one-third of urban housing units had complete facilities; 60% of urban households lacked running water; 71% did not have their own kitchen; and two-thirds did not have sanitation facilities (World Bank, 1992).
2. *Hukou* is the registered residency in the government monitoring system.
3. The theory of policy networks stresses the close interdependence between different governmental agencies and other institutions in policymaking and implementation (Klijn and Koppenjan, 2000).
4. In the political literature, contingent neoliberalism emphasizes that there is no need to stick too much to the textbook principles of liberalism (for example, the economy should be fully market-oriented and government intervention should be as little as possible). Alternatively, there is no unique form of liberalism that is effectively applicable to all countries and all times; instead, contingent neoliberalism theory argues that liberalism should be adjusted to local conditions and able to change over time, while ideal neoliberalism sticks to some invariant principles (Wilson, 2004).
5. The intuition behind this is that after having t continuous periods of positive abnormal return, without a bubble, the probability of having a negative abnormal return increases.
6. House price/(monthly rent × 12 months).
7. Hedonic regression decomposes the value of housing into its constituent characteristics and obtains estimates of the marginal implicit value of each characteristic.
8. General Office of the State Council of the People's Republic of China.
9. The other work unit categories with lower status include the local-level state-owned work units, urban collective work units, and other (nonpublic) work units.
10. The imputed rent was estimated as the self-reported monthly rental value of owner-occupied housing, deducting the cost of mortgage loans.
11. In the 1990s, the majority of urban households that previously rented housing became owners of their own houses through disposal of public-owned housing at discounted prices.
12. The People's Republic of China conducts population census every 10 years. Between two censuses, there is one 1% sampled survey, which is commonly called by-census.
13. The estate which is walled and gated and provides collective amenities such as security, exercise facilities, schools, and sometimes even hospitals.
14. A model that simultaneously determines raw material demand for housing construction and waste generation through estimations of the population and its lifestyle, which is manifested in the stocks of dwellings, their composition and lifetimes.
15. Presale is a popular practice in many Asian property markets (Chan *et al.*, 2010). Under a presale contract, a developer can sell a property before its completion and the buyer makes a series of payments according to the scheduled progress of construction.
16. The Asian Development Bank recognizes China as the People's Republic of China.

References

Adams, B. (2009) Macroeconomic implications of China urban housing privatization, 1998–1999. *Journal of Contemporary China* 18(62): 881–888.

Ahuja, A., Cheung, L., Han, G., Porter, N. and Zhang, W. (2010) Are house prices rising too fast in China? IMF Working Paper WP/10/274. Retrieved from http://www.imf.org/external/pubs/ft/wp/2010/wp10274.pdf

Barros, C.P., Chen, Z. and Gil-Alana, L. (2013) Duration of housing project sales in urban Beijing. *Habitat International* 39(1): 36–42.

Chan, S.H., Wang, K. and Yang J. (2010) Presale contract and its embedded default and abandonment options. *Journal of Real Estate Finance and Economics* 44(1–2): 116–152.

Chen, A. (1996) China's urban housing reform: price-rent ratio and market equilibrium. *Urban Studies* 33(7): 1077–1092.

Chen, X. and Funke, M. (2013) Real-time warning signs of emerging and collapsing Chinese house price bubbles institute for economies in transition. *National Institute Economic Review* 223(1): R39–R48.

Chen, X. and Gao, X. (1993) Urban economic reform and public-housing investment in China. *Urban Affairs Quarterly* 29(1): 117–145.

Chen, J., Guo, F. and Wu, Y. (2011) One decade of urban housing reform in China: urban housing price dynamics and the role of migration and urbanization, 1995–2005. *Habitat International* 35(1): 1–8.

Chen, J., Guo, F. and Zhu, A. (2011) The housing-led growth hypothesis revisited: evidence from the Chinese provincial panel data. *Urban Studies* 48(10): 2049–2067.

Chen, J., Hao, Q. and Stephens, M. (2010) Assessing housing affordability in post-reform China: a case study of Shanghai. *Housing Studies* 25(6): 877–901.

Chen, J., Stephens, M. and Man, J.Y. (2013) *The Future of Public Housing: Ongoing Trends in the East and the West*. Berlin: Springer-Verlag.

Chen, J., Yang, Z. and Wang, Y.P. (2014) The new Chinese model of public housing: a step forward or backward? *Housing Studies* 29(4). doi: 10.1080/02673037.2013.873392.

Cheng, Z. (2012) The changing and different patterns of urban redevelopment in China: a study of three inner-city neighborhoods. *Community Development* 43(4): 430–450.

Cheng, Y., Dagsvik, J.K. and Han, X. (2014) Real estate market policy and household demand for housing. *Pacific Economic Review* 19(2): 237–253.

Cheng, Y. and Han, X. (2013) Does large volatility help?—stochastic population forecasting technology in explaining real estate price process. *Journal of Population Economics* 26(1): 323–356.

Coulson, N. E. and Tang, M. (2013) Institutional and demographic influences on the presence, scale and geographic scope of individual Chinese real estate investment. *Regional Science and Urban Economics* 43(2): 187–196.

Deng, Y. and Fei, P. (2008) The emerging mortgage markets in China. In D. Ben-Shahar, C.K.Y. Leung and S.E. Ong (eds.) *Mortgage Markets Worldwide*, (pp.1–33). Oxford: Blackwell.

Deng, X., Huang, J., Rozelle, S. and Uchida, E. (2008) Growth, population and industrialization, and urban land expansion of China. *Journal of Urban Economics* 63(1): 96–115.

Deng, Y. and Liu, P. (2009) Mortgage prepayment and default behavior with embedded forward contract risks in China's housing market. *Journal of Real Estate Finance and Economics* 38(3): 214–240.

Deng, Y., Morck, R., Wu, J. and Yeung, B. (2011) Monetary and fiscal stimuli, ownership structure, and China's housing market. NBER Working Paper 16871.

Deng, L., Shen, Q. and Wang, L. (2011) The emerging housing policy framework in China. *Journal of Planning Literature* 26(2): 168–183.

Deng, Y., Zheng, D. and Ling, C. (2005) An Early assessment of residential mortgage performance in China. *Journal of Real Estate Finance and Economics* 31(2): 117–136.

Ding, C. (2003) Land policy reform in China: assessment and prospects. *Land Use Policy* 20(2): 109–120.

Ding, C. and Lichtenberg, E. (2011) Land and urban economic growth in China. *Journal of Regional Science* 51(2): 299–317.

Douglass, M., Wissink, B. and van Kempen, R. (2012) Enclave urbanism in China: consequences and interpretations. *Urban Geography* 33(2): 167–182.

Dowall, D.E. (1994) Urban residential redevelopment in the People's Republic of China. *Urban Studies* 31(9): 1497–1516.

Dreger, C. and Zhang, Y. (2013) Is there a bubble in the Chinese housing market. *Urban Policy and Research* 31(1): 27–39.
Fawley, B.W. and Wen, Y. (2013) The great Chinese housing boom. Federal Reserve Bank of St. Louis Economic Synopses (13), May 3, 2013.
Fleisher, B.M., Yin, Y. and Hills, S.M. (1997) The role of housing privatization and labor-market reform in China's dual economy. *China Economic Review* 8(1): 1–17.
Fu, Y. and Somerville, C.T. (2001) Site density restrictions: measurement and empirical analysis. *Journal of Urban Economics* 49(2): 404–423.
Fu, Y., Tse, D.K. and Zhou, N. (2000) Housing choice behavior of urban workers in China's transition to a housing market. *Journal of Urban Economics* 47(1): 61–87.
Gan, L., Yin, Z. and Zang, W. (2010) The impact of housing reform on durables consumption in China. *China Economic Review* 21: S55–S64.
Han, Q. (1999) The dilemma and solution in China's housing financial system. *China's Real Estate (in Chinese)* (1): 58–61.
Han, X. (2010) Housing demand in Shanghai: a discrete choice approach. *China Economic Review* 21(2): 355–376.
Hao, P., Geertman, S., Hooimeijer, P. and Sliuzas, R. (2012) Spatial analyses of the urban village development process in Shenzhen, China. *International Journal of Urban and Regional Research* 37(6): 2177–2197.
He, S. and Wu, F. (2005) Property-led redevelopment in post reform China: a case study of Xintiandi redevelopment project in Shanghai. *Journal of Urban Affairs* 27(1): 1–23.
He, S. and Wu, F. (2009) China's emerging neoliberal urbanism: perspectives from urban redevelopment. *Antipode* 41(2): 282–304.
Hu, M., Bergsdal, H., van der Voet, E., Huppes, G. and Muller, D.B. (2010) Dynamics of urban and rural housing stocks in China. *Building Research & Information* 38(3): 301–317.
Hu, J., Su, L., Jin, S. and Jiang, W. (2006) The rise in house prices in China: bubbles or fundamentals? *Economic Bulletin* 3(7): 1–8.
Huang, Y. (2013) Low-income housing in Chinese cities: policies and practices. *China Quarterly* 212(2012): 941–964.
Huang, W., Boeteng, A. and Wang, S. (2011) Ownership structure and firm performance: evidence from Chinese listed real estate companies. *SSRN Electronic Journal*. Retrieved from http://papers.ssrn.com/sol3/papers.cfm?abstract_id=1852905
Huang, Y. and Clark, W.A.V. (2002) Housing tenure choice in transitional urban China: a multilevel analysis. *Urban Studies* 39(1): 7–32.
Huang, Y. and Jiang, L. (2009) Housing inequality in transitional Beijing. *International Journal of Urban and Regional Research* 33(4): 936–956.
Hui, E.C. (2001) Home purchase in China: a case study of Guangzhou from in-kind allocation to cash subsidy. *Journal of the Asia Pacific Economy* 6(1): 47–60.
Hui, E.C. and Yue, S. (2006) Housing price bubbles in Hong Kong, Beijing and Shanghai: a comparative study. *Journal of Real Estate Finance and Economics* 33(4): 299–327.
Klijn, E.H. and Koppenjan, J.F.M. (2000) Public management and policy networks: foundations of a network approach to governance. *Public Management: An International Journal of Research and Theory* 2(2): 135–158.
Lai, O.-K. (1998) Governance and the housing question in a transitional economy, the political economy of housing policy in China reconsidered. *Habitat International* 22(3): 231–243.
Lee, J. and Zhu, Y.-P. (2006) Urban governance, neoliberalism and housing reform in China. *The Pacific Review* 19(1): 39–61.
Li, S.-M. (2012) Housing inequalities under market deepening: the case of Guangzhou, China. *Environment and Planning A* 44(12): 2852–2866.
Lim, G.-C. and Lee, M.-H. (1990) Political ideology and housing policy in modern China. *Environment and Planning C: Government and Policy* 8(4): 477–487.
Lim, G.-C. and Lee, M.-H. (1993) Housing consumption in urban China. *Journal of Real Estate Finance and Economics* 6(1): 89–102.
Logan, J.R., Bian, Y. and Bian, F. (1999) Housing inequality in urban China in the 1990s. *International Journal of Urban and Regional Research* 23(1): 7–25.

Logan, J.R., Fang, Y. and Zhang, Z. (2009) Access to housing in urban China. *International Journal of Urban and Regional Research* 33(4): 914–935.

Logan, J.R., Fang, Y. and Zhang, Z. (2010) The winners in China's urban housing reform. *Housing Studies* 25(1): 101–117.

Mak, S.W.K., Choy, L.T.H. and Ho, W.K.O. (2012) Region-specific estimates of the determinants of real estate investment in China. *Urban Studies* 49(4): 741–755.

Man, J.Y. (ed.) (2011) *China's Housing Reform and Outcomes*. Cambridge, MA: Lincoln Institute of Land Policy.

Man, J.Y. and Hong, Y.-H. (eds.). (2011) *China's Local Public Finance in Transition*. Cambridge, MA: Lincoln Institute of Land Policy.

Peng, W., Tam, D.C. and Yiu, M.S. (2008) The property market and the macroeconomy of mainland China: a cross region study. *Pacific Economic Review* 13(2): 240–258.

Qu, W. and Liu, X. (2012) Assessing the performance of Chinese land lease auctions: evidence from Beijing. *Journal of Real Estate Research* 34(3): 292–310.

Ren, Y., Xiong, C. and Yuan, Y. (2012) House price bubbles in China. *China Economic Review* 23(4): 786–800.

Sato, H. (2006) Housing inequality and housing poverty in urban China in the late 1990s. *China Economic Review* 17(1): 37–50.

Shaw, V.N. (1997) Urban housing reform in China. *Habitat International* 21(2): 199–212.

Shen, Y., Hui, E.C. and Liu, H. (2005) Housing price bubbles in Beijing and Shanghai. *Management Decision* 43(4): 611–627.

Shin, H.B. (2009) Residential redevelopment and the entrepreneurial local state: the implications of Beijing's shifting emphasis on urban redevelopment policies. *Urban Studies* 46(13): 2815–2839.

Song, Y.-L., Chiang, L.-H. N. and Li, S.-M. (2012) The place attachment of residents displaced by urban redevelopment projects in Shanghai. *Issues & Studies* 48(3): 43–73.

Song, W. and Wu, Q. (2010) Gentrification and residential differentiation in Nanjing, China. *Chinese Geographical Science* 20(6): 568–576.

Stephens, M. (2010) Locating Chinese urban housing policy in an international context. *Urban Studies* 47(14): 2965–2982.

Tang, B.-S., Wong, S.-W. and Liu, S.-C. (2006) Property agents, housing markets and housing services in transitional urban China. *Housing Studies* 21(6): 799–823.

Wang, S.-Y. (2011) State misallocation and housing prices: theory and evidence from China. *American Economic Review* 101(5): 2081–2107.

Wang, S., Chan, S.H. and Xu, B. (2012) Estimates of the price elasticity of new housing supply, and their determinants: evidence from China. *Journal of Real Estate Research* 34(3): 312–344.

Wang, D. and Li, S.-M. (2004) Housing preferences in a transitional housing system: the case of Beijing, China. *Environment and Planning A* 36(1): 69–87.

Wang, D. and Li, S.-M. (2006) Socio-economic differentials and stated housing preferences in Guangzhou, China. *Habitat International* 30(2): 305–326.

Wang, Y.P. and Murie, A. (1996) The process of commercialisation of urban housing in China. *Urban Studies* 33(6): 971–989.

Wang, Y.P. and Murie, A. (1999) Commercial housing development in urban China. *Urban Studies* 36(9): 1475–1494.

Wang, Y.P. and Murie, A. (2011) The new affordable and social housing provision system in China: implications for comparative housing studies. *International Journal of Housing Policy* 11(3): 237–254.

Wang, Y.P., Shao, L., Murie, A. and Cheng, J. (2012) The maturation of the neo-liberal housing market in urban China. *Housing Studies* 27(3): 343–359.

Wang, H. and Wang, K. (2012) What is unique about Chinese real estate markets? *Journal of Real Estate Research* 34(3): 275–289.

Wang, Y.P., Wang, Y. and Wu, J. (2009) Urbanization and informal development in China: urban villages in Shenzhen. *International Journal of Urban and Regional Research* 33(4): 957–973.

Wang, S., Yang, Z. and Liu, H. (2011) Impact of urban economic openness on real estate prices: evidence from thirty-five cities in China. *China Economic Review* 22(1): 42–54.

Wang, F., Yin, H. and Zhou, Z. (2012) The adoption of bottom-up governance in China's homeowner associations. *Management and Organization Review* 8(3): 559–583.
Wei, L. and Shao, L. (2013) Evaluation on the financial competitiveness of Chinese listed real estate companies based on entropy method. *Cornell University Library* arXiv:1302.2493.
Wei, S.-J., Zhang, X. and Liu, Y. (2012) Status competition and housing prices: some evidence from China. NBER Working Paper 18000.
Whalley, J. and Zhang, S. (2007) A numerical simulation analysis of (Hukou) labour mobility restrictions in China. *Journal of Development Economics* 83(2): 392–410.
Wilson, D. (2004) Toward a contingent urban neoliberalism. *Urban Geography* 25(8): 771–783.
World Bank. (1992) *China: Implementation Options for Urban Housing Reform.* Report No. 10315. Washington DC: The World Bank.
World Bank and DRC. (2013) *China 2030: Building a Modern, Harmonious, and Creative High-Income Society*. Washington, DC: The World Bank.
Wu, F. (1996) Changes in the structure of public housing provision in urban China. *Urban Studies* 33(9): 1601–1627.
Wu, F. (2001) China's recent urban development in the process of land and housing marketisation and economic globalisation. *Habitat International* 25(3): 273–289.
Wu, F. (2004) Intraurban Residential relocation in Shanghai: modes and stratification. *Environment and Planning A* 36(1): 7–25.
Wu, F. (2005) Rediscovering the 'gate' under market transition: from work-unit compounds to commodity housing enclaves. *Housing Studies* 20(2): 235–254.
Wu, J., Gyourko, J. and Deng, Y. (2012) Evaluating conditions in major Chinese housing markets. *Regional Science and Urban Economics* 42(3): 531–543.
Yang, Y.-R. and Chang, C.-H. (2007) An urban regeneration regime in China: a case study of urban redevelopment in Shanghai's Taipingqiao area. *Urban Studies* 44(9): 1809–1826.
Ye, L. (2011) Urban regeneration in China: policy, development, and issues. *Local Economy* 26(5): 337–347.
Ye, J. and Wu, Z. (2008) Urban housing policy in China in the macro-regulation period 2004–2007. *Urban Policy and Research* 26(3): 283–295.
Yu, Z. (2006) Heterogeneity and dynamics in China's emerging urban housing market: two sides of a success story from the late 1990s. *Habitat International* 30(2): 277–304.
Zhang, X.Q. (1997) Chinese housing policy 1949–1978: the development of a welfare system. *Planning Perspectives* 12(4): 433–455.
Zhang, X.Q. (2000a) Privatization and the Chinese housing model. *International Planning Studies* 5(2): 191–204.
Zhang, X.Q. (2000b) The restructuring of the housing finance system in urban China. *Cities* 17(5): 339–348.
Zhang, X.Q. (2006) Institutional transformation and marketisation: the changing patterns of housing investment in urban China. *Habitat International* 30(2): 327–341.
Zhang, Y. and Chen, J. (2014) The changing prevalence of housing overcrowding in post-reform China: the case of Shanghai, 2000–2010. *Habitat International* 42(2): 214–223.
Zhang, D, Cheng, W. and Ng, Y.-K. (2013) Increasing returns, land use controls and housing prices in China. *Economic Modelling* 31: 789–795.
Zhao, Y. and Bourassa, S.C. (2003) China's urban housing reform: recent achievements and new inequities. *Housing Studies* 18(5): 721–744.
Zheng, S., Fu, Y. and Liu, H. (2006) Housing-choice hindrances and urban spatial structure: evidence from matched location and location-preference data in Chinese cities. *Journal of Urban Economics* 60(3): 535–557.
Zheng, S., Long, F., Fan, C.C. and Gu, Y. (2009) Urban villages in China: a 2008 survey of migrant settlements in Beijing. *Eurasian Geography and Economics* 50(4): 425–446.
Zhou, J. (2011) Uncertainty and housing tenure choice by household types: evidence from China. *China Economic Review* 22(3): 408–427.
Zhou, M. and Logan, J.R. (1996) Market transition and the commodification of housing in urban China. *International Journal of Urban and Regional Research* 20(3): 400–421.
Zhu, Y.-P. (2013) Policy networks and policy paradigm shifts: urban housing policy development in China. *Journal of Contemporary China* 22(82): 554–572.

6

URBANIZATION AND URBAN SYSTEMS IN THE PEOPLE'S REPUBLIC OF CHINA: RESEARCH FINDINGS AND POLICY RECOMMENDATIONS

Ming Lu
Shanghai Jiao Tong University and Fudan University

Guanghua Wan

Asian Development Bank

1. Introduction

The People's Republic of China (PRC) had 171.3 million urbanites in 1978, accounting for 17.9% of the total population. The urbanization level increased to 52.6% in 2012,[1] implying a total of 710.5 million urban residents. The speed of urbanization in the PRC has gained momentum over time. From 1978 to 2012, the urbanization rate grew annually by 1 percentage point on average. The annual rate of urbanization was only 0.6 percentage points from 1978 to 1995 but jumped to 1.4 percentage points for 1995–2012. It seems that the pace of urbanization is picking up, rather than slowing down as some expected.

It is important to point out that the PRC's urbanization has proceeded apace despite various stringent constraints imposed by the infamous household registration or *Hukou* system. The *Hukou* system was implemented initially in Chinese cities in 1951 after the founding of the People's Republic. It was extended to rural areas in 1955. *Hukou* has been used to control or prevent free movement of the population not only between countryside and cities but also across locations since 1958 and remains in effect today. Although recent reforms have been implemented to allow migrants to change their *Hukou* status after they have been employed in a city for a certain period, this only applies to medium and small cities.[2]

Rapid urbanization is a result of rural-to-urban migration, but the urbanization level quoted above is based on official statistics and it includes migrants without household registration (*Hukou*) in the city where they live (Tao and Xu, 2005; Li, 2008). According to the Sixth

Population Census, more than 220 million residents do not have local *Hukou*, most being rural-to-urban migrants.[3] The real urbanization rate defined as the proportion of urban *Hukou* residents in the total is only about 35%. This means a significant proportion of the total urban population cannot enjoy the same benefits as local *Hukou* residents. It is in this context that the PRC's urbanization is said to be incomplete, with serious ramifications as discussed later in the paper.

The PRC's urbanization strategy can be characterized as prosmall or antibig cities, although larger cities have recently been enjoying more support from central and local governments. The rigid *Hukou* system or incomplete urbanization and contradictory urbanization strategy have led to a series of abnormalities: urbanization lagging behind development and industrialization status; urban land expanding much faster than urban population growth; open discrimination against migrants; a significant proportion of urban residents being excluded from urban society; and serious distortions in the urban system with too many small cities and too few big cities (Lu, 2013).

This paper takes stock of the literature on the PRC's urbanization, focusing on the incomplete nature of urbanization and three major abnormalities: open discrimination; lagging urbanization levels; and skewed distribution of city size. The following section gathers evidence on the extent to which urbanization has been lagging behind, the segregation caused by *Hukou*, and how distorted the urban system is. This is followed by discussion in Section 3 of the impacts of these abnormalities in terms of exclusion, efficiency loss and adverse impacts on equity. In Section 4, policy recommendations are proposed. Finally, Section 5 concludes.

2. The PRC's Urbanization and Urban System: Segregation, Repression and Distortion

2.1 *Intraurban Segregation*

According to Lewis (1954), urbanization is driven by capital accumulation in urban industries. Underlying this model are two implicit assumptions: (1) rural-to-urban migration is frictionless and (2) the urban labor market is competitive, without discrimination against migrants. Thus, urbanization is simply a result of industrialization.

However, both assumptions are invalid in the case of the PRC. The infamous *Hukou* seriously impedes migration and legitimizes all kinds of discrimination against migrants. It also restricts access to most welfare entitlements and basic public services for the majority of migrants (Zhu, 2003, 2004), even for small benefits such as purchasing a city bus pass (Chan and Buckingham, 2008). As *Hukou* determines many important aspects of life, the *Hukou* book which records the location and attributes of households has been dubbed the PRC's 'No. 1 document' (Chan, 2009). Migrants are excluded from many urban jobs (Chan and Buckingham, 2008; Wang *et al.*, 2009; Friedman and Lee, 2010) and face many formal and informal obstacles to securing jobs (Li, 2003).

As urbanization proceeds apace, more migrants enter cities without local urban *Hukou*. It can be said that a new 'dual society' driven by *Hukou* has emerged in Chinese cities (Lu *et al.*, 2013) where migrants are segregated from the native urbanites. A study using survey data in Shanghai, the largest city in the PRC, shows that residential segregation between *Hukou* and non-*Hukou* people has occurred (Chen, Lu, and Chen, 2012). Another indicator of segregation is the income gap between *Hukou* and non-*Hukou* groups. According to Démurger *et al.*

(2009), on average, native urban residents earned 30% more than long-term rural migrants in 2002. Furthermore, migrants often do not get paid on time. Using 2005 population census data, after controlling for origin of migration and whether migrants came from regions where a different dialect is spoken, Chen *et al.* (2013) found that those without local urban *Hukou* face difficulties in entering service sectors and gaining better paid positions. For a long period, the wages of urban *Hukou* workers kept increasing, while migrants' incomes did not grow significantly, implying worsening income gaps (Meng and Bai, 2007; Zhang and Meng, 2007). More specifically, from 2001 to 2005, for those with comparable education, migrants' wages decreased by 4% while the average real wage of urban workers rose by 7% (Knight *et al.*, 2011). This finding is consistent with more recent data from the National Bureau of Statistics (NBS), which show that the ratio of average wages for migrants compared to native urban workers has declined from 76% to 65%. This decline was also found by The Research Group in Survey and Statistics Department of the People's Bank of China in Shanghai (2011). In another study, using four rounds of data from Shanghai, Yan (2007) estimated that from 1995 to 2003, increases in returns on education differed between migrants and local residents. This was confirmed by Zhang and Meng (2007) who showed an increasing wage gap between rural migrants and urban residents, mainly due to a relative decline in migrants' educational returns.

However, there are research findings showing a moderation of labor market discrimination or segregation. Using data from Shanghai, Yan (2011) finds that the proportion of migrants in the formal employment sector[4] is rising and migrants' educational returns are increasing. The gap in educational returns between migrants and local residents is narrowing, implying gradual integration of the urban labor market for migrants and native workers, where the differences in incomes and jobs are mainly attributable to resident-migrant differences in human capital and institutional discrimination in job attainment and social security. Cai and Du (2011) showed that the effect of *Hukou* status on wages is shrinking gradually, but this finding should be interpreted with caution. It does not necessarily suggest improvement in segmentation. Cai and Du (2011) also reported that when dividing samples into 10 quantiles, the wage gap between migrants and residents shrinks in the low-income quantiles, while the gap widens in the high-income group. Our interpretation of their findings is: The high-income migrant group may accept low wages to obtain urban *Hukou*, but it is the low-income workers who really face labor mobility barriers. This is the fundamental cause of the recently emerged shortage of labor supply, and rising wages in coastal areas.

The *Hukou*/non-*Hukou* segmentation in cities is not only seen in the labor market, but also in social dimensions. The *Hukou* system and the accompanying discrimination against migrants impede social integration (Zhang and Lei, 2008) and social harmony (Chen and Lu, 2008). Furthermore, once a dualistic urban society is formed, it hampers urban development. The discriminations related to *Hukou* in the labor market directly lead to intraurban inequality and social conflicts (Chen and Lu, 2008). Chen, Liu, and Lu (2013) pointed out that, even if labor market discrimination is removed, *Hukou* status still leads to inequality in public services, and consequently social conflicts and unproductive waste. Using data from Shanghai, Wang, Chen, and Lu (2009) found that, compared with local residents, migrants have significantly lower trust scores in terms of within-community trust, social trust and public trust. Income and education do not change the trust difference between migrants and local residents. Furthermore, migrants with low trust scores live close to each other, so they impact each other and reduce their trust levels further. The income inequality between migrants and local residents also reduces happiness. Chen, Xu, and Liu (2012) find that migrants have lower happiness scores.

Even urban residents with advantageous social status feel unhappy with the inequality related to *Hukou* (Jiang, Lu, and Sato, 2012).

2.2 *Repressed Urbanization*

Intraurban segregation and unequal access to social security increase labor mobility costs for rural-to-urban migration and repress urbanization, and the urban economy becomes more reliant on capital accumulation (Chen and Lu, 2008; Chen, Liu and Lu, 2013). Underurbanization can also be attributed to policies that restrict the growth of large cities but encourage the growth of small- and medium-sized cities (Wang, 2010). Furthermore, capital deepening as experienced by the PRC has contributed to slow employment growth in the urban sector. Real interest rates have been seriously repressed to boost investment and capital accumulation. Thus, more capital has been used to substitute labor, especially in the manufacturing sector. For example, Chen and Lu (2013) find that the lower the PRC's real interest rate is, the slower urban employment growth, relative to industrial value-added growth, becomes.

Consequently, urbanization is repressed and lags behind industrialization (Chang and Brada, 2006; Sridhar and Wan, 2010; Lu *et al.*, 2013). There is no standard indicator for measuring under- or overurbanization. One possibility is to compare sector GDP shares. The PRC's secondary industry accounts for about 50% of GDP, and the sum of secondary and tertiary industries account for about 90%. In contrast, the urbanization rate in 2012 was only 52.6%, which included migrants without local urban *Hukou*. Another possibility is to take the global norm as a benchmark. Lu *et al.* (2013) used cross-country data to fit an urbanization per capita GDP model. Compared with the model's predictions, the PRC's urbanization ratio is about 10 percentage points lower than the norm.

2.3 *Distorted Urban System*

Urbanization is not just about the rising proportion of urban population, but also about spatial distribution of population across different cities. Natural drivers such as income growth (Deng *et al.*, 2008) and human capital externality (Glaeser and Lu, 2013) are important in affecting the spatial distribution of population. According to Glaeser and Lu (2013), a 1-year increase in city-level schooling leads to 22.7% higher individual incomes. Also, the 1982 and 2000 census data show a positive correlation between the 1982 university graduate ratio and population growth across Chinese cities over the period from 1982 to 2000 (Chen and Lu, 2012). On the other hand, a 1% rise in city size increases employment probability by 0.044–0.050 percentage points. In particular, unskilled workers benefit more than college graduates in finding jobs in large cities, if their labor is supplementary to that of skilled workers (Lu *et al.*, 2012).

The most influential theory of urban system development is the core-periphery model, which rationalizes how a monocentric urban system is formed. Under the interaction of centripetal and centrifugal forces, the relationship between a region's market potential and its distance to the core is of a '∽' shape. As the distance to the core rises, the market potential declines, then rises, and finally falls again. Whether the second peak occurs or not depends on distance and trade costs. If the distance to the core is large and trade costs are high enough, the centrifugal forces will drive population dispersion and form a secondary urban center. If the population number increases, the market potential of the secondary center also grows (Fujita and Krugman, 1995; Fujita, Krugman, and Mori, 1999; Fujita, Krugman, and Venables, 1999).

The Chinese urban system fits the core-periphery model. Ho and Li (2010) found that the coastal area and big cities were growing faster compared with other regions. Xu *et al.* (2010) provided evidence for the '∽' shape using city-level panel data. Within about 600 km from Shanghai and Hong Kong, China, city-level economic growth declines as distance increases. The growth-distance relationship becomes positive at about 600 to 1500 km from the two biggest seaports, and becomes negative again for cities more than 1500 km away from the two biggest seaports. The authors also found the growth rate falls first and then rises with the distance to the nearest large city.[5]

One may ask: Will the urban system become more dispersed when domestic demand becomes more important in the PRC? Lu and Xiang (2012) compared the effects of distance to a port on labor productivities in manufacturing and services. They found '∽'-shaped cubic curves for both. The slope of the distance-productivity curve for manufacturing is negative almost everywhere, but a secondary peak shows up for the service sector. Therefore, when services become more important, the regions closer to seaports still have geographic advantages of agglomeration. Although the secondary urban centers will play a stronger role, the trend of economic agglomeration won't change substantially.

An empirical regularity in relation to urban systems is Zipf's Law, which states that a city of rank r in the (descending) order of cities has a size S equal to 1/r times the size of the largest city in that country. That is, the size of the second largest city should be half the size of the largest city; the size of the third largest city should be one-third the size of the largest city and so on. Most of the empirical studies find that city-size distributions for the PRC follow Zipf's Law (Song and Zhang, 2002; Zhang and Li, 2007; Gangopadhyaya and Basu, 2009; Schaffar, 2009; Ye and Xie, 2012; Soo, 2013), or at least are not far from Zipf's law or a scale-ranking pattern (Peng, 2010).

Although the PRC's urban system largely shows both a core-periphery and a scale-ranking pattern, many find that the size distribution of Chinese urban systems is distorted. It is noteworthy that both the core-periphery theory and Zipf's Law are based on both a frictionless market and free mobility of labor, which is far from true in the case of the PRC. The central government has always emphasized the development of the inland region. In support of this, the so-called Third Front Projects (*Sanxian Jianshe*) were launched in 1964 and continued until 1980. Ever since the 1980s, the central government has adopted a strategy of encouraging the development of small- and medium-sized cities, while the population of big cities is seriously controlled, especially in mega-cities like Beijing and Shanghai. More recently, the central government has directed economic resources toward inland areas, by giving them increased land quotas[6] to develop industries, and more fiscal transfers and subsidies. One consequence of these policies is a lack of population concentration across cities. The concentration actually declined in the postreform period (Fan, 1999; Anderson and Ge, 2005). While Xu and Zhu (2009) found that Chinese city size distribution evened out during the 1990s, with small cities expanding more rapidly than large cities, others report a parallel growth pattern of Chinese cities in the long run (Wang and Zhu, 2013). Policies restricting land supply and the development of large cities may have contributed to the flattening distribution of the manufacturing sector across regions, causing economic underagglomeration (Fan and Shao, 2011).

If labor mobility is free across regions, spatial equilibrium is reached, as people are indifferent about where to live, but policies restricting labor mobility have prevented the PRC from reaching this spatial equilibrium. Desmet and Esteban (2013) decompose the determinants of city size distribution into three main components: efficiency (productivity gain); amenities; and friction. Higher efficiency and better amenities lead to larger cities, but also to greater friction through congestion and other negative effects of agglomeration. When the economy reaches spatial equilibrium, an efficient urban system consists of several big cities and a much greater number of medium- and small-sized cities.

Therefore, the PRC's big cities are underdeveloped, and population distribution across cities is compressed. Bosker *et al.* (2012) claimed that the PRC's core-periphery urban system will be strengthened by freer mobility if the *Hukou* system is removed. Their model predicts that increased labor mobility will substantially strengthen the dominant position of the PRC's largest cities (Beijng, Shanghai, Guangzhou and Chongqing). But, it will also give rise to other large cities, either due to their central location with respect to the currently most populated provinces, or by virtue of their relatively peripheral location, which increases migration costs for workers and trade costs for firms, effectively shielding them from competition with existing main centers of production.[7]

Henderson (2007) points out that compared with other countries, Chinese cities are relatively small, and that the PRC particularly lacks cities with populations between 1 and 12 million. Wang (2010) also suggests that the PRC lacks large cities with populations of over 1 million. He predicts that the proportion of the Chinese population living in cities with over 1 million inhabitants may reach 30% by 2020 and 39% by 2030. This will require 100 or 150 additional large cities in the PRC.

Distribution of city size can be measured via Gini coefficients. With population data for each city, a Gini coefficient of city-level population can be computed. A higher Gini means more unequal spatial distribution of population. In 2000, the Gini coefficient of city-level population for the PRC was 0.43, much lower than for other large countries, including Brazil (0.65), Japan (0.65), Indonesia (0.61), UK (0.60), Mexico (0.60), Nigeria (0.60), France (0.59), India (0.58), Germany (0.56), USA (0.54) and Spain (0.52). Only countries of the former USSR have similar Gini coefficients: Russian Federation (0.45) and Ukraine (0.40) (Fujita *et al.*, 2004). In the PRC, the Gini coefficient of city-level population is smaller than its counterparts in terms of built-up areas, and much smaller than that measured using city-level GDP. Between 1990 and 2006, inequality in GDP, as measured by Gini coefficients, kept rising, while that of built-up areas and population grew at a slower pace. In fact, the latter inequalities even narrowed in some years. Therefore, economic activities are agglomerating, while population agglomeration is hindered (Lu, 2011).

3. Impacts of Repressed and Distorted Urbanization

The consequences of *Hukou*, lagging urbanization and distorted urban systems are serious. For example, large numbers of rural surplus laborers remain in the countryside with no work available, industrial restructuring has slowed down, and cities' roles in economic agglomeration are being limited. The PRC has suffered a great loss in efficiency due to the control of migration, the distortion of urbanization and the underdevelopment of large cities (Au and Henderson, 2006a, 2006b). This section briefly summarizes the impacts on efficiency and then discusses the distributional impacts in more detail.

3.1 *Efficiency Loss*

Au and Henderson (2006a) obtained an inverted U-shape linking city scale and productivity. They found that when a city grows, its real output per worker increases rapidly, indicating a great productivity gain from urbanization. Thus, distortions in urban systems result in substantial efficiency and growth loss. It is estimated that 51–62% of Chinese cities are too small. In a typical city, this amounts to about a 17% loss in worker productivity. For a quarter of the cities included in the estimations, the loss is as high as 25–70%. Jiang, Okui, and Xie (2008) found that deviations in the provincial-level Zipf's coefficient from its standard equilibrium value of 1 have negative impacts on economic growth. Wang (2010) also argues that the policy of restricting city size has harmed economic growth. Wang and Xia (1999) estimated how city population size contributes to productivity and how much population size affects government expenditure in infrastructure, management and individual living costs. Correspondingly, they assessed the difference between the benefits and costs of urbanization, and found that large cities with populations between 1 and 4 million have the highest economies of scale in the PRC, equivalent to 17–19% of the cities' GDP. Above this size, the net benefits declined gradually, while for cities with less than 100,000 residents, there were no net benefits.

Not only is labor productivity lost, but macroeconomic structure is also distorted. The Chinese economy is known to be driven by a very high investment to GDP ratio, while the consumption to GDP ratio is less than 50%, which is very low from an international perspective (Chen, Lu, and Zhong, 2010, 2013). The repressed consumption can partly be explained by the *Hukou* system. Without urban *Hukou*, urban life is very expensive for migrants, since they do not get equal access to social security and public services. According to Chen, Jiang, Lu, and Sato (2013), the probability of rural-to-urban migration rises then falls with age. The turning point of the inverted U-shape is 33 years of age. So, for a representative migrant, he/she does not have the expectation that he/she will live in a city for a lifetime, thus his/her future income will decline after returning home. Migrants receive much less social security cover, so they need to save more to cover aging and health care. Furthermore, migrants won't spend much on durable goods, if they expect that they won't stay permanently in the city where they work. Consequently, compared with an urban *Hukou* resident, rural-to-urban migrants would have significantly lower consumption due to higher expectations of returning home with lower future incomes, higher precautionary savings motivation, and lower demand for durable goods (Chen, Lu, and Zhong, 2010, 2013).

3.2 *Urban-Rural Gaps and Interregional Inequality*

In the PRC, since most transprovince migration largely involves rural-to-urban population flow, lagging urbanization is expected to contribute to the worsening of both rural-urban income gaps and interregional income inequality. Urban-rural gaps account for 70–80% of interregional inequality, because usually a poor region has a higher proportion of rural population (Wan, 2006). In a normal market economy, full mobility of labor will help narrow urban-rural income gaps and interregional inequality. Thus, urban-rural inequality usually narrows during urbanization (Henderson, 2007). For example, the Republic of Korea eliminated urban-rural inequality in 1994, and Sri Lanka and Taipei,China brought down their urban-rural income ratio to under 1.4 by 1995 (Henderson, 2007).

There are two channels by which urbanization reduces urban-rural inequality. First, rural surplus laborers who are underemployed or unemployed can achieve higher productivity when they migrate to cities. Second, when more rural laborers move into cities, those staying behind have more land and other resources and can expand their scale of production. In the PRC, urbanization reduces the urban-rural income gap (Lu and Chen, 2006; Wan *et al.*, 2006), and if the PRC can remove its labor mobility barriers, the two mechanisms for narrowing urban-rural inequality will function better. Whalley and Zhang (2007) modeled the relationship between labor mobility and income inequality. They concluded that removal of the *Hukou* system would reduce inequality. Liu (2005) found that people who obtained urban *Hukou* later in their lives fared significantly less well than other urban residents. They had fewer years of education, were less likely to hold state sector jobs or to have employer-provided health care benefits, and were more likely to be self-employed or unemployed. In addition, because many migrants don't stay in the cities permanently and return home when they grow older, their agricultural land cannot be reallocated efficiently due to this incomplete migration, thus limiting the scale of agricultural production.

3.3 *Interhousehold Inequality*

Urbanization means a reduction in the rural population, whose members are usually poorer than urbanites. Thus, urbanization is considered inequality-reducing. Zhou (2009) provided both theoretical and empirical analyses of the relationship between urbanization, the urban-rural income gap and overall income inequality in the PRC. He showed that the PRC's overall income inequality exhibits an inverted-U pattern and noted that the PRC was expected to pass the peak point between 2006 and 2009. He also found that urbanization helps to contain rises in rural inequality. Tang and Zhang (2011) also discovered an inverted-U pattern between inequality and urban employment. A policy implication of this study is that to reduce inequality, it is vital to generate jobs in urban areas, which means promotion of urbanization.

More recently, Wan (2013) derived a relationship between urbanization and inequality using the Theil index and obtained $\partial T/\partial W_u = (T_u - T_r) + [(Y_u - Y_r)/Y - \ln(Y_u/Y_r)]$, where T = Theil index, W = population share, u and r represent urban and rural values, and Y = per capita income. Clearly, considering the urban-rural gap (the second term on the right-hand side of the equation), urbanization helps reduce inequality if and only if urban inequality T_u is lower than rural inequality T_r. But for given urban and rural inequalities (the first term), the relationship between inequality and urbanization is nonlinear. It can be demonstrated that urbanization leads to worsening income distribution initially and after passing through a threshold point, it helps reduce inequality. The peak point is determined by four variables: urban/rural average income and urban/rural inequalities.

When applied to the PRC, Wan (2013) found that: (1) urbanization led to higher inequality from 1988 to 1994 but inequality has been reducing since 1995, and in particular, after 2003, urbanization has helped to narrow urban-rural gaps; (2) the peak points vary over time but correspond to 24–39% urbanization rates. As the PRC is approaching a 55% urbanization rate, urbanization is expected to drive down inequality in the future; and (3) inequality-reducing effects were conditional on urban inequality being lower than rural inequality, a legacy of the planning era. However, urban inequality has been rising faster than rural inequality and they became almost identical in 2010. Thus, the PRC must strive to contain rising urban inequality in order to maximize the benign effect of urbanization on income distribution.

4. Policy Suggestions

The *Hukou* or household registration system and the land system are the main barriers to urbanization and interregional mobility of production factors. Because public services provided by local governments are usually linked with *Hukou* status, the public services system also becomes a barrier to migration. The deeper institutional roots of this issue are:

(1) the fiscal arrangements between central government and local government, under which local governments shoulder a heavy burden of local expenditure, but local tax revenue is much less than their expenditure responsibilities; and (2) evaluation of the performance of local government officials is biased toward local economic growth. Therefore, local officials are motivated to increase local investments and cut social expenditure. Though migrants can find jobs in rich areas, local governments do not have incentives to provide public services to them. Therefore, to facilitate migration, a series of parallel reforms must be enacted; and the starting point is the reform of the *Hukou* system.

4.1 *Four Principles to Guide Reform of the Hukou System*

The first principle is to phase out the disparities in public services created by *Hukou*, including education, health care, public housing, and social security. These disparities between regions and between the rural and urban PRC have historical origins and also stem from different levels of regional economic development. From a longer-term perspective, the right to obtain local public services should be based on local residence and taxation, with *Hukou* gradually evolving into an identity verification and permanent residence registration system.

In order to prevent labor migration solely for gaining access to better public services, *Hukou* reforms should be simultaneously advanced on two fronts. First, the thresholds for nonlocal residents to obtain local urban *Hukou* should be gradually lowered. Second, steady, moderate equalization in urban-rural and interregional basic public services should be promoted through central fiscal transfers.

The second principle is to emphasize *Hukou* reform in the big cities. Getting urban *Hukou* in small and midsized cities has become relatively easier but most migrants move to big cities. Permanent nonlocal labor without local *Hukou* has already exceeded a third of the total urban population in the big cities of the eastern region, and is over 50% in Guangdong (Canton). Ongoing expansion of city size is inevitable, which in the absence of accelerated *Hukou* reforms will result in a new generation of migrant workers (i.e. second-generation migrant workers) who find it hard to settle in the city or return to the countryside. This will create progressively worse social conflicts. Future *Hukou* reform must therefore be directed toward facilitating *Hukou* settlement of labor at the location of employment, especially in the big cities.

The third principle in *Hukou* reform is that the entry requirements for gaining urban *Hukou* in big cities should be gradually lowered. As long as public services and *Hukou* are somewhat linked, and local *Hukou* residents in big cities benefit from greater quotas to enter local universities, future reforms cannot eliminate *Hukou* or adopt a free registration system immediately. If reforms are overly radical, the huge interregional/intercity gap in public services, especially education, will cause large numbers of migrants to flood the cities in a short period of time, putting intolerable pressure on the cities, especially the big ones. Yet, if the *Hukou* system is not abolished immediately, setting entry requirements or criteria remains a thorny issue. Who should be granted local urban *Hukou?* The key is to give priority to those pursuing employment over those pursuing public services. Therefore, the criteria should mainly be employment and social security contribution records. One could use years of work and unbroken residence in one area as conditions for conferring *Hukou*. At the same time, educational level and professional qualifications should be removed from the list of requirements. For university graduates, their actual employment status, not their educational qualifications, should be used as conditions for entry.

The fourth principle in *Hukou* reform is to undertake a series of parallel reforms in social security and public services. Portability of social security benefits is urgently needed, and the link between local *Hukou* and social security benefits needs to be weakened. The gap in social services between permanent residents with and without local *Hukou* should be narrowed through central fiscal transfers. Because most high-quality kindergartens, primary and secondary schools are concentrated in the downtown area, there should be steady, moderate equalization of education resources among different areas within big cities. Most of the PRC's elite universities and high education resources are historically concentrated in the eastern big cities, and these cities give local students larger entrance quotas to these elite universities. The Ministry of Education has already proposed lowering the proportion of local student enrollment – a useful step in weakening the connection between *Hukou* and social services.

Of course, a better approach to reducing the gaps between supply and demand for high-quality education resources is to increase supply and not to decrease demand. For example, big cities should give incentives to attract high-quality foreign education resources (especially in vocational education), thereby increasing the quality of urban labor and providing high quality and broad choices in vocational education for the nonlocal population.

4.2 *The Linking of Land Reform and Hukou Reform Will Ensure a Win-Win Outcome*

How can public services resources in population-inflow regions be increased so that urban expansion does not elicit opposition from the original residents? How should the land system be reformed? How should land (including contracted agricultural land and residential land) owned by peasants who have moved to the city be dealt with? How should suburban land gained by urban expansion be distributed to suburban peasants? Linking land reform with *Hukou* reform offers the most effective way to solve these problems.

The core of our proposal is to enable long-term migrants to convert their rural residential land into construction-use land quotas which are then transferred to the city of their employment for urban expansion. The residential land at the origin is then restored into farmland. The migrants win as they obtain urban *Hukou* and associated benefits. The native urbanites also win because some of the gains from the appreciation of suburban land (as it becomes construction-use land) can be used to fund public services and social security for themselves as well as for new migrants. In fact, all parties involved will win: the original suburban peasants, peasants entering the city, suburban land users, the population-inflow region's government and the population-outflow region's government. The suburban peasants in the population-inflow region and the peasants who enter the city both obtain urban *Hukou* and reasonable compensation. Users of suburban land obtain new space. The population-inflow region's government represents local residents in obtaining a portion of the land appreciation gains while the population-outflow region's government also shares part of the gains as they restore abandoned residential land to farmland for productive use, which in turn provides revenues for funding local public services to be enjoyed by those staying behind. To make this win-win proposal a reality, a nation-wide construction-use land quota trading system could be established, to maximize the gains from construction-use land usage rights while preserving sufficient land for farming or food security.

The reform proposal separates land usage rights from land ownership. Under unchanged land ownership, in which land belongs to the rural collective by law, the proposal enables land usage rights owned by rural households to become interspatially reallocable. Consider the case of a peasant working in the city, whose hometown is in an inland region or in the countryside far from the city. The ownership of residential land in his hometown is worth little to him. But if the land can be converted into construction-use land quota, and be used in cities, it will be very valuable. He will be better off without making anyone else worse off. His contracted agricultural land can be transferred to the rural collective for a price, or he can continue to enjoy future agricultural profits by subcontracting or sharecropping.

The 'land-coupon' trade that is being tested in Chengdu and Chongqing is essentially a 'linked land and *Hukou* reform' but its implementation is limited to the municipal boundary. In comparison, what is proposed here goes beyond any administrative boundaries. This is consistent with the fact that most migrants are interregional and the huge disparities in land use efficiency across regions can be utilized to maximize the value of usage rights for construction-use land quotas, achieving an efficient use of labor and land.

Opponents claim that economically developed regions have land that is more fertile than the economically underdeveloped areas in the population-outflow regions. This may undermine food security. One solution is to apply a conversion coefficient that equals the ratio of the average yield in the inflow region to the average yield in the outflow region when converting residential land into construction land quotas.

Opponents also claim that the exchange of land may lead to unemployment for peasants if they 'lose' their land but cannot find jobs. However, modern economies are dominated by secondary and tertiary industries. In the PRC, the agricultural share of total GDP has fallen to 10% and will continue to fall. The secondary and tertiary industries in the PRC are mainly located in urban areas and they are the main job creators for peasants. Big cities are more capable of creating jobs, especially for low-skilled laborers (Lu *et al.*, 2012). Also, only those who have permanent residence, stable employment and social security in the city are allowed to participate in this scheme. Thus, it does not necessarily lead to unemployment.

Some argue that rural land must be used as a safety net for the peasants. In our proposal, peasants are selling their hometown land user rights voluntarily to obtain urban *Hukou* with multiple benefits, including pension, health care, housing and unemployment benefits. In this case, land will no longer need to function as a safety net, as in the past when the country lacked a social security system.

Our proposal is essentially a mechanism to enable the trading of land usage rights. In such a process, the transaction costs of multiple entities negotiating together are too high and the government must play a role to establish the necessary institutional infrastructure and trading environment. Forced requisitions and demolition should be avoided during the conversion of urban suburban collective land into urban construction-use land. To adequately guarantee landless peasants' interests, a reasonable portion of land appreciation gains should be shared with new migrant entrants.

Our proposal is essentially only a marginal reform to the current land system. If clear rural land user rights are defined for peasants then the nature of land ownership need not be changed. When it comes to the PRC's urbanization and land system issues, many academics have placed their hope on land privatization reforms. While not denying the advantages of land privatization reform such as efficiency gains, protection of the interests of peasants, and facilitation of industrialization and urbanization, there are three potential problems with land privatization, which can be avoided in the trading of construction-use land quotas.

First, it will be hard to push forward *Hukou* reform under the land privatization reform proposal. If land system and *Hukou* system reforms are decoupled, it may lead the PRC into an awkward situation where the government of a population-inflow region purchases the land owned by local peasants and converts it to nonagricultural land. Land appreciation gains will mainly be enjoyed by local peasants and not by the numerous migrants, who will also find it hard to settle there.

Second, land privatization will expand inequality between rural residents. It must be noted that different locations have experienced different land value appreciations because location is a primary determinant of industry and services enterprises (Sridhar and Wan, 2010). Under land privatization reforms, peasants in different regions own land with different appreciation potential, and this creates de facto wealth inequality.

Third, the goals of the PRC's construction-use land quota system are consistent with farmland protection. But land privatization may create risks for future Chinese farmland protection goals.

Therefore, if the government adopts land privatization reform measures, schemes to reduce inequality and food security risks should be carefully designed.

4.3 *Other Parallel (Matching) Reform Measures*

For the proposed reforms to work effectively, there must be parallel reforms of the performance review system for local officials and of the fiscal system (especially funding mechanisms for local public services). Local governments should be incentivized to pursue not only short-run local economic growth through investment, but also long-run per capita GDP growth based on human capital formation, which is crucial in allowing laggard regions to catch up.

The performance review system for local government officials should give different weights to aggregate GDP growth and to per capita GDP growth, and these two weights should be different for different regions.[8] If interregional mobility of labor and interregional reallocation of construction-use land quotas are realized, the total GDP for population-outflow regions will inevitably grow more slowly even if GDP per capita grows faster. If the performance review for local officials is based on total GDP growth, then a unified nationwide regional development strategy will not be supported by the population-outflow regions. Furthermore, the more economically developed a region is, the higher the weight for aggregate GDP growth; and the less economically developed a region is, the higher the weight for GDP per capita growth.

Needless to say, fiscal reforms are urgently needed. First, government taxation as a share of GDP is quite high by international standards. Reducing the taxation burden will permit market forces more leeway in determining a reasonable scale and interregional layout of cities. Second, ever since 1994, when the PRC launched its tax sharing reform, central government has received an increasingly higher share of the tax revenue, while its expenditure share has not risen accordingly. Therefore, local governments' share of taxes under the tax sharing system framework should be increased to pay for local public services, and the responsibility of the central government for providing local public goods, especially those with interregional positive externality, like education and roads, should be increased. Third, more central-to-local fiscal transfer payments should be directed toward local public services and infrastructure, especially in regions which lag behind the rest, to narrow interregional disparity in quality of living. The quality and availability of public services across regions should be 'equalized' to avoid public services-induced migration.

As more and more rural people migrate to cities and become permanent urbanites, the central government should reform the current education financing system. If local governments shoulder the educational expenditure, they do not have the incentive to invest in education, which brings positive externalities to the population-receiving regions. The population-receiving regions won't invest in education and training for migrants, if the migrants cannot obtain local *Hukou* and stay permanently. Giving migrants local *Hukou* can change the expectations of the migrants and prompt governments to invest in human capital. Along with this, the central government should take more responsibility for education and training. The allocation of central-to-local transfer for education and training should be based on the number of permanent residents, including migrants without local *Hukou*. Another way to reform the system is to make the education fiscal transfer portable so that migrants can take education coupons to where they work and live.

Acknowledgments

The authors gratefully acknowledge financial support from China's National Natural Science Funds (71133004, 71063022) and National Social Science Funds (13&ZD015 and 12AZD045). We are also grateful for helpful comments from Zhao Chen, Iris Claus, Les Oxley, and research support from the Fudan Lab for China Development Studies.

Notes

1. Wang and Wan (2014) dispute the official urbanization rate, arguing that recent rates have been underestimated, for example, by 3 percentage points in 2012.
2. Much literature provides an introduction to both the history and the reform of the *Hukou* system. Please refer to Liu (2005), Chan and Buckingham (2008), Chan (2009), and Lu *et al.* (2013).
3. Please refer to the report at http://www.stats.gov.cn/zgrkpc/dlc/yw/t20110428_402722384.htm
4. Formal sector employment usually refers to employment with formal contract, not including self-employment or jobs in mini businesses.
5. Since the distance to the regional core city is not far enough, a complete cubic curve for the relationship between growth and distance cannot be seen, but the first half, a U-shaped curve is shown (Xu *et al.*, 2010).
6. To preserve agricultural land for food security, a land quota system is adopted in the PRC. Each city or county should have a quota to convert agricultural land into nonagricultural use.
7. It is worth mentioning that geographers, using a geographic information database, a digital elevation model, and socioeconomic data, have identified nine existing Chinese urban clusters, whose locations are highly consistent with the prediction by Bosker *et al.* (2012) for the emergence of other large cities.
8. The 'National Major Function-Oriented Zone Plan' also proposes implementing different performance review mechanisms for government officials in different regions, but this is mainly directed at the balancing of economic development and other objectives.

References

Anderson, G. and Ge, Y. (2005) The size distribution of Chinese cities. *Regional Science and Urban Economics* 35(6): 756–776.

Au, C.C. and Henderson, J.V. (2006a) Are Chinese cities too small? *Review of Economic Studies* 73(3): 549–576.

Au, C.C. and Henderson, J.V. (2006b) How migration restrictions limit agglomeration and productivity in China. *Journal of Development Economics* 80(2): 350–388.

Bosker, M., Brakman, S., Garretsen, H. and Schramm, M. (2012) Relaxing Hukou: increased labor mobility and China's economic geography. *Journal of Urban Economics* 72(2–3): 252–266.

Cai, F. and Du, Y. (2011) Wage increases, wage convergence, and the Lewis turning point in China. *China Economic Review* 22(4): 601–610.

Chan, K.W. (2009) The Chinese Hukou system at 50. *Eurasian Geography and Economics* 50(2): 197–221.

Chan, K.W. and Buckingham, W. (2008) Is China abolishing the Hukou system? *The China Quarterly* 195(1): 582–605.

Chang, H.G. and Brada, J.C. (2006) The paradox of China's growing under-urbanization. *Economic Systems* 30: 24–40.

Chen, B.K. and Lu, M. (2013) Toward balanced growth: financial repression, multi-dimensional imbalances and reform strategy. (in Chinese) Working Paper, Central University of Finance and Economics and Shanghai Jiaotong University.

Chen, B.K., Chen, Z., Freeman, R. and Lu, M. (2013) Language as a bridge: the effects of dialect on labor market performance in urban China. Paper presented at the *International Conference on Chinese Labor Market, Zhejiang University, Hangzhou, China, June 5–6, 2013*.

Chen, B.K., Lu, M. and Zhong, N.H. (2010) Consumption constrained by Hukou. (in Chinese) *Economic Research Journal*, special issue on consumption and finance: 62–71.

Chen, B.K., Lu, M. and Zhong, N.H. (2013) Institutional constraints, identity and household consumption heterogeneity in China. In J. Whalley (ed), *China's Trade, Exchange Rate and Industrial Policy Structure* (pp. 121–149). Singapore: World Scientific Publishing.

Chen, Z., Jiang, S.Q., Lu, M. and Sato, H. (2013) China's labour market, rural-urban migration and growth pattern: future prospect. In J. Zhang (ed), *Unfinished Reforms in the Chinese Economy* (pp. 83–123). Singapore: World Scientific Publishing.

Chen, Z., Liu, X.F., Lu, M. (2013) Beyond Lewis: rural-to-urban migration with endogenous policy change. *China Agricultural Economic Review* 5(2): 213–230.

Chen, Z. and Lu, M. (2008) From segmentation to integration. (in Chinese) *Economic Research Journal* 1: 21–32.

Chen, Z. and Lu, M. (2012) Ensuring efficiency and equality in China's urbanization and regional development strategy. In W.T. Woo, M. Lu, J.D. Sachs and Z. Chen (eds), *A New Economic Growth Engine for China: Escaping the Middle-Income Trap by Not Doing More of the Same* (pp. 185–212). Singapore: Imperial College Press and World Scientific.

Chen, Z., Lu, M. and Chen, J.M. (2012) Hukou system and residential segregation: a new challenge of urban public administration in China. (in Chinese) *Fudan Journal* 5: 77–86.

Chen, Z., Xu, T. and Liu, X.F. (2012) Hukou identity, demonstration effects, and happiness: evidence from Shanghai and Shenzhen. (in Chinese) *The Journal of World Economy* 4: 79–101.

Démurger, S., Gurgand, M., Li, S. and Yue, X.M. (2009) Migrants as second-class workers in urban China? A decomposition analysis. *Journal of Comparative Economics* 37(4): 610–628.

Deng, X.Z., Huang, J.K., Rozelle, S. and Uchida, E. (2008) Growth, population and industrialization, and urban land expansion of China. *Journal of Urban Economics* 63(1): 96–115.

Desmet, K. and Esteban, R.H. (2013) Urban accounting and welfare. *American Economic Review* 103(6): 2296–2327.

Fan, C.C. (1999) The vertical and horizontal expansions of China's city system. *Urban Geography* 20(6): 493–515.

Fan, J.Y. and Shao, T. (2011) Housing price, location of diversified product and urban system. (in Chinese) *Economic Research Journal* 2: 87–99.

Friedman, E. and Lee, C.K. (2010) Remaking the world of Chinese labor: a 30-year retrospective. *British Journal of Industrial Relations* 48(3): 507–533.

Fujita, M., Henderson, J.V., Kanemoto, Y. and Mori, T. (2004) Spatial distribution of economic activities in Japan and China. In V. Henderson and J.F. Thisse (eds), *Handbook of Urban and Regional Economics*, (Vol. 4 pp. 2911–2977). Amsterdam: North-Holland.

Fujita, M. and Krugman, P.R. (1995) When is the economy monocentric? von Thünen and Chamberlin Unified. *Regional Science and Urban Economics* 25: 505–528.

Fujita, M., Krugman, P.R. and Mori, T. (1999) On the evolution of hierarchical urban systems. *European Economic Review* 43(2): 209–251.

Fujita, M., Krugman, P.R. and Venables, A.J. (1999) *The Spatial Economy: Cities, Regions and International Trade*. Cambridge, MA: MIT Press.

Gangopadhyaya, K. and Basu, B. (2009) City size distributions for India and China. *Physica A* 388: 2682–2688.

Glaeser, E.L. and Lu, M. (2013) Human capital externalities in China. Working Paper, Harvard University and Shanghai Jiao Tong University.

Henderson, J.V. (2007) Urbanization in China: policy issues and options, Report for the China Economic Research and Advisory Program. Available at http://www.econ.brown.edu/faculty/henderson/finalfinalreport-2007050221.pdf (accessed 22 June 2014).

Ho, C.Y. and Li, D. (2010) Spatial dependence and divergence across Chinese cities. *Review of Development Economics* 14(2): 386–403.

Jiang, S.Q., Lu, M. and Sato, H. (2012) Identity, inequality, and happiness: evidence from urban China. *World Development* 40(6):1190–1200.

Jiang, T., Okui, R. and Xie, D.Y. (2008) City size distribution and economic growth: the case of China. Working Paper, The Hong Kong University of Science and Technology.

Knight, J., Deng, Q.H. and Li, S. (2011) The puzzle of migrant labor shortage and rural labor surplus in China. *China Economic Review* 22(4): 585–600.

Lewis, W.A. (1954) Economic development with unlimited supplies of labour. *The Manchester School of Economics and Social Studies* 22(2): 139–191.

Li, S. (2003) The review and outlook on research of personal income distribution. (in Chinese) *China Economic Quarterly* 2(2): 379–404.

Li, S. (2008) Rural migrant workers in China: scenario, challenges and public policy. Working Paper 89, Policy Integration and Statistics Department International Labor Office, Geneva.

Liu, Z.Q. (2005) Institution and inequality: the Hukou system in China. *Journal of Comparative Economics* 33(1): 133–157.

Lu, M. (2011) The interregional reallocation of construction land use right: a new impetus of Chinese economic growth. (in Chinese) *The Journal of World Economy* 1: 107–125.

Lu, M. (2013) *The Power of Space: Geography, Politics and Urban Development*. (in Chinese) Shanghai: Shanghai People's Press.

Lu, M. and Chen, Z. (2006) Urbanization, urban–biased policies and urban–rural inequality in China: 1987–2001. *Chinese Economy* 39(3): 42–63.

Lu, M., Chen, Z., Wang, Y.Q., Zhang, Y., Zhang, Y. and Luo, C.Y. (2013) *China's Economic Development: Institutions, Growth and Imbalances*. Northampton, MA: Edward Elgar.

Lu, M., Gao, H. and Sato, H. (2012) City scale and inclusive employment. (in Chinese) *Social Science in China* 10: 47–66.

Lu, M. and Xiang, K.H. (2012) Geography and service: will domestic demand disperse urban system? (in Chinese) *China Economic Quarterly* 11(3): 1079–1096.

Meng, X. and Bai, N.S. (2007) How much have the wages of unskilled workers in China increased: data from seven factories in Guangdong. In R. Garnaut and L.G. Song (eds), *China: Linking Markets for Growth* (pp. 151–175). China: Asia Pacific Press.

Peng, G.H. (2010) Zipf's law for Chinese cities: rolling sample regressions. *Physica A: Statistical Mechanics and Its Applications* 389(18): 3804–3813.

Schaffar, A. (2009) On Zipf's law: testing over China's and India's city size distribution. Working Paper, Université de La Réunion.

Song, S.F. and Zhang, K.H. (2002) Urbanization and city size distribution in China. *Urban Studies* 39(12): 2317–2327.

Soo, K.T. (2013) Zipf, Gibrat and geography: evidence from China, India and Brazil. *Papers in Regional Science* 93(1): 159–181. doi: 10.1111/j.1435-5957.2012.00477.x.

Sridhar, K.S. and Wan, G.H. (2010) Firm location choices in China, India and Brazil. *China Economic Review* 21(1): 113–122.

Tang, D. and Zhang, J. (2011) Kuznets process of Chinese economic growth, urbanization and income distribution: theory and empirics. (in Chinese) *World Economic Papers* 5: 15–34.

Tao, R. and Xu, Z.G. (2005) Urbanization, rural land system and migrants' social security. (in Chinese) *Economic Research Journal* 12: 45–56.

The Research Group in Survey and Statistics Department of People's Bank of China in Shanghai. (2011) A Study on Lewis turning point: trend, forecast and policy. (in Chinese) *Review of Financial Development* 6: 29–47.

Wan, G.H. (2006) *Economic Growth and Income Inequality: In the Aspects of Methods and Evidence*. (in Chinese) Shanghai: Shanghai People's Press.

Wan, G.H. (2013) The urbanization-inequality nexus: method and application to China. (in Chinese) *Economic Research Journal* 5: 73–86.

Wan, G.H., Lu, M. and Chen, Z. (2006) The inequality–growth nexus in the short and long runs: empirical evidence from China. *Journal of Comparative Economics* 34(4): 654–667.

Wang, H.Y., Appelbaumb, R.P., Degiulib, F. and Lichtenstein, N. (2009) China's new labour contract law: is China moving towards increased power for workers? *Third World Quarterly* 30(3): 485–501.

Wang, H., Chen, Z. and Lu, M. (2009) Household registration, social segmentation and trust: the empirical studies from Shanghai. (in Chinese) *The Journal of World Economy* 10: 81–96.

Wang, X.L. (2010) Urbanization path and city scale in China: an economic analysis. (in Chinese) *Economic Research Journal* 10: 20–32.

Wang, X.L. and Wan, G.H. (2014) China's urban employment and urbanization rate: a re-estimation. *China & World Economy* 22(1): 30–44.

Wang, X.L. and Xia, X.L. (1999) The optimization of city scales to push economic growth. (in Chinese) *Economic Research Journal* 9: 22–29.

Wang, Z. and Zhu, J. (2013) The evolution of China's city size distribution: empirical evidence from 1949 to 2008. *Chinese Economy* 46(1): 38–54.

Whalley, J. and Zhang, S.M. (2007) A numerical simulation analysis of (Hukou) labour mobility restrictions in China. *Journal of Development Economics* 83: 392–410.

Xu, Z., Chen, Z. and Lu, M. (2010) The core-periphery model of China's urban system, an empirical study of geography and economic growth. (in Chinese) *The Journal of World Economy* 7: 144–160.

Xu, Z.L. and Zhu, N. (2009) City size distribution in China: are large cities dominant? *Urban Studies* 46(10): 2159–2185.

Yan, S.P. (2007) Human capital, systems and differences in wages: a case study on the dual labor-markets in large cities. (in Chinese) *Management World* 6: 4–13.

Yan, S.P. (2011) The structural transformation of the labor markets in China's large cities. (in Chinese) *Management World* 9: 53–62.

Ye, X.Y. and Xie, Y.C. (2012) Re-examination of Zipf's law and urban dynamic in China: a regional approach. *The Annals of Regional Science* 49:135–156.

Zhang, D.D. and Meng, X. (2007) Assimilation or disassimilation? The labour market performance of rural migrants in Chinese cities. *The 6th Conference on Chinese Economy, CERDI-IDREC, Clermont-Ferrand, France.*

Zhang, T. and Li, B. (2007) A study on urbanization in China. (in Chinese) *Comparative Journal* 31: 20–32.

Zhang, W.H. and Lei K.C. (2008) The urban new immigrants' social inclusion: internal structure, present situation and influential factors. (in Chinese) *Sociological Studies* 5: 117–141, 244–245.

Zhou, Y.B. (2009) Urbanization, urban–rural income gap and overall income inequality in China: an empirical test of the inverse-U hypothesis. (in Chinese) *China Economics Quarterly* 8(4): 1239–1256.

Zhu, Y. (2003) The floating population's household strategies and the role of migration in China's regional development and integration. *International Journal of Population Geography* 9(6): 485–502.

Zhu, Y. (2004) Workers, unions and the state: migrant workers in China's labour-intensive foreign enterprises. *Development and Change* 35(5): 1011–1035.

7

INCOME INEQUALITY IN THE PEOPLE'S REPUBLIC OF CHINA: TRENDS, DETERMINANTS, AND PROPOSED REMEDIES

Chen Wang
Leiden University

Guanghua Wan
Asian Development Bank

Dan Yang
Southwest University

1. Introduction

The prereform People's Republic of China (PRC) is perceived to be an egalitarian society despite the existence of a significant urban–rural gap and inequality across rural households. In 1978, the PRC began reforms with the introduction of the agricultural production responsibility system. Under this system, farming land was decollectivized and allocated to individual households based on household labor force and household size. Any surpluses above the state taxes and procurement quota were kept by individual farmers rather than pooled for distribution across households as in the past. These introduced incentives into the rural economy which were previously absent, leading to inclusive growth due to fairly equal distribution of land (Wan, 2007).

Inequality[1] started to rise in the mid 1980s when the government shifted its reform focus to the urban sector (Wan, 2008a, 2008b). Faster urban growth implies a widening urban–rural gap. Meanwhile, urban production relies more on investment and fixed assets such as machinery and equipment which, unlike farm land, are not divisible. These assets were leased or sold to a

China's Economy: A Collection of Surveys, First Edition. Edited by Iris Claus and Les Oxley. Published 2015 by John Wiley & Sons, Ltd.

minority when state- or collective-owned enterprises were reformed, causing inequality hikes among urban residents. It is important to note that investment or asset-induced inequality tends to self-reinforce over time. Finally, the open-door strategy implemented around the mid-1980s raised regional inequality as it came with preferential policies biased toward the coastal region, which already had location and cultural advantages[2] to enable engagement in international trade and the attraction of Foreign Direct Investment (FDI).

Consequently, the PRC went from a relatively egalitarian society to one of the most unequal countries in the world within a short period of three decades. According to Wan and Sebastian (2011), there were still more than 100 million Chinese surviving on no more than $1.25 a day (purchasing power parity or PPP-adjusted) in 2008. In the same year, the number of Chinese living on under $2.00/day (PPP-adjusted) was estimated to be 336 million. On the other hand, the PRC had 960,000 millionaires in 2010, each with more than 10 million Yuan ($1.6 million) in personal wealth. In 2011, there were 146 billionaires in the PRC, each with more than $1 billion in assets.[3]

This high and rising inequality has had many profound repercussions. It has dampened domestic consumption, having generated pressures on the PRC's exports and contributed to the trade imbalance. As noted by Milanovic (2005), inequality trends and patterns in the PRC determine, to a large extent, the profile and changes of global inequality and poverty. From the perspective of the Chinese government, high inequality undermines social cohesion and political stability. Some of the most widely reported crimes were related to inequality (Tian *et al.*, 2009). Historically, lessons abound where unequal distribution has led to civil unrest and the demise of governments.

In addition, growth effects on poverty reduction become smaller when inequality is high. In other words, in a more equal society, the same growth rate leads to larger poverty reduction than in an unequal society. In a highly unequal economy, growth benefits may accrue to the rich only, with little impact on poverty. On the other hand, rising inequality offsets the poverty-reducing impacts of growth (Zhang and Wan, 2006). This is because any given poverty reduction can be decomposed into growth and redistribution effects. The redistribution effect is poverty-increasing if distribution worsens, and vice versa. As Wan (2008c) demonstrates, redistribution is more important than growth in combating poverty in the PRC.

Finally, rising inequality hinders economic growth in the PRC (Wan *et al.*, 2006). Besides the various arguments presented in the preceding two paragraphs, high inequality means those at the bottom of society cannot afford investment in financial or human capital. Health, as a major component of human capital, is shown to be adversely affected by inequality (Li and Zhu, 2006). Moreover, high inequality exerts pressure for redistribution which may distort incentive mechanisms in the economy and induce considerable transaction costs. Worst of all, high inequality may be strengthened and reinforced by alliances between the rich and the politically powerful, eroding efficiency, equity and even justice.

It is thus not surprising that inequality has been ranked among the top three socioeconomic issues in the PRC for many years. In response, the Chinese government launched the Great Western Development Strategy in 2000 to tackle the regional divide. This was followed, in the mid 2000s, by the 'socialist new countryside development' movement to reduce urban–rural gaps. In 2006, 'building a harmonious society' became a central development goal in the 11th Five-Year Plan, 2006–2010. More recent interventions include expansion of social protection to the rural population, improvement of the living conditions of migrant workers, and increases in public funding for education and health services. In November 2013, the Third Plenum of the 18th Central Committee of the Chinese Communist Party outlined a systematic approach to improve income distribution through reforms in areas including the household registration system (*hukou*), social protection, access to public services, taxation, and governance.

This paper aims at providing a nonexhaustive literature review of the PRC's inequality trends and determinants and suggested government interventions. Section 2 will focus on inequality profiles, starting with interhousehold disparity, then examining regional divides and urban–rural disparity. Section 3 presents research findings on drivers or causes of these inequalities. This is followed by a summary of suggested policy interventions in Section 4. Section 5 concludes.

2. Inequality Profiles

To construct an inequality profile, the popular Gini and/or Theil indices are commonly estimated using observations on consumption, income, or salary. In theory, the smallest unit of a distribution study is an individual. Individual or interperson inequality consists of interhousehold and intrahousehold gaps. In practice, however, the smallest unit is usually a household, particularly when analyzing inequalities in developing economies, because of the lack of data for individuals. Interhousehold inequality encompasses regional or urban–rural inequalities as its components. In this section, we will start with interhousehold disparity and then move on to regional inequality and urban–rural gaps.

2.1 *Profile of Interhousehold Inequality*

To date, no official estimates of interhousehold inequality exist for consecutive years over a long period as the central government does not permit the release of household survey data, collected by the National Bureau of Statistics (NBS). This is why early literature on the PRC's income distribution largely focused on regional disparity or urban–rural gaps.

In 1986, the Chinese Academy of Social Sciences surveyed 5,000 urban households in 28 provinces and 5,000 rural households in 10 provinces.[4] After data checking, 7,464 household observations (3,811 urban and 3,653 rural) were used by Hussain *et al.* (1994) to derive the earliest interhousehold inequality estimates for the PRC. They computed the Theil indices for the urban (0.0931) and rural (0.1805) PRC. Both indices were found to be dominated by the intraprovincial component. Interprovincial components only accounted for 5% (urban) and 15% (rural) of the total. They also estimated Gini indices for individual provinces, ranging from 0.19 to 0.22 for urban provinces, and 0.19 to 0.28 for rural provinces. It is not surprising that urban inequalities were lower than their rural counterparts as egalitarian distribution was only applicable in the urban PRC in the prereform period. Clearly, these findings are subject to considerable sampling errors as the survey sample is far too small for the PRC.

In 1988, the first phase of the Chinese income distribution project (later known as the China Household Income Project or CHIP) was conducted.[5] The project covered 10,258 rural and 9,009 urban households. The sampling framework followed that of the NBS. Different survey instruments and different sampling strategies were used for urban and rural areas because of the difference in the composition of urban and rural incomes (Eichen and Zhang, 1993). The CHIP widens the definition of income to include noncash income such as in-kind payments and agricultural products for self-consumption. Based on this data set, Khan *et al.* (1992) produced the first comprehensive Gini estimates: 0.382 for the PRC, 0.338 for the rural PRC, and 0.233 for the urban PRC. They also decomposed the Gini estimates by income sources. The results indicate that the most important sources of nation-wide income inequality are urban wages and in-kind subsidies to urban workers, contributing 36% and 32% to the nation-wide Gini estimate, respectively. For urban inequality, the two most important contributors are wages (34%) and housing subsidies (24%). On the other hand, income from production activities explains more than 60% of rural income inequality.

The CHIP has provided household data for 1988, 1995, 2002, and 2007. Rural-to-urban migrants were added to the 2002 and 2007 CHIPs. In 2007, the sample sizes increased to 13,000 rural households, 10,000 urban households, and 5,000 rural-to-urban migrant households. Using 1988 and 1995 CHIP data, Zhao (2001) and Gustafsson and Li (2001) discovered increases in inequality. The latter study concluded that the rise in inequality is general, not limited to a particular region or population group. Li *et al.* (2011) analyzed the 2002 and 2007 CHIP data, showing that when rural-to-urban migrants are included the 2002 Gini estimate drops slightly to 0.460 from 0.462. The same happens to the 2007 Gini estimate: 0.483 with migrants included and 0.487 without migrants.

Other studies using the CHIP data include Griffin and Zhao (1993), Khan and Riskin (1998, 2005), Gustafsson and Li (1998, 2001), Zhao (2001), Fleisher *et al.* (2005), Sicular *et al.* (2007), Gustafsson *et al.* (2010), and Li *et al.* (2011).

Ravallion and Chen (2007) obtained yearly Gini coefficients for 1980–2001 using grouped income data published by the NBS (various years). Lin *et al.* (2010) followed a similar approach. As tabulated in Table 1, both studies came up with two sets of estimates: one with and one without adjusting income observations by spatial price differences. Since the affluent regions have higher prices, such an adjustment leads to smaller inequality estimates, as Wan (2001) discovered earlier. The upward bias is about 15% according to Ravallion and Chen (2007) or Lin *et al.* (2010), but much larger according to Sicular *et al.* (2007). In addition to using different data, Sicular *et al.* (2007) used disaggregated deflators to capture price differences between urban and rural areas in each province and also among provinces while the other two studies only differentiated the urban and rural PRC.

In early 2013, the Chinese government released official Gini estimates for the years 2003–2011, which were later updated.[6] The NBS estimates show a broadly stable trend. Inequality peaked in 2008 with a Gini estimate of 0.491, and has since been declining marginally each year, reaching its lowest level of 0.473 in 2013. Whether this represents the beginning of the end of worsening income distribution is debatable.

Table 1 presents eight sets of estimates of the Gini coefficient for interhousehold inequality in the PRC. The World Income Inequality Database (WIID) set was collected from different publications and may be based on different data sets, which could explain why they vary considerably from one year to another. The Gini estimates from the World Development Indicators (WDI) database are inconsistent because post-1989 estimates are expenditure- or consumption-based, while the earlier estimates are income-based. Furthermore, WDI estimates are likely to be biased downward as they are weighted averages of rural and urban estimates. Technically, such weighted averages fail to consider the urban–rural gap, which has been rather substantial. Consequently, these two sets of estimates will be discarded hereafter. Among the remaining six sets of estimates, two were obtained after adjusting for spatial price differences. Since most researchers, particularly the government, do not consider spatial price differences, it seems appropriate to focus on the unadjusted estimates. Note, however, that the adjusted and unadjusted estimates share the same trends.

The four sets of estimates in columns 3, 6, 7, and 9 of Table 1 are compatible. Ravallion and Chen (2007) and Lin *et al.* (2010) used NBS data in grouped form. The CHIP data piggy-backed on the NBS surveys. However, the inequality estimates based on the CHIP

Table 1. Interhousehold Inequality for the Whole PRC: Gini Estimates

		Ravallion and Chen (2007)				Lin *et al.* (2010)		
Year	WDI[a]	Data not adjusted by spatial price index	Data adjusted by spatial price index	WIID	CHIP[b]	Data not adjusted by spatial price index	Data adjusted by spatial price index	NBS
1978	...	...	...	0.317	...	...	...	...
1979	...	...	...	...	...	...	...	...
1980	...	...	...	...	...	...	...	...
1981	0.291	0.310	0.280	...	...	...	...	...
1982	...	0.285	0.259	...	...	...	...	...
1983	...	0.283	0.260	0.284	...	...	...	...
1984	0.277	0.291	0.269	...	...	...	...	...
1985	...	0.290	0.265	0.224	...	...	...	...
1986	...	0.324	0.292	...	...	...	...	...
1987	0.299	0.324	0.289	...	...	...	...	...
1988	...	0.330	0.295	0.382	0.395	...	...	...
1989	...	35.2	0.318	...	...	...	...	...
1990	0.324	0.349	0.316	...	...	0.345	0.287	...
1991	...	0.371	0.331	0.341	...	...	...	...
1992	...	0.390	0.342	...	...	...	...	...
1993	0.355	0.420	0.367	...	...	...	...	...
1994	...	0.433	0.376	...	...	...	...	...
1995	...	0.415	0.365	0.290	0.469	0.397	0.329	...
1996	0.357	0.398	0.351	0.390	...	...	...	...
1997	...	0.398	0.350	...	...	...	...	...
1998	...	0.403	0.354	...	...	...	...	...
1999	0.392	0.416	0.364	...	...	...	...	...
2000	...	0.438	0.385	0.390	...	0.411	0.347	...
2001	...	0.447	0.395	...	...	...	...	...
2002	0.426	...	...	0.454	0.468	...	...	...
2003	...	...	...	0.449	...	...	...	0.479
2004	...	...	...	...	...	...	...	0.473
2005	0.425	...	...	...	...	0.457	0.388	0.485
2006	...	...	...	...	...	...	...	0.487
2007	...	...	...	...	0.497	...	...	0.484
2008	0.426	...	...	...	...	...	...	0.491
2009	0.421	...	...	...	...	...	...	0.490
2010	...	...	...	...	...	...	...	0.481
2011	...	...	...	...	...	...	...	0.477
2012	...	...	...	...	...	...	...	0.474
2013	...	...	...	...	...	...	...	0.473

Note. ... = data not available, WIID = World Income Inequality Database of UNU-WIDER.
[a]Based on income (1981–1987) and consumption (1990–2009).
[b]China Household Income Project.
Sources: Gustafsson *et al.* (2010) and Li *et al.* (2011) for CHIP data; Lin *et al.* (2010); Ravallion and Chen (2007); National Bureau of Statistics, *Provincial Statistical Yearbooks* in various years; and World Bank, *World Development Indicators*.

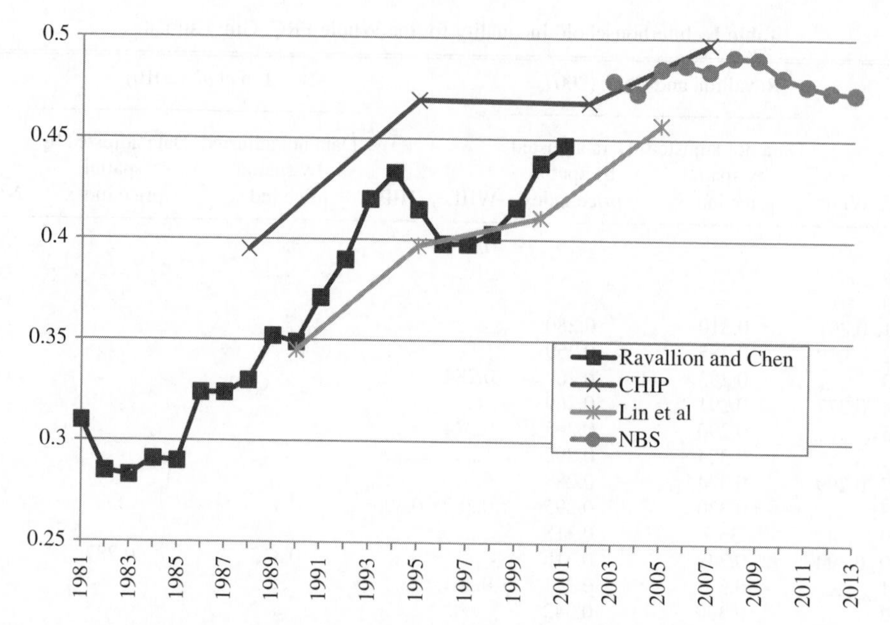

Figure 1. Gini Coefficients Based on Household Survey Data. CHIP = Chinese Household Income Project; NBS = National Bureau of Statistics.

Note: Gini coefficients from Ravallion and Chen (2007) and Lin *et al.* (2010) are based on nonadjusted data.

Sources: Gustafsson *et al.* (2010) and Li *et al.* (2011) for CHIP data; Lin *et al.* (2010); Ravallion and Chen (2007); and National Bureau of Statistics, *Provincial Statistical Yearbooks*.

data are consistently larger and Lin *et al.*'s are consistently smaller than other estimates. The discrepancies can be attributed to the approximation Lin *et al.* (2010) used to obtain unit-record data from grouped data. The CHIP data have a smaller coverage or sample size than the data used by others.

Figure 1 plots the four compatible sets of inequality estimates, all showing a rising trend of income inequality. It is interesting to note that the unadjusted estimates of Ravallion and Chen (2007) appear to be fairly consistent with the official estimates. Thus, one can combine the two sets of estimates to form a more complete time series. Doing this shows that income inequality declined from the onset of economic reform until the mid 1980s and since then has been rising amid some fluctuations. Over a short period of 30 years, inequality as indicated by the Gini coefficient grew by more than 50% from 0.283 in 1983 to 0.491 in 2008 or 0.473 in 2013.

Apart from these nation-wide estimates, researchers attempted to estimate interhousehold inequality at the subnational level. These studies, all using the CHIP data, include Zhao (2001) and Li *et al.* (2011) on rural inequality and Khan *et al.* (2001), Demurger *et al.* (2006), and Li *et al.* (2011) on urban inequality. Zhao (2001) found that the Gini coefficient for the rural PRC rose from 0.338 in 1988 to 0.416 in 1995. This inequality dropped to 0.354 in 2002 and 0.358 in 2007 (Li *et al.*, 2011). Turning to urban inequality, Khan *et al.* (2001) estimated the Gini coefficient to be 0.233 in 1988 and 0.332 in 1995. Demurger *et al.* (2006) accounted for spatial price differences and their Gini estimates are 0.191 in 1988, 0.298 in 1995, and 0.284 in 2002. Li *et al.* (2011) produced Gini estimates of 0.331 in 2002 and 0.340 in 2007.

2.2 *Profile of Regional Inequality*

Balanced regional development has been a major government goal in the PRC for hundreds of years. This is not surprising as underdevelopment of border areas has been considered a major threat to national security or sovereignty. Looking back at the PRC's long history, the authority has frequently encountered revolutions or uprisings arising from unequal distributions and relied on border prosperity to enhance national sovereignty.[7] Also, regional inequality is closely related to ethnic tensions. Today, around 75% of the PRC's minorities live in the poor inland areas which are home to only 22% of the national population. Rising regional gaps may undermine national unity. This is one of the major considerations underlying the massive west development campaign launched in late 1999.

Regional inequality usually refers to interprovincial gaps. Lardy (1978) estimated Coefficients of Variation (CVs) using provincial data on Gross Values of Industrial Output (GVIO) for the years 1952, 1957, and 1974. The results showed declining inequality. There are two problems with this analysis. The CV is not an appropriate inequality measure as it violates the important transfer axiom which states that any progressive transfer leads to a reduction in inequality. Also, the variable of GVIO used to represent living standard or welfare failed to include agricultural output, which comprised a large proportion of national output until the late 1970s. To rectify the second problem, Paine (1981) compiled the gross value of agricultural output data for 1952 at the provincial level, and discussed inter-provincial output differentials. However, he did not estimate inequality by any indices.

Lyons (1991) extended the work of Lardy (1978) by estimating CVs and standard deviations (SDs) using provincial accounts data from 1952 to 1987. Instead of gross output, he used the variables of per capita consumption and Net Material Product (NMP).[8] He found that the CV of NMP declined from 1952 to 1967, was stable from 1967 to 1976, and resumed the declining trend from 1976 to 1987. On the other hand, SDs increased almost continuously since 1962, accelerating in the 1980s. This is not surprising as SD is not only scale-dependent but also mean-dependent. It is very rare to use SD to measure inequality. When the consumption variable was used, its CV displayed a clear downward trend over the period under study, at least until the early 1980s.

Tsui (1991) employed the Gini, Theil, and CV indices to estimate regional inequality from 1952 to 1985, using NMP and NIU (National Income Utilized) data. Discrepancies in inequality based on these two data sets reflect the redistributional effects of government transfers (T) as $NIU = NMP_{agri} + NMP_{nonagri} + T$. Regional inequality had no apparent long-term trend before the 1970s but has since been increasing, and not surprisingly, government transfers led to lower inequality. The inequality trends by different indicators are very similar, which is understandable as inequality estimates based on different inequality indicators are highly correlated (Sharrocks and Wan, 2005).

Kanbur and Zhang (2005) updated regional inequality estimates using consumption data from 1953 to 2000. This period can be divided into six sub-periods: (1) Presocialism (1949–1956), (2) the Great Leap Forward and the Great Famine (1957–1961), (3) Post-famine recovery (1962–1965), (4) Cultural Revolution (1966–1978), (5) Rural reform (1979–1984), and (6) Post-rural reform and opening up (1985–2000).

Figure 2 plots the estimates by Tsui (1991) and Kanbur and Zhang (2005). Their estimates share a similar trend, including peaks. While Kanbur and Zhang's estimates are slightly higher during the first and third periods, estimates from both studies became almost identical for the period of the Cultural Revolution. For the post-reform period, Tsui's estimates became higher.

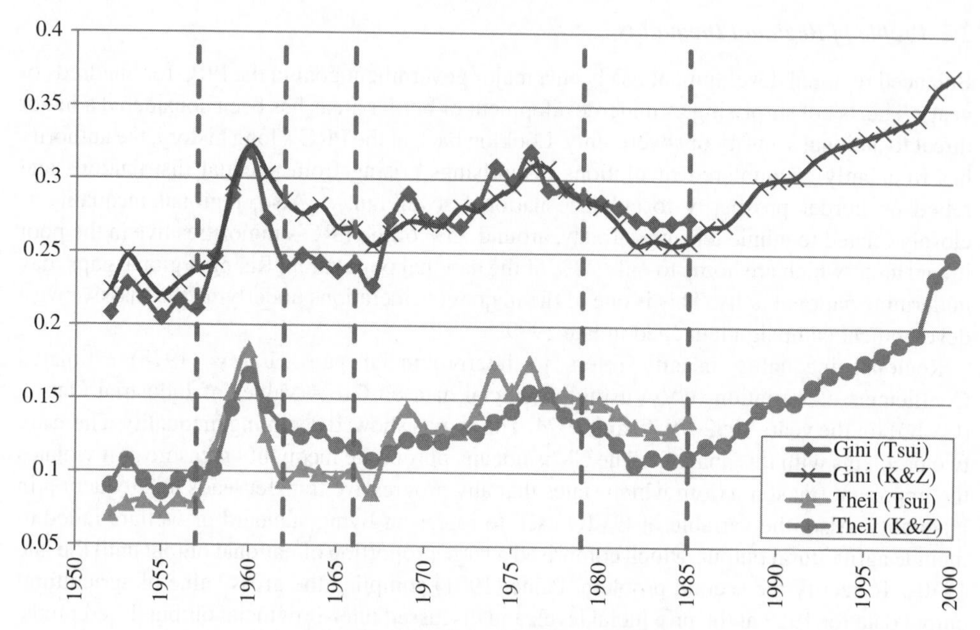

Figure 2. Regional Inequality in the PRC.

Source: Based on Kanbur and Zhang (2005) and Tsui (1991) using NMP.

Figure 2 demonstrates an overall upward trend of regional inequality in the PRC. It was low during the early years of communist rule but increased sharply during the Great Leap Forward, peaking in 1960. It then started steadily declining until the postfamine recovery. The Cultural Revolution saw inequality rise, peaking before the start of the rural reform. Possible reasons include the disruption of central planning, stagnation of agricultural regions, and continued industrialization pushing in the northeast and the east (Zhang and Zou, 2012).

In the first few years of the postreform period, regional inequality declined because of the improvements in agricultural productivity and procurement prices of grains. Rapid development of Township and Village Enterprises (TVEs) also helped boost rural income (Zhou *et al.*, 1992). Rapid rural growth led to the narrowing of the urban–rural gap, a large component of overall regional inequality (Wan, 2007). But regional inequality rose from the mid-1980s, by which time the reform focus had shifted to urban areas while the impacts of the household production responsibility system leveled off.[9] Meanwhile, region-biased policies were instituted to attract FDI and promote trade in coastal areas. In 2000, regional inequality reached its highest level in the People's Republic era.

The latest regional inequality estimates are provided by Wan (2013), as shown in Figure 3. Wan (2013) used income data (net income for rural residents and disposable income for urban residents) at provincial level to estimate the Theil index over the period 1978–2010. Again, Figures 2 and 3 share a broadly similar trend for the overlapping years although the Theil indices in Figure 3 are more conservative than those of Kanbur and Zhang (2005). Also, Kanbur and Zhang's estimates are consistently on the uptrend for the latest period while Wang and Wan's Theil values exhibited a downward trend from 1994 to 1998. The decrease in inequality from 1995 to 1998 can be attributed to the major reform to the taxation system in 1994 which corrected some of the regional imbalances, the provincial governor grain-bag responsibility

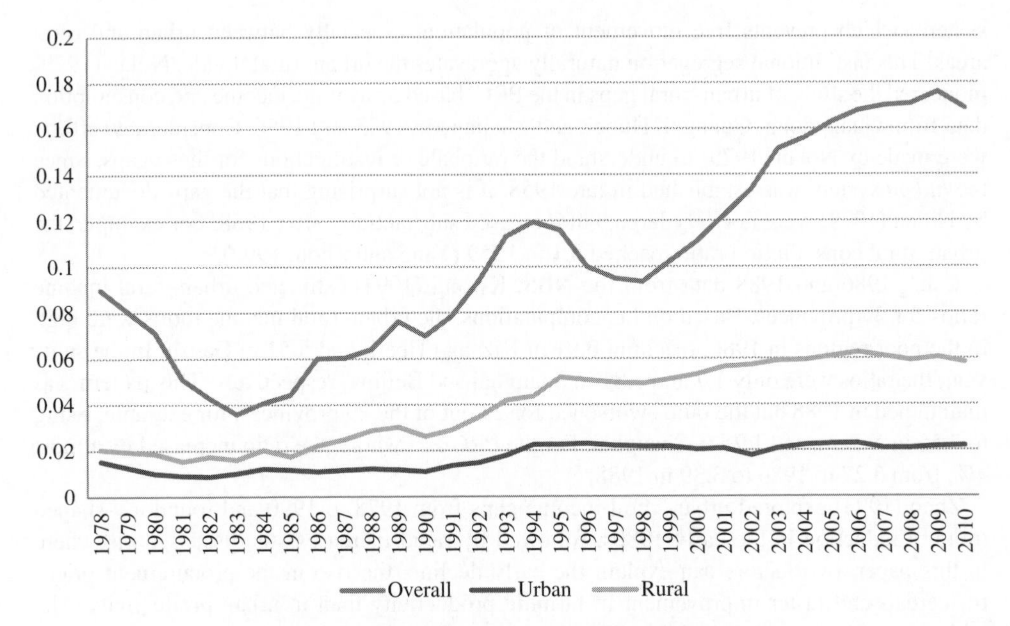

Figure 3. Regional Inequality in the PRC: Theil Index.

system[10] implemented in 1995 (Wan and Zhou, 2005) which helped raise rural income, and the Asian financial crisis which adversely affected rich regions more.

Figure 3 also shows regional inequality within the rural and urban PRC. Very much like interhousehold inequality, rural inequality across provinces has always been higher than the urban counterpart. However, unlike interhousehold inequality, where urban inequality has been growing faster and has approached its rural counterpart, regional inequality within the rural PRC has diverged away from its urban counterpart.

A commonly discussed component of regional inequality is the east-central-west divide. The PRC's provinces are often classified into three groups geographically.[11] How important is this divide to total regional inequality? As demonstrated by Wan (2007), this divide contributed around 30% of total regional inequality and the contribution is fairly stable over time. Another widely discussed component of regional inequality is the coast–inland disparity, where the central and west provinces are merged to form the inland area and the east is taken as the coastal area. In addition to its location advantages, the latter had better infrastructure and economic bases even before the reform (Song *et al.*, 2000). These were exacerbated from the mid-1980s when the opening up strategy was implemented, providing the coastal provinces with favorable fiscal, investment, and taxation policies. Consequently, the coast–inland gap increased over time. According to Zhang and Zhang (2003), the coast–inland ratio in terms of per capita GDP rose from 1.12 in 1985 to 1.45 in 1998. In terms of per capita domestic capital investment, the ratio increased by 26%, from 1.2 in 1985 to 1.52 in 1998.

2.3 *The Profile and Importance of the Urban–Rural Disparity*

The urban–rural gap is a common feature in many developing economies (Shorrocks and Wan, 2005). However, it takes on special significance in the PRC because of the notorious *hukou* system, which prevents free movement of population, especially between urban and rural areas. This institutional segregation naturally aggravates the urban–rural divide. Nolan (1979) pioneered the study of urban–rural gaps in the PRC, based on average income and consumption data from Guangdong, Guangxi, Hubei, and Zhejiang in 1955 and 1956. Considerable efforts were made by Nolan (1979) to understand the rationale or justifications for these gaps. Since the *hukou* system was established in late 1958, it is not surprising that the gaps documented by Nolan (1979) were not very large, but increased substantially after 1958. For example, the urban–rural consumption ratio reached 3.1 in 1959 (Yang and Zhou, 1999).

Using 1986 and 1988 data from the NBS, Kwong (1994) estimated urban–rural income ratios for 29 provinces. Based on his computations, the urban–rural income ratios were high in the poor regions in 1986, reaching 6.91 in Xizang (Tibet), and 5.51 in Gansu. In the same year, the ratios were only 1.7 and 1.81 in Shanghai and Beijing, respectively. This pattern was maintained in 1988 but the ratios worsened for 23 out of the 29 provinces, for example, rising to 7.55 in Xizang and 1.75 in Shanghai. For the PRC as a whole, the ratio increased by almost 4%, from 3.27 in 1986 to 3.39 in 1988.

Zhao (1993) explored urban–rural income gaps from 1978 to 1990 and found a v-shaped trend: a reduction in the early 1980s, followed by rapid increases. As discussed elsewhere in this paper, two factors can explain the early decline: the rise in the procurement prices for cereals and faster improvement in farming productivity than in urban productivity. The widening of the gap after the mid-1980s was due to the shift of reform focus to urban sectors and the waning effects of policy shocks on the rural economy. Instead of income, Yang and Zhou (1999) explored urban–rural consumption ratios. They found that the ratio reached its lowest level of 2.2 in 1985 and started increasing after that. Using the 1995 and 2002 CHIP data, Sicular *et al.* (2007) computed urban–rural income ratios. Adding housing-related income (an income component not included in the NBS definition),[12] the urban–rural income ratio rose from 3.11 in 1995 to 3.18 in 2002. These values are 10% and 6% higher than those with housing-related income excluded. After adjusting for spatial price differences, the ratio became 2.24 in 1995 and 2.27 in 2002.

Wan *et al.* (2012) obtained urban–rural income ratios for individual provinces for the period 1978–2009. The ratio declined from 1978 to 1985 but has generally risen since 1985. The correlation between overall inequality and the urban–rural ratio is quite clear. In particular, the ratio was low for 1983 and 1984, forcefully demonstrating the impact on rural income of government support in terms of grain price rises in the early years of reform. The declines after the mid-1990s can be attributed to the introduction of the so-called ‘provincial governor grain bag responsibility system’. Despite this policy shock, the urban–rural income ratio maintained a generally increasing trend until 2009. At the national level, the ratio almost doubled from 1.9:1 in 1985 to 3.3:1 in 2009.

Figure 4 shows the ratio of average urban disposable income to average rural net income from 1952 to 2012 and the urban–rural consumption ratio from 1952 to 1992. Clearly, the gaps have widened since the mid-1980s. It was close to 3 in 1995 and has moved beyond 3 since 2002. By international standards, and even after various adjustments such as spatial price deflation and including migrants in the urban sample, the PRC's urban–rural inequality is high (Sicular *et al.*, 2007).

The PRC's urban–rural income gap has a distinct regional dimension. It is present in all provinces, rich or poor, eastern, central, or western. In 2007, it was largest in the western and eastern PRC, with ratios of 3.85 and 3.44, respectively. Sicular (2013) observed that between 2002 and 2007, excluding large municipalities such as Beijing and Shanghai, this ratio rose

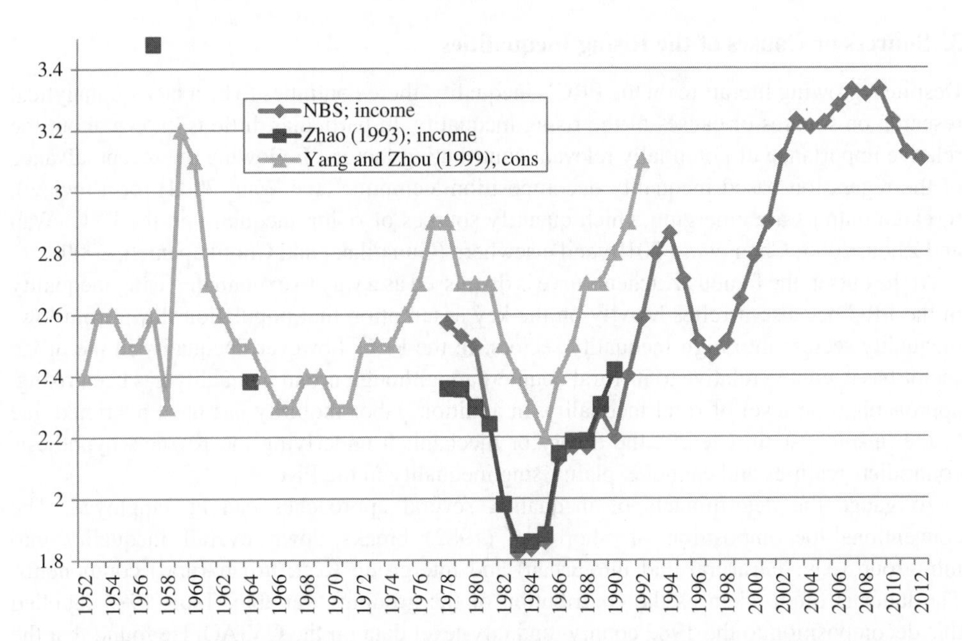

Figure 4. The PRC's Urban–Rural Income and Consumption Ratios, 1952–2012.

Sources: National Bureau of Statistics (various years); urban–rural consumption ratio from Yang and Zhou (1999).

by a remarkable 43% in the east, as compared to 27% in the central PRC, and only 3% in the west. The reason for these regional differences merits further investigation.

It is worth noting that Figures 1–4 share a similar trend. This highlights the importance of the urban–rural gap in both regional and interhousehold inequalities. In fact, it is possible to gauge the contribution of the urban–rural gap to total regional and nation-wide interhousehold inequalities. For example, according to Wan (2007), the PRC's urban–rural income gap has been a central factor underlying regional income inequality, contributing 70–80% of total regional inequality. Using the NBS data of cities and counties for the year 1994, Lee (2000) found that the urban–rural disparity accounted for 26% of overall regional inequality in per capita gross value of industrial and agricultural output (GVIAO), and 37.7% of per capita consumption. These contributions are smaller than those produced by Wan (2007) and Liu (2010). Similar to Wan (2007), Liu (2010) showed that in terms of regional income inequality, the contribution of the urban–rural gap was 57.98% in 1997, increasing over time and reaching 72.84% in 2006. In terms of regional consumption inequality, the gap contributed no less than 75% over the entire period of 1995–2006, reaching as high as 79.46% in 2006.

The contribution of the urban–rural gap to total interhousehold inequality was investigated by Sicular *et al.* (2007), using CHIP data. Without adjusting for spatial price differences, the urban–rural gap accounted for about 40% of regional income inequality in 1995, rising to 45% in 2002. Adjusting for spatial price differences, however, reduces the contribution noticeably, to less than 30% in 1995 and about 30–32% in 2002. This is consistent with Gustafsson and Li (1998) who concluded that if average income in rural and urban was equalized, holding inequality within urban and rural unchanged, almost one-third of inequality in the PRC would disappear.

3. Sources or Causes of the Rising Inequalities

Despite a growing literature on the PRC's inequality, there continues to be a lack of analytical research on sources or causes of the rising inequality. In particular, little is known about the relative importance of potentially relevant contributing factors. Following the recent advance of the regression-based inequality decomposition technique (see Wan (2004) for a review), research outputs are emerging which quantify sources of rising inequality in the PRC (Wan and Zhou, 2005; Chen *et al.*, 2010) and elsewhere (Gunatilaka and Chotikapanich, 2009).

At the outset, the famous Kuznets curve is dismissed as a way to explain the rising inequality in the PRC because it relies heavily on the key assumption that population flows from low-inequality sectors into high-inequality sectors. In the PRC, however, inequality in the urban sector has been low relative to its rural counterpart, although urban inequality has been rising, approaching the level of rural inequality. In addition, labor mobility has been restricted due to the *hukou* system. Clearly, the theory or mechanism underlying the Kuznets hypothesis contradicts realities and cannot explain rising inequality in the PRC.

To gauge the determinants of inequality, several approaches can be employed. The conventional decomposition of Shorrocks (1982) breaks down overall inequality into intragroup (e.g., intrarural and intraurban) and intergroup (e.g., urban–rural) components. The latter is often taken as the contribution of the grouping variable. Tsui (1993) applied this decomposition to the 1982 county- and city-level data on the GVIAO. He found that the interprovince component constituted only 36% of the total. Grouping the data into rural and urban areas, total inequality consisted of 52% from urban–rural gaps, 40% from intrarural gaps, and 8% from intraurban gaps.

Using the same approach, Kanbur and Zhang (1999), Bhalla *et al.* (2003), and Wan (2007) confirmed the dominance of the rural–urban component in total regional inequality. However, this component was found to be increasing over time by Wan (2007) but stable by Kanbur and Zhang (1999). On the contrary, the contribution of the inland–coastal gaps to total regional inequality was found to be stable over time by Kanbur and Zhang (1999) but increasing by Wan (2007). These different results may arise from the use of different data. Generally speaking, the income data used by Wan (2007) is better than GDP or other gross output variables as a well-being measure.

Figure 5a provides an update to Wan (2007). It shows the dominance of the urban–rural component throughout the entire period. Figure 5b confirms the constancy of the east-central-west divide in terms of its contribution to total regional inequality, implying that it is a less important contributor relative to the urban–rural gap.

However, the conventional decomposition is problematic for identifying fundamental determinants of inequality. For example, if one uses gender to group a sample and finds a very large between-sex component, this component cannot be exclusively attributed to gender discrimination unless everything else remains the same for the male and female subsamples. If males possess higher human capital, its impact on income would be captured by the 'between' component. In other words, the between-group component is usually contaminated.

The use of conditional convergence modeling requires estimation of growth regressions, with variables such as location, physical and human capital, infrastructure, institutions, and policies controlled for (Chen and Fleisher, 1996). These conditioning variables, which represent the heterogeneous steady states, are considered to drive income inequality. Ding *et al.* (2008) provided evidence on conditional convergence in the PRC over the period 1986–2002. According to them, it would take 40–60 years to eliminate half of the gap between the lagging

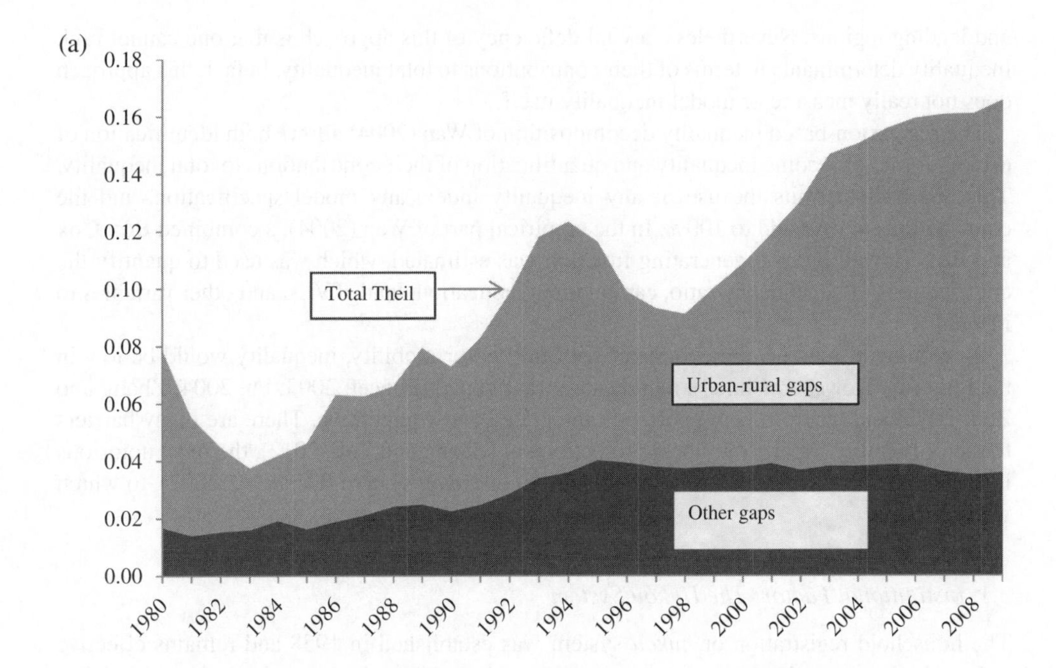

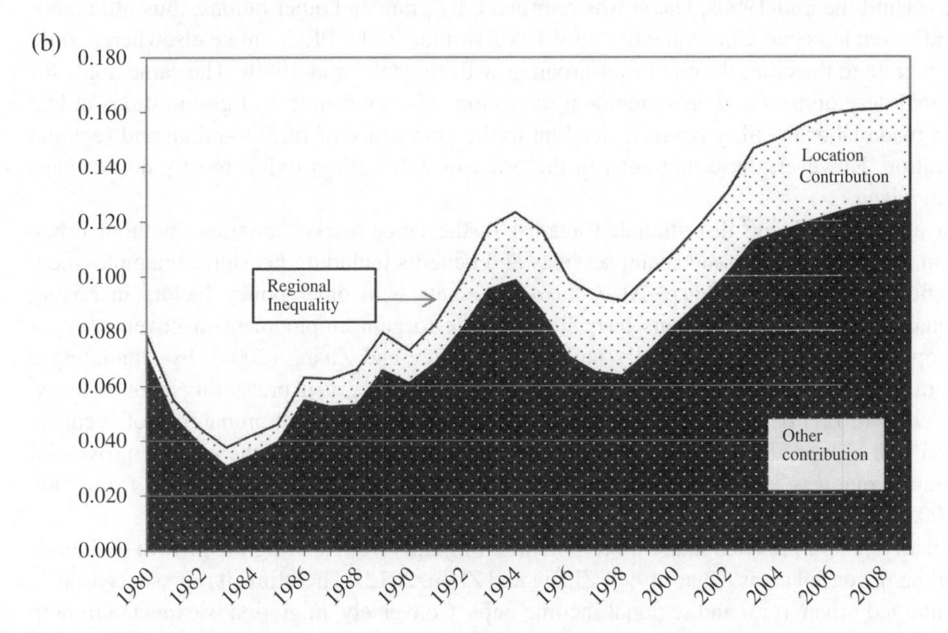

Figure 5. (a) Contribution of Urban–Rural Gap to Regional Inequality in the PRC, 1980–2009
(b) Contribution of Location to Regional Inequality in the PRC, 1980–2009.

and leading regions. Nevertheless, a vital deficiency of this approach is that one cannot rank inequality determinants in terms of their contributions to total inequality. In fact, this approach does not really measure or model inequality itself.

The regression-based inequality decomposition of Wan (2004) allows both identification of driving forces of income inequality and quantification of their contributions to total inequality. This approach permits the use of any inequality index, any model specification, and the contributions always add to 100%. In the empirical part of Wan (2004), a combined Box-Cox and Box-Tidwell income-generating function was estimated, which was used to quantify the contributions of dependency ratio, capital input, education, land, TVEs, and other variables to inequality.

Assuming all markets are complete, with full factor mobility, inequality would be low in the long run. However, Chinese markets are fragmented (Poncet, 2003; Fu, 2004; Zhang and Zou, 2012) and far from being perfectly integrated and competitive. There are many barriers to factor mobility. Apart from local protectionism (Zhang and Zou, 2012), the most notorious institutional barrier is the household registration or *hukou* system (Cai *et al.*, 2002), to which we now turn.

3.1 *Institutional Factor: The Hukou System*

The household registration or *hukou* system was established in 1958 and remains effective today. Until the mid-1990s, *hukou* was reinforced by grain and other rations, thus little labor mobility could occur. Consequently, rural labor surplus in the PRC, unlike elsewhere, could not migrate to the cities despite faster urban growth since the mid-1980s. The same holds for regional development and cross-regional migration. The abolishment of grain rations in late 1993 made labor mobility possible, leading to the emergence of rural-to-urban and regional migration. However, these migrants, in the order of 260 million today, mostly do not have urban *hukou*.

In addition to being discriminated against in the labor market, migrants without urban *hukou* are denied most basic social services and benefits including pensions, unemployment benefits, and health insurance. Also, *hukou* interacts with other policy factors in raising inequality. Even today, migrants have little chance to gain employment in government or monopoly industries which usually pay well. Whalley and Zhang (2007), by simulating a general equilibrium model, confirmed the significant role of *hukou* in preventing labor mobility. Bao *et al.* (2011) demonstrated that a 1% increase in the perceived probability of securing *hukou* will induce an 11.85% increase in the migration rate whereas the average provincial migration rate was 3.775 from 1985 to 1990, 3.589 from 1995 to 2000, and 3.655 from 2000 to 2005.

Clearly, *hukou* prevents many more potential migrants from sharing the growth dividends in urban or coastal areas (Zhao, 1999; Zhang and Zhou, 2012). Therefore, it represents a cause of enlarged urban–rural and regional income gaps. Conversely, migration is expected to help moderate these gaps as it not only offers migrant workers better job opportunities and allows them to share urban outputs, but also helps lessen the pressure of land shortage in the rural areas and allows those left behind more work and investment opportunities (Zhu and Luo, 2010). Moreover, remittance from migrants helps raise rural incomes and promote investment and consumption in the rural PRC (Sicular, 2013).

However, Sicular *et al.* (2007) noted that overall inequality shows no clear upward or downward trend as the migrant population share increases. They argue that migrants tend to have characteristics more similar to urban residents (younger, better educated, smaller households), so relocation of this subset of the rural population does not significantly alter the urban–rural gap as much as would movement of 'average' rural residents. However, their inference holds all other factors constant and does not take into account the effects of migration on the incomes of those remaining behind in rural areas or those with urban *hukou*. Also, Ito (2008) suggested that the removal of *hukou* may not help eradicate rural–urban inequality, because migration may lead to the decline of the rural industrial sectors. It is not clear if the decline of TVEs in terms of their output share in the rural economy from 52% in 1995 to 28% in 2000 as documented by Ito (2008) is caused by migration. The decline may be driven by business relocations or competition from urban industries.

3.2 *Policy Issues*

Regional development policies and the opening up of the coastal cities contributed directly to rising inequalities (Zhang and Zou, 2012). Preferential investment, taxation, and banking policies for the coastal region expedited its economic growth and technological leadership. Industrial agglomeration then took place. By comparison, it was not until 1991 that the government opened up inland areas. By then, the inland areas may have already lost the capability to compete with the coast (Feng, 2004).

The fiscal system in the PRC is dis-equalizing. Before the reforms, the PRC had a highly centralized fiscal system where the central government alone prepared budgets and collected revenue. Even the State-Owned Enterprises (SOEs) were part of the state financial system. After the major decentralization reform of the fiscal system in 1994 (Lin and Liu, 2000), aimed at arresting the free fall of the ratio of government revenue to GDP and the share of central government in total government revenue (Wang, 1997), fiscal disparities have increased (Zhao, 2009). In 1995, the government introduced an equalization grant to curb the fiscal disparity. Unfortunately, the grants and other discretionary transfers failed to redistribute resources. The grants, instead of targeting the poorer provinces, were used to reward local governments who were loyal to upper levels of government (Shen *et al.*, 2012).

Now, the PRC has one of the most decentralized fiscal systems in the world, particularly on the spending side. More than half of all expenditure takes place at the subprovincial level. Poor areas have very little tax revenue and hence cannot fund basic social services. The richest province has more than eight times the per capita public spending of the poorest province. The situation is worse at the subprovincial level. The richest county (the level that is most important for service delivery) has about 48 times the level of per capita spending of the poorest county (Dollar and Hofman, 2008). These differences in public spending translate into differences in social outcomes such as health and school enrolment rates, with profound implications for current and future inequalities.

The *hukou*-related urban biases represent another determinant of inequality (Yang, 1999). For example, rural households received much less in terms of transfers and subsidies than did urban households. Although removing the agriculture tax in 2006 was a step in the right direction, tax and subsidy payments still favor urban residents (Wang and Piesse, 2010). The urban biases also interact with biases toward SOEs because few rural residents can gain employment in SOEs. The latter biases, particularly in terms of energy and credit subsidies, reinforce intersector gaps which have risen significantly over time (Chen *et al.*, 2010).

3.3 *Location or Geographic Factors*

Geography matters. In addition to preferential policies, coastal provinces benefit from location advantages for exports, better infrastructure, and more human capital, although the inland areas have more natural resources and higher population growth rates (Lu, 2008). Demurger *et al.* (2002) quantified the effect of both policy (preferential policy index) and geography (ability to participate in international trade) variables, finding that geography and policy had about equal influence on coastal growth. Geography also plays a major role in determining the urban–rural income gap (Gustafsson and Li, 1998). According to Sicular *et al.* (2007), about 46% of the urban–rural gap in 1995 could be attributed to location dummy variables and constant terms: that contribution increased to 81% in 2002.

Nevertheless, the contribution of location to regional inequality may be declining over time. According to Wan *et al.* (2007), the contribution of east-central-west gaps in composing regional inequality has dropped from almost 18% in 1987 to just over 15% in 2001. These results are broadly in line with the decomposition results shown in Figure 5b. The between component (largely indicating location impacts) is small and may decline further as infrastructure develops, labor mobility improves, and urbanization proceeds. This finding corroborates the findings of Chen and Zheng (2008), who used data from 100 villages in nine provinces to study rural inequality. They found that less than half of inequality was due to between-village factors.

3.4 *External Factors: Trade and FDI*

The benefits of trade and capital flows to economic development are well-known and they can be amplified indirectly via the multiplier effect. Of course, the coastal PRC gained much more than the inland area (and urban areas more than rural) from the open-door policies (Fujita and Hu, 2001). In 1999, the degree of openness, (imports + exports + FDI)/GDP, was 64.47% for the 11 coastal provinces, but under 10% for the 8 central and 12 western provinces (Yin, 2004). It is thus not surprising for Wei *et al.* (2009) to have found that FDI generated a consistent and positive effect on growth differences between regions. In addition, firms with FDI usually offer higher salaries, thus FDI contributes to the wage gap between firms and individuals (Wu, 2005; Tian *et al.*, 2011). Furthermore, Kanbur and Zhang (2005) regressed the coastal–inland inequality component on various determinants and showed that openness and decentralization contributed to the rapid increase in inland–coastal disparity in the reform period of the 1980s and 1990s.

According to Wan *et al.* (2007), trade accounted for 12% of regional inequality in the late 1980s and grew to more than 14% in early 2000s. The contribution of FDI also rose, from 5% to almost 7% from 1987 to 2001. Adding these two together, globalization has contributed more than 20% to total regional inequality in the PRC since 1999, overtaking capital as the sole most important driver of inequality. These findings are consistent with those of Zhang and Zhang (2003) who used CV as a measure of inequality.

3.5 *Other Factors*

Education and skills are the major means for obtaining earnings, thus inequalities in these areas must help drive inequality. Ito (2008) noted that human capital-related factors are largely responsible for the increased rural–urban disparity, more than 25% of which can be explained by the schooling variable (Sicular *et al.*, 2007). Based on the 2002 CHIP data, educational inequality accounts for as much as 36% of self-employment income inequality, but it only accounts for 2% of rural inequality (Liu and Sicular, 2009). Thus, as urbanization proceeds, education is expected to play a much more significant role in affecting inequality.

Unfortunately, regional gaps in human capital are large. As Yin (2004) highlighted, in 2000, the eastern region had 5.98% of its population with college or higher degrees, relative to only 2.97% in the western region. As another example, 7.4% of employees were illiterate in the eastern region in 1999, much lower than the 16.25% in the western region. Using enrolment data, Lee (2008) found increasing educational inequality across provinces and the disparity became worse at higher levels of the educational ladder. Meanwhile, returns on education were found to be on the rise in the PRC, further aggravating the inequality impacts of educational endowments.

Worse still, educational attainment is highly correlated with provincial innovation activities (Chi and Qian, 2010). Controlling for a set of variables, Wang and Zhang (2003) found a significant correlation between knowledge disparity (particularly in public spending on knowledge advancement and educational attainment) and economic inequalities.

Finally, a number of studies have indicated that households headed by a member of the Communist party are on average better off than others, but decomposition results show that gaps in average household income between households headed by party members and those by nonparty members contributed little to total interhousehold inequality. The same can be concluded regarding ethnicity (Gustafsson and Li, 1998).

4. Suggested Interventions

As far as policy options are concerned, the urban–rural gap and regional inequality deserve priority consideration. Eliminating the former is possible and will cut interhousehold inequality by one-third. While it is not possible to eliminate regional inequality, encouraging migration and developing transport and telecommunication infrastructure can help lower inequality considerably. When combined with other interventions, the PRC can contain and eventually reverse the rising trend of inequality.

4.1 *Tackling the Urban–Rural Gaps: Urbanization*

Since the urban–rural gap has been the largest component of income inequality in the PRC, tackling this should be a policy priority. It is important to point out that fiscal policy intervention or redistribution alone would not be sufficient because only a little more than one-third of the PRC's population can be classified as being urban, with the absolute majority of the PRC's population being poor rural residents. Thus, the government must abolish the *hukou* so as to alleviate various kinds of discrimination and allow migrants to enjoy some social protection.

However, abolishing *hukou* is only a necessary but not sufficient condition for bridging the urban–rural gap. In other words, the urban–rural gap will not automatically disappear after abolishing *hukou*. This is demonstrated by the persistence of urban–rural disparity in India, Mexico, and many other countries where labor and population movement is free. Other policy measures (fiscal policy, taxation policy, social protection programs) are needed to support urban settlement of rural residents. In this context, the inability to sell or mortgage rural land represents an obstacle to urbanization. Allowing farmers to trade their land plots not only helps facilitate permanent migration but also helps defray the cost of urban settlement and promote agricultural development. In addition, migrants must be provided with education and training opportunities to enable them to acquire or upgrade skills so they can compete with native urban residents.

To minimize the social and environmental problems potentially associated with massive migration, a step-by-step procedure is necessary where migrants with long-term jobs or secure housing should be given priority. Those with better education should also enjoy concessions. In fact, some cities such as Shenzhen have recently adopted a scoring system, with demographic and other characteristics of potential migrants being taken into consideration. To ease fiscal pressure, new migrants may be provided with limited access to financial assistance in housing, education, health care, and other welfare provisions. Community colleges could be set up in the cities to provide training and education to temporary and long-term migrants and their family members.

4.2 *Tackling Regional Inequality*

Underlying regional inequality are cross-regional differences in human and physical capital endowments and other economic conditions (such as proximity to the global market). According to Wan *et al.* (2007), equalization of domestic capital on a per capita basis across regions will cut regional inequality by 20%. To narrow these gaps, greater public investment in infrastructure, and productive capabilities in the lagging regions should be prioritized. In particular, continued financial reform is necessary in order to improve access to finance in inland provinces and rural areas. While various government entities and financial institutions are experimenting with microcredit schemes, such schemes must cater for capital formation.

Meanwhile, it is important to promote trade and FDI in the inland PRC. Policy biases that helped expand trade and FDI but are gradually being phased out in the coastal PRC should be implemented in inland provinces to create a better environment for attracting and absorbing FDI (Wei *et al.*, 2009). Since firms are attracted to locations with better infrastructure (Sridhar and Wan, 2010), infrastructure investment in the PRC should continue in the more backward regions (Ding *et al.*, 2008; Demurger *et al.*, 2002). Such public infrastructure investments are effective in reducing regional disparities (Vijverberg *et al.*, 2011). Zou *et al.* (2008) found that reducing roading inequality would lead to a reduction of income inequality. Infrastructure investment, particularly in the rural areas, could facilitate rural–urban migration and achieve more rapid technological progress in the rural sector (Liu and Zou, 2011).

Fundamental changes are needed in the collection and allocation of fiscal resources across regions (Gao, 2008). An equalization in fiscal support would lead to an almost 15% drop in regional inequality and a progressive fiscal scheme would result in a much larger impact (Wan *et al.*, 2007). Fiscal transfers should be conditional, geared toward capital formation and education of the young. Public research and development investment in agriculture should be increased to improve farming productivity, as agriculture has been the major part of the economy of the inland areas. Special attention shall be paid to the quality of schooling in poor areas, where school fees in compulsory education have been abolished since 2005.

Reform of the fiscal system should include centralization of public spending on basic services to eliminate disparities. In the USA, the poorest state has about 65% of the revenue of the average state, and in Germany, any state falling below 95% of the average level is subsidized through the '*Finanzausgleich*', while any receiving more than 110% are taxed (Dollar and Hofman, 2008).

4.3 *Hukou Reform and Social Protection*

There is consensus that the *hukou* system must be reformed, as highlighted in the *Decision on Major Issues Concerning Comprehensively Deepening Reforms* that was adopted at the Third Plenum of the 18th Central Committee of the Chinese Communist Party. While experiments have been undertaken in a couple of provinces, they are largely designed to reform *hukou* for residents within provincial borders. How to reform *hukou* at the national level remains a daunting task.

Besides ensuring a minimum living standard for all, which is already in place, a well-functioning social protection system helps the poor and the vulnerable to invest in human and possibly physical capital, which is essential for improving income distribution in the long run. This will become increasingly important as aging and migration gain momentum. While social protection in terms of pension, health care, and unemployment benefits are more advanced in urban areas, the rural sector is significantly lagging behind, not only in terms of breath and depth of coverage, but also in terms of level of benefits. Similar differences also exist between provinces which may adversely affect labor mobility across provincial borders. These differences must be addressed.

One of the most serious problems lies in the nonportability of various benefits. Overcoming this problem calls for a centralized social welfare system where individuals can have access irrespective of their location of residence and *hukou* status. While there is still a long way to go as far as social protection is concerned, it is important not to develop into a welfare state. The lessons of overshooting experienced by Australia and Canada ought to be borne in mind.

4.4 *Other Proposed Remedies*

It is widely accepted that job creation will help moderate income inequality as the poor and vulnerable mainly have labor as their only resource, while the rich often have capital and other resources. To enhance job creation, growth must be maintained, particularly in the labor-intensive tertiary sector. At present, the services sector contributes about 40% of GDP and around 35% of total employment, both low. If international experience is any guide, the services sector should account for 50–60% of national GDP and total employment at the current stage of development. A simple calculation projects the need for 400–456 million jobs in the services sector, implying a gap of 150–200 million. It must be pointed out that these calculations have not taken into account new jobs to be generated by economic growth, which is expected to remain high and sustainable for the next 20–30 years.

The roles of central and local governments should be clear and properly defined to help in the reallocation of fiscal resources (Shen *et al.*, 2012). Local governments should focus on public services and social development while the national government should focus on regional equalization.

Further ownership reform is needed to break down state monopoly by removing various subsidies to SOEs and introducing private investment in currently protected sectors (Feng, 2004). As the state sector still accounts for a major share of the economy in the inland PRC, such ownership reforms are expected to boost growth more in the inland areas and help bridge regional inequality (Yin, 2004). Also, concerted effort should be made to promote the private sector as the rapid economic growth of the eastern region has been closely associated with the development of the private sector (Hao and Wei, 2010).

Meanwhile, antiprotection regulations should be enacted to remove inter-regional trade protection (Zhang and Zou, 2012). An integrated domestic market with less government intervention not only helps promote economic development but also facilitates mobility and improvement of income distribution (Hao and Wei, 2010).

5. Summary and Areas for Future Research

In the prereform PRC, egalitarian distribution was only implemented in the urban sector and within production teams of the rural sector. Thus, sizable income inequality existed, largely attributable to urban–rural gaps and disparities within the rural sector. Economic reforms broke the 'iron rice bowl' in the urban areas and the egalitarian distribution within production teams. Consequently, intrarural and intraurban inequalities have been increasing until recently. However, overall inequality declined in the first few years of reform due to the narrowing of the urban–rural gap, which represents a dominant component of overall inequality. From the mid-1980s until the early 2000s, inequalities in all dimensions in the PRC exhibited increasing trends, leading to a voluminous literature and policy interventions. To what extent these interventions have been effective in containing the rising inequalities requires further research.

Further research is also needed on the impacts of inequality on growth, consumption, crime, health, and human capital formation. There is a lack of analytical work on the consequences of inequality in general, particularly in the PRC. Unless these consequences are properly documented and brought to the attention of policy makers, the urgency and significance of tackling income inequality may be underestimated.

Of course, before appropriate policy interventions can be initiated, it is vital to pin down the causes or sources of worsening income distribution. To this purpose, many studies have employed conventional decomposition techniques to quantify the components of inequality or its changes in the PRC, as reviewed in this paper. Unfortunately, such decompositions cannot identify fundamental determinants of inequality and the results are likely to be contaminated. The more recently advanced regression-based inequality decomposition offers a promising alternative (see Wan, 2004), but its empirical applications in the PRC are limited and should be expanded.

One important research area which so far has attracted little attention relates to the evaluation of various policy interventions. These include the introduction in 2000 of the great western development strategy to tackle the regional divide and in 2005 of the "socialist new countryside development" movement aimed at reducing the urban–rural gaps. In 2006, the government adopted the goal of "building a harmonious society" in its 11th Five-Year Plan. In November 2013, the Third Plenum of the 18th Central Committee of the Chinese Communist Party outlined a systematic approach to tackling the issue of income distribution, through reforms in a wide range of areas including the *hukou* system, social protection, access to public services (particularly education and health care), taxation, and governance.

Acknowledgment

We are grateful to Kristine Briones for research assistance, and Iris Claus and Les Oxley for constructive comments and suggestions. This paper is part of the research output of the PRC's National Natural

Science Foundation Projects 71133004 and 71063022, and Yunnan province's Bairen Jihua (top 100 scientists program).

Notes

1. In this paper, the words gap, divide, and disparity are used as synonyms for inequality.
2. Coastal residents are known to be more business-minded and have more trade and entrepreneurship skills. Most overseas Chinese are from the coastal areas and they provide a significant share of FDI.
3. www.chinadaily.com.cn/bizchina/2012--02/07/content_14549447.htm
4. There are 34 province-level administrative units in the PRC, including 23 provinces, 5 autonomous regions, 4 metropolitan municipalities, and 2 special districts (Hong Kong, China and Macao, China).
5. CHIP was initiated by the Chinese Academy of Social Sciences and later transferred to Beijing Normal University.
6. http://www.stats.gov.cn/english/PressRelease/201401/t20140120_502079.html
7. The PRC had frequently been invaded, particularly from the north and west. Border prosperity was expected to nurture the loyalty of border residents and could help raise border populations, which formed the basis for national defense.
8. This is equivalent to value added in the first or secondary industry. The service sector was not considered to produce material outputs.
9. The household production responsibility system was the very first step in igniting the PRC's reforms. It replaced the inefficient commune system by allocating land to individual farmers and households who became decision makers for agricultural production, marketing, and output distribution. By the end of 1986, all households in the rural PRC had adopted the household production responsibility system.
10. Introduced for food security reasons and also called the "rice bag" system, it mandates that provincial leaders are responsible for maintaining an overall balance of grain supply and demand within their provinces, stabilizing grain production area, output, and stocks, and using local reserves to regulate grain markets and stabilize grain prices (OECD, 1999).
11. The west includes Sichuan, Shannxi, Guizhou, Xinjiang, Tibet, Yunan, Gansu, Qinghai, and Ningxia. The Central provinces include Heilongjiang, Jilin, Inner-Mongolia, Shanxi, Henan, Anhui, Jiangxi, Hubei, and Hunan. The east includes Beijing, Tianjin, Liaoning, Shanghai, Hebei, Shandong, Zhejiang, Jiangsu, Fujian, Guangdong, Hainan, and Guangxi (Zhang and Zou, 2012).
12. This refers to the imputed rental value of owner-occupied housing and imputed subsidies on publicly owned rental housing.

References

Bao, S., Bodvarsson, O., Hou, J. and Zhao, Y. (2011) The regulation of migration in a transition economy: China's Hukou system. *Contemporary Economic Policy* 29(4): 564–579.

Bhalla, A., Yao, S. and Zhang, Z. (2003) Causes of inequalities in China, 1952 to 1999. *Journal of International Development* 15: 939–955.

Cai, F., Wang, D. and Du, Y. (2002) Regional disparity and economic growth in China: the impact of labor market distortions. *China Economic Review* 13(2): 197–212.

Chen, J. and Fleisher, B. (1996) Regional income inequality and economic growth in China. *Journal of Comparative Economics* 22(2): 141–164.

Chen, M. and Zheng, Y. (2008) China's regional disparity and its policy responses. *China and World Economy* 16(4): 16–32.
Chen, Z., Lu, M. and Wan, G. (2010) *Inter-Industry Wage Differentials: An Increasingly Important Contributor to Urban China Income Inequality*. Global COE Hi-Stat Discussion Paper Series gd09–139. Tokyo: Institute of Economic Research, Hitotsubashi University.
Chi, W. and Qian, X. (2010) The role of education in regional innovation activities: spatial evidence from China. *Journal of the Asia Pacific Economy* 15(4): 396–419.
Demurger, S., Fournier, M. and Li, S. (2006) Urban income inequality in China revisited (1988–2002). *Economics Letters* 93(3): 354–359.
Demurger, S., Sachs, J., Woo, W., Bao, S. and Chang, G. (2002) The relative contributions of location and preferential policies in China's regional development: being in the right place and having the right incentives. *China Economic Review* 13, 444–465.
Ding, L., Haynes, K. and Liu, Y. (2008) Telecommunications infrastructure and regional income convergence in China: panel data approaches. *Annals of Regional Science* 42: 843–861.
Dollar, D. and Hofman, B. (2008) Intergovernmental fiscal reforms, expenditure assignment, and governance. In J. Lou and S. Wang (eds), *Public Finance in China: Reform and Growth for a Harmonious Society* (pp. 223–250). Washington, DC: The World Bank.
Eichen, M. and Zhang, M. (1993) Annex: the 1988 household sample survey- data description and availability. In K. Griffin and R. Zhao (eds), *The Distribution of Income in China*. New York: St. Martin's Press.
Feng, J. (2004) Income disparities in China: a review of Chinese studies. In *OECD, Income Disparities in China: An OECD Perspective* (pp. 27–38). Paris, France: OECD Publications.
Fleisher, B.M., Li, H., Li, S. and Wang, X. (2005) Sorting, selection, and transformation of return to college education in China. Working Paper Nos. 05-07, Ohio State University.
Fu, X. (2004) Limited linkages from growth engines and regional disparities in China. *Journal of Comparative Economics* 32(1): 148–164.
Fujita, M. and Hu, D. (2001) Regional disparity in China 1985–1994: the effects of globalization and economic liberalization. *The Annals of Regional Science* 35: 3–37.
Gao, Q. (2008) Social benefits in urban China: determinants and impacts on income inequality in 1988 and 2002. In G. Wan (ed), *Understanding Inequality and Poverty in China: Methods and Applications*, New York: Palgrave Macmillan.
Griffin, K. and Zhao, R. (1993) *The Distribution of Income in China*. New York: St. Martin's Press.
Gunatilaka, R. and Chotikapanich, D. (2009) Accounting for Sri Lanka's expenditure inequality 1980–2002: regression-based decomposition approaches. *Review of Income and Wealth* 55(4): 882–906.
Gustafsson, B. and Li, S. (1998) Inequality in China at the end of the 1980s: locational aspects and household characteristics. *Asian Economic Journal* 12(1): 35–63.
Gustafsson, B. and Li, S. (2001) A more unequal China? Aspects of inequality in the distribution of equivalent income. In C. Riskin, R. Zhao, and S. Li (eds), *China's Retreat from Equality: Income Distribution and Economic Transition*. New York: M. E. Sharpe.
Gustafsson, B., Li, S. and Sicular, T. (2010) *Inequality and Public Policy in China*. New York: Cambridge University Press.
Hao, R. and Wei, Z. (2010) Fundamental causes of inland-coastal income inequality in post-reform China. *Annals of Regional Science* 45(1): 181–206.
Hussain, A., Lanjouw, P. and Stern, N. (1994) Income inequalities in China, evidence from household survey data. *World Development* 22(12): 1947–1957.
Ito, J. (2008) The removal of institutional impediments to migration and its impact on employment, production and income distribution in China. *Economic Change and Restructuring* 41: 239–265.
Kanbur, R. and Zhang, X. (1999) Which regional inequality? The evolution of rural-urban and inland-coastal inequality in China from 1983 to 1995. *Journal of Comparative Economics* 27(4): 686–701.
Kanbur, R. and Zhang, X. (2005) Fifty years of regional inequality in China: a journey through central planning, reform, and openness. *Review of Development Economics* 9(1): 87–106.
Khan, A. and Riskin, C. (1998) Income and inequality in China: composition, distribution and growth of household income, 1988 to 1995. *The China Quarterly* 154: 221–253.
Khan, A. and Riskin, C. (2005) China's household income and its distribution, 1995 and 2002. *The China Quarterly* 182: 356–384.

Khan, A., Griffin, K. and Riskin, C. (2001) Income distribution in urban China during the period of economic reform and globalization. In C. Riskin, R. Zhao, and S. Li (eds), *China's Retreat from Equality: Income Distribution and Economic Transition*, New York: M. E. Sharpe.

Khan, A., Griffin, K., Riskin, C. and Renwei, Z. (1992) Household income and its distribution in China. *The China Quarterly* 132: 1029–1061.

Kwong, T. (1994) Markets and urban-rural inequality in China. *Social Science Quarterly* 75(4): 821–837.

Lardy, N. (1978) *Economic Growth and Distribution in China*. New York: Cambridge University Press.

Lee, J. (2000) Changes in the source of China's regional inequality. *China Economic Review* 11(3): 232–245.

Lee, M.-D.P. (2008) Widening gap of educational opportunity? A study of the changing patterns of educational attainment in China. In G.H. Wan (ed), *Inequality and Growth in Modern China* (pp. 163–184). Oxford: Oxford University Press.

Li, H. and Zhu, Y. (2006) Income, income inequality, and health: evidence from China. *Journal of Comparative Economics* 34(4): 668–693.

Li, S., Luo, C. and Sicular, T. (2011) Overview: income inequality and poverty in China, 2002–2007. CIBC Working Paper Series 2011–10, Department of Economics, The University of Western Ontario.

Lin, J. and Liu, Z. (2000) Fiscal decentralization and economic growth in China. *Economic Development and Cultural Change* 49(1):1–21.

Lin, T., Zhuang, J., Yarcia, D. and Lin F. (2010) Decomposing income inequality: People's Republic of China, 1990–2005. In J. Zhuang (ed), *Poverty, Inequality, and Inclusive Growth in Asia: Measurement, Policy Issues, and Country Studies*, Manila: Asian Development Bank, London: Anthem Press.

Liu, X. (2010) Decomposition of China's income inequality, 1995–2006. *The Chinese Economy* 43(4): 49–72.

Liu, X. and Sicular, T. (2009) Nonagricultural employment determinants and income inequality decomposition. *The Chinese Economy* 42(4): 29–43.

Liu, Y. and Zou, W. (2011) Rural-urban migration and dynamics of income distribution in China: a non-parametric approach. *China and World Economy* 19(6): 37–55.

Lu, D. (2008) China's regional income disparity: an alternative way to think of the sources and causes. *Economics of Transition* 16(1): 31–58.

Lyons, T. (1991) Interprovincial disparities in China: output and consumption, 1952–1987. *Economic Development and Cultural Change* 39(3): 471–506.

Milanovic, B. (2005) Can we discern the effect of globalization on income distribution? Evidence from household surveys. *World Bank Economic Review* 19(1): 21–44.

Nolan, P. (1979) Inequality of income between town and countryside in the People's Republic of China in the mid-1950s. *World Development* 7(4–5): 447–465.

OECD (1999) *Agriculture in China and OECD Countries: Past Policies and Future Challenges (OECD Proceedings), China in the Global Economy*. Paris, France: OECD Publishing.

Paine, S. (1981) Spatial aspects of Chinese development: issues outcomes and policies, 1949–1979. *Journal of Development Studies* 17(2): 133–195.

Poncet, S. (2003) Measuring Chinese domestic and international integration. *China Economic Review* 14(1): 1–21.

Ravallion, M. and Chen, S. (2007) China's (uneven) progress against poverty. *Journal of Development Economics* 82(1): 1–42.

Shen, C., Jin, J. and Zou, H. (2012) Fiscal decentralization in China: history, impact, challenges and next steps. *Annals of Economics and Finance* 13(1): 1–51.

Shorrocks, A. (1982) Inequality decomposition by factor components. *Econometrica* 50(1): 193–201.

Shorrocks, A.F. and Wan, G.H. (2005) Spatial decomposition of inequality. *Journal of Economic Geography* 5(1): 59–82.

Sicular, T. (2013) The challenge of high inequality in China. *Inequality in Focus* 2(2): 1–5.

Sicular, T., Yue, X., Gustafsson, B. and Li, S. (2007) The urban-rural income gap and inequality in China. *Review of Income and Wealth* 53(1): 93–126.

Song, S., Chu, G. and Cao, R. (2000) Intercity regional disparity in China. *China Economic Review* 11: 246–261.

Sridhar, K. and Wan, G. (2010) Firm location choice in cities: evidence from China, India, and Brazil. *China Economic Review* 21(1): 113–122.
Tian, H., Wan, G. and Huo, X. (2009) Analysis of regional economic difference and crime rate. *Journal of Northwestern Polytechnical University (Social Sciences Edition)* 29(2): 220–236.
Tian, X., Lo, V., Lin, S. and Song, S. (2011) Cross-region FDI productivity spillovers in transition economies: evidence from China. *Post-Communist Economies* 23(1): 105–118.
Tsui, K. (1991) China's regional inequality, 1952–1985. *Journal of Comparative Economics* 15(1): 1–21.
Tsui, K. (1993) Decomposition of China's regional inequality. *Journal of Comparative Economics* 17(3): 600–627.
Vijverberg, W., Fu, F. and Vijverberg, C. (2011) Public infrastructure as a determinant of productive performance in China. *Journal of Productivity Analysis* 36: 91–111.
Wan, G. (2001) Changes in regional inequality in rural China: decomposing the Gini index by income sources. *Australian Journal of Agricultural and Resource Economics* 45(3): 361–381.
Wan, G. (2004) Accounting for income inequality in rural China: a regression-based approach. *Journal of Comparative Economics* 32(2): 348–363.
Wan, G. (2007) Understanding regional poverty and inequality trends in China: methodological issues and empirical findings. *Review of Income and Wealth* 53(1): 25–34.
Wan, G (2008a) *Inequality and Growth in Modern China*. Oxford: Oxford University Press.
Wan, G. (2008b) Introduction to the special section: poverty and inequality in China. *Review of Development Economics* 12(2): 416–418.
Wan, G. (2008c) *Poverty Reduction in China: Is High Growth Enough?* Policy Brief No. 4, 2008. UNU-WIDER: United Nations University Press.
Wan, G. (2013) Inequality and urbanization in China. *The Economic Research Journal* 5:73–86 (in Chinese).
Wan, G. and Sebastian, I. (2011) Poverty in Asia and the Pacific: an update. ADB Economics Working Paper 267, Manila: Asian Development Bank.
Wan, G. and Zhou, Z. (2005) Income inequality in rural China: regression-based decomposition using household data. *Review of Development Economics* 9(1): 107–120.
Wan, G., Lu, M. and Chen, Z. (2006) The inequality-growth nexus in the short and long run: empirical evidence from China. *Journal of Comparative Economics* 34(4): 654–667.
Wan, G., Lu, M. and Chen, Z. (2007) Globalization and regional income inequality: empirical evidence from within China. *Review of Income and Wealth* 53(1): 35–59.
Wan, G., Ye, J. and Zhuang, J. (2012) On regional and inter-household inequality in China. In W.T. Woo, M. Lu, J.D. Sachs and Z. Chen (eds), *A New Economic Growth Engine for China: Escaping the Middle-Income Trap by Not Doing More of the Same*. London: World Scientific.
Wang, S. (1997) China's 1994 fiscal reform. *Asian Survey* 37(9): 801–817.
Wang, D. and Zhang, L. (2003) Knowledge disparity and regional inequality in post-reform China. *Post-Communist Economies* 15(3): 383–399.
Wang, X. and Piesse, J. (2010) Inequality and the urban-rural divide in China: effects of regressive taxation. *China and World Economy* 18(6): 36–55.
Wei, K., Yao, S. and Liu, A. (2009) Foreign direct investment and regional inequality in China. *Review of Development Economics* 13(4): 778–791.
Whalley, J. and Zhang, S. (2007) A numerical simulation analysis of (*hukou*) labour mobility restrictions in China. *Journal of Development Economics* 83(2): 392–410.
Wu, X. (2005) Will foreign capital inflow alleviate income inequality? *Journal of the Asia Pacific Economy* 10(4): 528–550.
Yang, D. (1999) Urban-biased policies and rising income inequality in China. *American Economic Review Papers and Proceedings* 89(2): 306–310.
Yang, D. and Zhou, H. (1999) Rural-urban disparity and sectoral labour allocation in China. *Journal of Development Studies* 35(3): 105–133.
Yin, Y. (2004) Disparities between urban and rural areas and among different regions in China. *Income Disparities in China: An OECD Perspective*. Paris, France: OECD Publications.
Zhang, Q. and Zou, H. (2012) Regional inequality in contemporary China. *Annals of Economics and Finance* 13(1): 113–137.
Zhang, X. and Zhang, K. (2003) How does globalization affect regional inequality within a developing country? Evidence from China. *The Journal of Development Studies* 39(4): 47–67.

Zhang, Y. and Wan, G. (2006) The impact of growth and inequality on rural poverty in China. *Journal of Comparative Economics* 34(4): 694–712.

Zhao, R. (1993) Three features of the distribution of income during the transition to reform. In K. Griffin and R. Zhao (eds), *The Distribution of Income in China*. New York: St. Martin's Press.

Zhao, R. (2001) Increasing income inequality and its causes in China. In C. Riskin, R. Zhao and S. Li (eds), *China's Retreat from Equality: Income Distribution and Economic Transition* (pp. 25–43). New York: M. E. Sharpe.

Zhao, Y. (1999) Labor migration and earnings differences: the case of rural China. *Economic Development and Cultural Change* 47(4): 767–782.

Zhao, Z. (2009) Fiscal decentralization and provincial-level fiscal disparities in China: a Sino-US comparative perspective. *Public Administration Review* 69(Suppl 1): S67–S74.

Zhou, Z., Dillon, J. and Wan, G. (1992) Development of township enterprise and alleviation of the employment problem in rural China. *Agricultural Economics* 6(3): 201–215.

Zhu, N. and Luo, X. (2010) The impact of migration on rural poverty and inequality: a case study in China. *Agricultural Economics* 41: 191–204.

Zou, W., Zhang, F., Zhuang, Z. and Song, H. (2008) Transport infrastructure, growth, and poverty alleviation: empirical analysis of China. *Annals of Economics and Finance* 9(2): 345–371.

8

THE EVOLVING GEOGRAPHY OF CHINA'S INDUSTRIAL PRODUCTION: IMPLICATIONS FOR POLLUTION DYNAMICS AND URBAN QUALITY OF LIFE

Siqi Zheng, Cong Sun, and Ye Qi
Tsinghua University

Matthew E. Kahn
UCLA and NBER

1. Introduction

Growing at a nearly 10% average annual rate for three decades, China has become the second largest economy in the world since 2010. Industrialization and urbanization have reinforced each other in this rapid economic development of China. For example, 40% of the world's clothes are 'Made in China'.[1] The proportion of the population living in urban areas increased from less than 20% in 1980 to 52% in 2012. As the 'World's Factory', China's industrialization has largely been driven by the fast growth of export-oriented and labor-intensive industries in the coastal areas in Eastern China. In the mid-2000s, more than 90% of total exports and roughly 60% of industrial output were produced in those coastal cities (National Bureau of Statistics of China, NBSC[2]).

Since the mid-2000s, the rising congestion costs associated with the industrial agglomeration in large coastal cities began to drive the shift of the nation's industrial geography. Labor and land costs have been increasing dramatically in these cities. The 2008 global financial crisis shrank international demand. As a result, many large cities in China's Eastern Region have undergone de-industrialization, while the less developed inland cities in the Central and Western Regions are experiencing fast industrialization. Many labor-intensive firms in large coastal cities either upgraded their capital and technology, or moved to nearby small cities and inland cities such as Wuhan and Zhengzhou. The manufacturing share of gross domestic product (GDP) in the

China's Economy: A Collection of Surveys, First Edition. Edited by Iris Claus and Les Oxley. Published 2015 by John Wiley & Sons, Ltd.

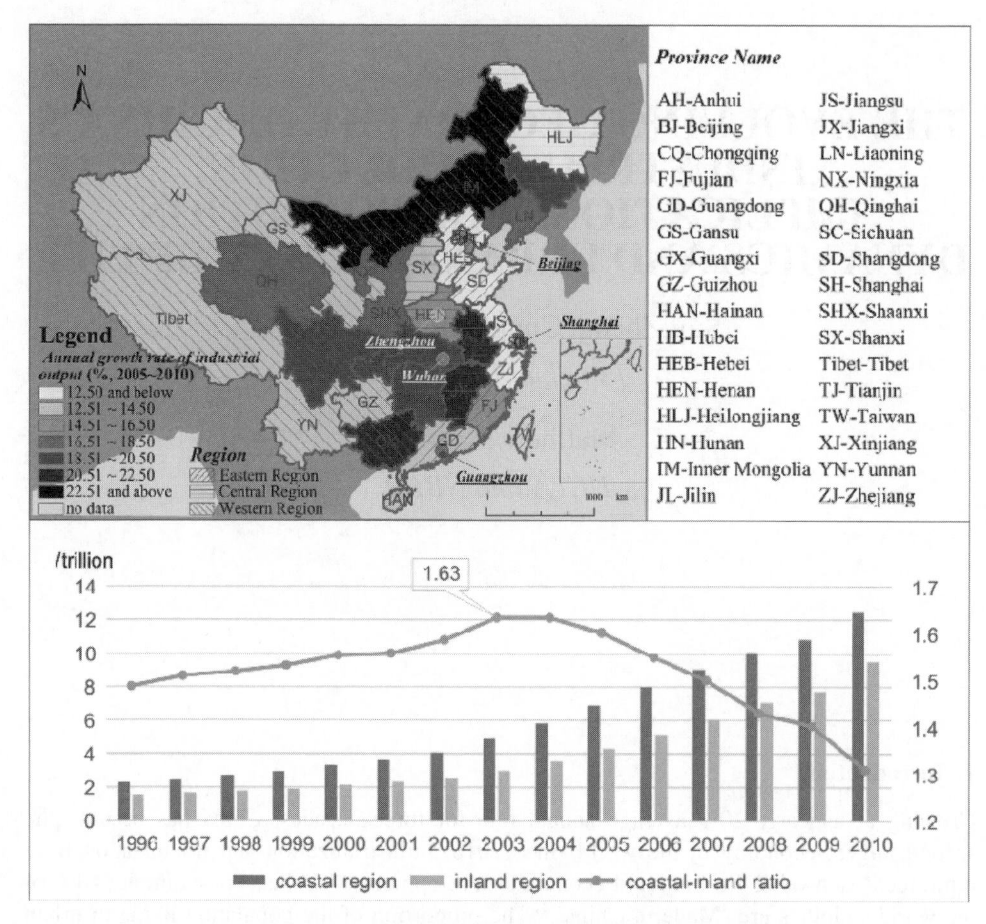

Figure 1. Manufacturing Output in the Coastal and Inland Regions.
Source: NBSC.

Central and Western Regions (inland region or inland area) grew from 36% in 2004 to 44% in 2010, but declined in the Eastern Region (coastal region or coastal area) after 2008 (Figure 1).

This changing geography of industrial production has important urban implications. In China, industrial production is the main source of both local and global pollution. In 2011, the industrial sector was responsible for 89.3% of total end-use energy consumption while the residential sector only consumed the rest 10.7% (NBSC). Industrial production contributes emissions to air and water, therefore industrial relocation and migration change the economic geography of industrial pollution. Public health researchers have documented the health consequences of exposure to pollution (Ratcliffe *et al.*, 1996), and environmental and urban economists have also documented that urban pollution is a major component of local quality of life (QOL) (Gyourko and Tracy, 1991; Zheng and Kahn, 2013a).

Real estate price differentials across cities reflect people's willingness-to-pay for the different QOL levels in those cities (Chen and Han, 2013). Cities featuring high air and water pollution must pay compensating differentials measured in terms of higher wages and lower real estate rents in order to attract workers to live in such cities (Roback, 1982; Rosen,

2002). Empirical studies have documented that, all else equal, real estate prices across and within Chinese cities are higher in areas that are less polluted (Zheng and Kahn, 2008; Zheng *et al.*, 2013a). Given that a clean environment is a normal good, the richer and more educated urban households in China's Eastern Region value it more than their counterparts in Western and Central Regions.

The economic geography of industrial pollution is an emergent property of the locational choice of industrial plants. Where firms locate is both a function of the natural advantages of different geographic areas and the regulatory policies and incentives offered by different local governments. Local governments who are aware of this strategic dynamic must decide whether to enforce regulations and pay the price of losing some footloose dirty jobs while enjoying the environmental gains of deindustrializing. In richer coastal cities, the local governments are enforcing stricter environmental regulations. A US literature on regulation's unintended consequences has documented that differential enforcement of pollution regulation encourages industrial migration to areas featuring more lax regulation (Kahn, 1997; Becker and Henderson, 2000; Greenstone, 2002; Kahn and Mansur, 2013).

Booming industrial activity brings new economic opportunities but can cause environmental deterioration in China's inland region. This paper surveys recent research to understand this trade-off between regional economic convergence and the spatial distribution of industrial pollution. How does the relocation of industrial activity alter the spatial distribution of pollution and local QOL? We review the related literature and present new evidence on these key questions related to China's changing urban standard of living.

A series of studies investigate how China's exports affect importing nations (Broda *et al.*, 2009; Feenstra and Wei, 2009; Bloom *et al.*, 2011; Atristain, 2012; Cheng, 2012; Autor *et al.*, 2013). Those studies focus on the external effects of China's industrial production dynamics. In contrast, we focus on how China's spatial equilibrium is affected by its industrial production dynamics.

The remainder of the paper is organized as follows. Section 2 presents the spatial dynamics of industrial location in the last 30 years in China. Section 3 discusses the urban implications of the recent geographic change in industrial activities on spatial disparities in pollution and local QOL. Section 4 concludes.

2. The Changing Geography of China's Industrial Production

2.1 *Market Fundamentals and the Geographic Dynamics of Industrial Production*

Starting from the 1980s, with the transition in China from the central-planned economy to a market economy, transportation costs have played a key role in determining profit maximizing firms' locational choice. Consistent with the New Economic Geography theory (see Krugman, 1991; Neary, 2001), China's coastal cities in the Eastern Region with good access to the global market became the most attractive location for private manufacturing firms (Sridhar and Wan, 2010).[3]

In the mid-2000s, more than 65% of manufacturing employment in above-scale (with annual sale above 5 million renminbi, RMB.) industrial firms was located in the coastal region, as compared to 42% in 1980. The bar graph in Figure 1 shows the manufacturing sector's value-added in both the coastal and inland regions between 1996 and 2010 (at constant 2010 RMB). The coastal region had a higher growth rate than the inland region during the years 1996–2004, but this trend flipped since 2005 and the ratio of these two has kept declining since then.

Many empirical studies show that during the early years of China's industrial export growth, the economic activity was highly spatially concentrated. Based on the calculation of industrial local Gini coefficients for three-digit manufacturing industries, Wen (2004) finds that industrial concentration rose from 1980 to 1995 and most industries were clustered in the Guangdong and Jiangsu provinces. Using three measures of industrial concentration, Long and Zhang (2012) find similar patterns between 1995 and 2004, especially for those export-oriented industries. The initial geographic concentration in coastal cities brought increasing returns to scale and generated regional specialization among firms (He and Pan, 2013; Lu *et al.*, 2013). Such geographic concentration not only decreases delivered prices for inputs based on proximity to suppliers, but also encourages more specialization and less vertical integration (Goldstein and Gronberg, 1984; Helsley and Strange, 2007; Li and Lu, 2009).

Since the mid-2000s, the Chinese labor market has witnessed a great change. The prominent feature is the growing labor scarcity, as shown by the shortage of unskilled workers and their fast growing wages (Ogawa and Chen, 2013; Du and Yang, 2014). The sharply rising wages in coastal cities has pushed labor-intensive manufacturing firms either to upgrade their capital and technology or to move out. The average wage ratio between coastal cities and inland cities grew to 1.5 in the mid-2000s. Qu *et al.* (2012) use the Annual Survey of Industrial Firms data set from 1998 to 2008 covering 31 provinces and 30 manufacturing industries to show that, from 2004, the size of new rural migrants has significantly decreased, and the large coastal cities started to face labor shortages and faster rising labor cost.

It is also not surprising that these land-intensive manufacturing industries were bid out by high-tech, finance, and other high-skilled industries which attract more international capital inflows and are able to pay much higher land rent. Large coastal cities face a large opportunity cost for manufacturing activity in their cities. Such manufacturing land could be used for higher value commercial and residential towers. But in inland cities, there is not such a demand for residential and commercial real estate. Figure 2 highlights the growing land price gap for industrial use in different regions after 2008. Gao *et al.* (2012) find that rising real estate prices is one important factor explaining why manufacturing firms are moving from coastal areas and relocating to inland areas.

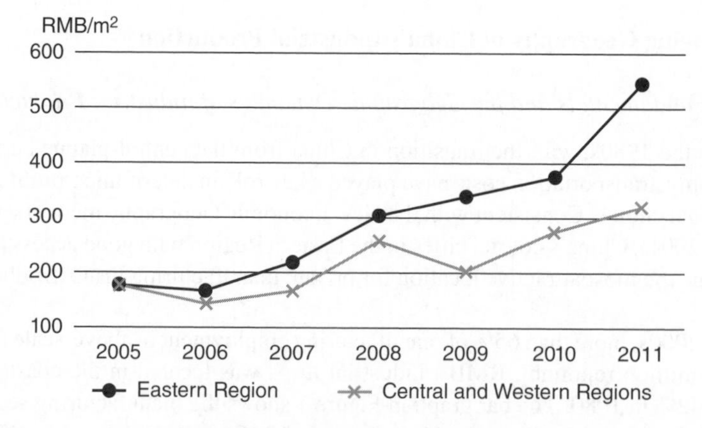

Figure 2. The Annual Auction Price (at Constant 2010 RMB) for Industrial Land Across China's Regions (2005–2011).
Source: China Land and Resources Statistical Yearbook.

In addition, the inland cities have a cost advantage in electricity price. For instance, the industrial electricity price in Zhejiang province is roughly 15% and 7% higher than Henan province and Shaanxi province, respectively in 2012 (National Development and Reform Commission). US-based research has documented that energy intensive firms, such as steel plants, are more likely to locate in geographic areas where electricity prices are lower (Kahn and Mansur, 2013).

Given these push factors, the second-tier and third-tier inland cities have become increasingly attractive destinations for labor and energy intensive industries. The annual growth rates of manufacturing value-added (at constant 2010 RMB) in the coastal and inland regions between 2004 and 2010 were 19% and 25%, respectively, and the ratio of these two switched from increasing in 1996–2003 to declining in 2004–2011 (see Figure 1). Qu *et al.* (2012) report that the share change in employment, assets, and output values for all manufacturing industries (especially for labor-intensive industries) in the coastal area have slowed down or even decreased since 2004.

2.2 *The Role of Government in Determining the Geography of Industrial Production*

A distinctive feature of Chinese cities is that the central and local governments both have a 'visible' hand in influencing firm location choices, with fiscal and land policies as basic policy tools. At the beginning of China's Economic Reform, China's central government recognized the coastal area's locational advantage and designed several favorable policies, such as setting up Special Economic Zones (SEZs) in this area. Favorable short-term tax deduction, and other favorable policies were set in those SEZs to attract foreign direct investments (FDIs) and foster industrial clusters (Gao, 2004; Du *et al.*, 2008).[4] Labor migration restrictions (*hukou* system) from the countryside to cities were gradually relaxed. This allowed a huge flow of migrant workers to move to coastal cities and thus provided sufficient cheap labor to those labor-intensive manufacturing industries located there (Ma *et al.*, 2013).

Local leaders have a strong incentive to foster the growth of their local economy. A booming economy increases local fiscal revenue, especially after taxation reform in 1994 (Lu and Tao, 2009). Local leaders compete with each other in their respective attempts to be promoted within the central government's promotion system (Qi, 2008). Each local leader knows that local GDP growth has been a key determinant of promotion (Qi and Zhang, 2014; Zheng *et al.*, 2013b). Given that the industrial sector contributed a large share of GDP and tax revenue, local governments competed for attracting FDI and other leading firms they prefer, by offering very cheap (or even free) industrial land,[5] initial tax deductions, good infrastructure, and favorable institutional environment. Those FDI firms and other large firms are expected to generate spillover effects to the whole city and contribute to GDP and tax revenue growth. In Broadman and Sun's (1997) study, FDI's location choice in China was determined by market size, proximity to port, infrastructure condition, and favorable policies. They find those subsidies in SEZs provided enough incentives to attract FDI and significantly decreased FDI firms' production cost in the initial years.

Some scholars argue that the changing geography of industrial production since the mid-2000s has been largely driven by government interventions (Lu and Xiang, 2013). Unlike many western countries, China's central government has been pursuing a well-defined set of regional growth policies. The Western Development Program and 'Rising of Central China' Program launched in 1999 and 2004, respectively, provide infrastructure aid and support for industrial adjustment to western and inland provinces. The Northeast Revitalization Program focuses on reinventing the poor cities in China's Northeast (Liaoning, Jilin, and Heilongjiang) that once benefited from the emphasis on heavy industry under central planning. The share of the land supply in inland regions had increased roughly 15% between 2003 and 2010 (Lu and Xiang, 2013), most of which came from taking agriculture land from farmers. Vast infrastructure investment in highways and high-speed railways has greatly shifted the industrial location patterns (Faber, 2013). Starting in 2007, China has introduced several new high-speed rails that connect large cities such as Beijing, Shanghai, Guangzhou, and Wuhan with nearby cities. Through facilitating market integration, high-speed rail stimulates the development of second- and third-tier cities and this will reduce discrepancies in income inequality across China's cities (Zheng and Kahn, 2013b).

Once China's inland cities were connected to the rest of the nation, the inland mayors there then aggressively started to build SEZs and offer the traditional packages of SEZ incentives to lure firms to inland area. Moreover, under China's household registration system, coastal city governments have no obligation to provide public service and social security for rural migrants (Ma *et al.*, 2013). This institutional arrangement lets this cheap labor force move back to inland cities and towns with a low cost of living.

Generous local government incentives can induce industry to move to less productive areas. By comparing several indicators including industrial output, labor distribution, firm size, capital–labor ratio, labor cost, and labor productivity by region and year, Cai *et al.* (2009a) find that many of these indicators did not show comparative advantage for industrial development in inland regions but industrial firms were moving there largely due to the favorable incentives provided by governments, such as favorable tax treatments. This highlights that there can be a tension between central government goals of fostering overall economic growth while simultaneously seeking to reduce spatial income inequality. If poor cities are inherently less productive (perhaps due to geographic factors), then investing in such areas may yield a relatively low rate of return relative to investing in areas with better fundamentals. Conversely, standard convergence arguments might predict that the marginal returns to investment in such areas may be high (Barro and Sali-i-Martin, 1991).

3. Implications for Spatial Variation of Pollution and Local QOL

Since the mid-2000s, the growth of industrial production in inland cities has contributed to the spatial income convergence. For instance, the annual wage growth was 16.7% for manufacturing workers in the Eastern Region during 2006–2010, while this rate was 20.4% and 19.3% in the Central and Western Regions in the same period, respectively (NBSC). The labor income gap between coastal cities and inland cities shrank slightly from 1.4 in 2005 to 1.3 in 2010 (NBSC). However, the income increase in those inland cities has been accompanied with more industrial pollution emission there.

3.1 *Pollution Production as a Consequence of Industrial Locational Choice*

The geographic concentration of manufacturing activity has significant local environmental impacts. During the 1980s, black smoke from smoke stacks became the characteristic of Chinese industrial cities; subsequently, many southern cities began to suffer from extremely high levels of acid rain pollution, and large cities' air quality was greatly deteriorated due to nitrous oxides (NOx), carbon monoxide (CO), and other pollutants due to the combustion of coal (He *et al.*, 2002). Cao *et al.* (2011) show that the Eastern Region experienced heavier

Table 1. Average Annual Percentage Change in Industrial SO_2 and COD (2004–2010).

	Industrial SO_2	Chemical oxygen demand (COD)
The Eastern Region (μ_1)	– 1.69%	– 1.87%
The Central and Western Regions (μ_2)	1.74%	0.33%
t-test (H_0: $\mu_2 = \mu_1$)	2.029**	1.578*

Notes: *$p < 0.10$, **$p < 0.05$.
COD is 'chemical oxygen demand'. The concentration of COD reflects the amount of organic compounds in water.
Data Source: NBSC.

emissions of such air pollutants than the rest of the country, due to the large share of industrial activities and power plants located there. As the World Bank reported, 12 of the 20 most polluted cities in the world were located in China (World Bank, 2007). Industrial activities also led to a severe deterioration in water quality, and roughly 70% of the river water was unsafe for human consumption (World Bank, 2006) at the beginning of the century. Industrial firms produced more than 35% of pollutant discharges into Chinese rivers in 2007, including heavy metal and organic pollutants.[6]

In Table 1, we present the annual percent change in different industrial emissions indicators for different Chinese regions. Between 2004 and 2010, both industrial SO_2 and chemical oxygen demand (COD) emissions declined in the Eastern Region, but increased in the Central and Western Regions. The *t*-tests show that this spatial variation in the annual growth rates is statistically significant for both industrial emission types.

Industrial pollution is highly correlated with energy consumption. Scale, composition, and technique effects work together to determine the total energy consumption from a city's industrial sector (Copeland and Taylor, 2004). Scale refers to the sheer count of jobs and output located in a city while composition refers to a city's set of industries and the vintage of its capital stock. Technique represents emissions per unit of economic activity. If technique effect keeps constant over time, the increases in both scale and share of energy-intensive manufacturing industries in China's inland cities will lead to rising energy consumption and energy intensity (energy consumption per GDP dollar). The scale of industrial production in inland cities has been rising faster than that in coastal cities. In Table 2 below, we do a simple decomposition exercise on energy intensity (energy consumption per GDP dollar) from the industrial sector in these two regions. The results reported in Table 2 show that the composition effect increases inland cities' energy intensity while it reduces that in coastal cities. Between 2006 and 2011, keeping technique effect constant, the change in manufacturing share in output contributed to a 3.17 tce (ton coal equivalent) decline and a 6.83 tce increase in coastal and inland cities, respectively. The good news is that, technology upgrading had made a major contribution to energy intensity decline in both regions (Rock *et al.*, 2013). Our own calculations show that the inland cities enjoyed a 19.8 tce energy intensity decrease, which outweighed the positive composition effect so that the net change in energy intensity is negative for the inland area.

This calculation highlights that the migration of industrial factories toward the west does induce a 'zero sum pollution game'. As coastal cities such as Shanghai grow cleaner due to deindustrialization, there are social marginal benefits from reducing the pollution exposure of millions of Shanghai wealthy residents to industrial pollution. A pessimist would posit that an

Table 2. Energy Consumption, Energy Intensity Changes in Coastal and Inland Cities.

	Year/period	Coastal cities	Inland cities
Manufacturing share in output	2006	46%	41%
	2011	44%	45%
Composition effect (tce per million RMB)	2006–2011	−3.17	6.83
Technique effect (tce per million RMB)	2006–2011	−22.4	−19.8

Notes: (1) When we calculate the composition effect, we assume sector-specific energy intensity is constant (use nationwide numbers in the initial year 2001) and let a city's industrial composition change over time. This means: Composition effect = $\sum_i (S_{ij,2011} - S_{ij,2006}) \times EI_{i,2006}$. Similarly, when we calculate the technique effect, we assume a city's industrial composition is constant (use numbers in initial year 2001) and let nationwide sector-specific energy intensity change over time. This means: Technique effect = $\sum_i (EI_{i,2011} - EI_{i,2006}) \times S_{ij,2006}$. Where subscript i and j denote industry and region respectively, EI_i denote nationwide energy intensity of industry i, S_{ij} denotes industry i's share in output in region j. (2) tce refers to 'ton coal equivalent', which is a standard unit of energy consumption used in Chinese statistics.
Data Source: NBSC.

equal amount of damage is created in the inland area where the factory moves. This logic is false because more people live in the large coastal cities such as Shanghai and thus exposing them to less pollution reduces the Pigouvian social cost of industrial production in China.

China's industrialization growth has taken place within a global economy. Access to global markets not only offers China export destinations and FDI but it also offers access to cleaner international technology. Such advanced technology offers the possibility of China's industry reducing its emissions per dollar of production, which may be the underlying reason for the large technique effects in both regions documented in Table 2. Some evidence is found in empirical studies. Wang and Jin (2007) find that foreign firms exhibit better environmental performance than state-owned and privately owned firms because the foreign firms use cleaner technology and are more energy efficient. Zheng *et al.* (2010) also report a negative correlation between a city's FDI inflows and its ambient air pollution level using IV regression strategy. Fisher-Vanden *et al.* (2013) examine the factors inducing the declining energy intensity in four Chinese industries (pulp and paper, cement, iron and steel, and aluminum). The factors include rising energy cost,[7] rising R&D investment, market-oriented reform, and the import of foreign technology.

3.2 *Energy Production as a Function of Industry Location*

Electricity generation has provided a crucial input for China's rapid industrialization in the past decades. In 2010, more than 70% of total electricity was consumed by the industrial sector (NBSC). China has the third largest coal reserves in the world, and 80% of China's electricity is generated using coal (NBSC). Therefore, pollution hotspots emerge as a by-product of the industrial production. When industrial production was concentrated in the coastal area, a large number of coal-fired power plants were located close to those industrial clusters to minimize transmission line loss. Since those industrial clusters are also large cities with high population density (Figure 3), this means that a large share of population has been exposed to the air pollution produced by the coal-fired plants.

With the evolving geography of industrial production, most of the newly built coal-fired power plants emerged nearby inland cities. In this way, those plants can minimize transmission

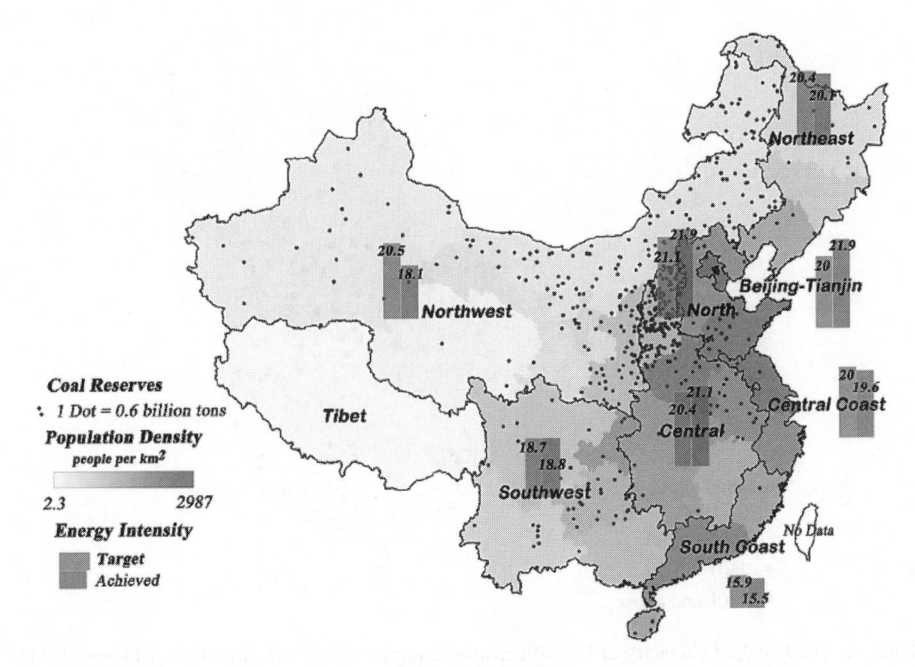

Figure 3. Population Density and the Distribution of Coal Reserves (2010).
Sources: Coal reserves and population density from NBSC, 2011; population density was calculated based on population and land area; energy intensity of eight regions is integrated based on provincial energy and gross regional product data.

cost and coal transport cost simultaneously (see Figure 3 for the spatial distribution of coal reserves in China). In addition, some coal-fired power plants in coastal cities were shut down due to the stricter pollution regulation there. Since the 2000s, new coal-fired power plants are not allowed to locate near coastal cities. It is predicted that more than 80% of newly built power plants will locate in inland cities in the near future.[9]

From an environmentalists' perspective, this is mixed news. On the positive side, the densely populated coastal area will be exposed to less pollution. Another piece of good news is that the central government has requested coal-fired power plants, especially the newly built ones, to install desulfurization equipment, such as SO_2 scrubbers (Xu *et al.*, 2009). Figure 4 shows the installed capacity of desulfurization equipment in coal-fired power plants. Unfortunately, with insufficient monitoring, there was much less focus on whether such SO_2 scrubbers are operated properly such that they actually reduce pollution. It was reported that, in some plants the equipment was left idle (Wang, 2013). The bad news, in terms of reducing China's greenhouse gas emissions, is that China is building new coal-fired power plants and these power plants have a high carbon emissions factor.

3.3 *Spatial Displacement Effects Caused by Differential Environmental Regulation*

Chinese urbanites differ with respect to their willingness to pay to avoid pollution. People in richer cities are willing to pay more to face less pollution and this incentivizes their local leaders to pursue more stringent environmental regulation (Zheng and Kahn, 2013a). As

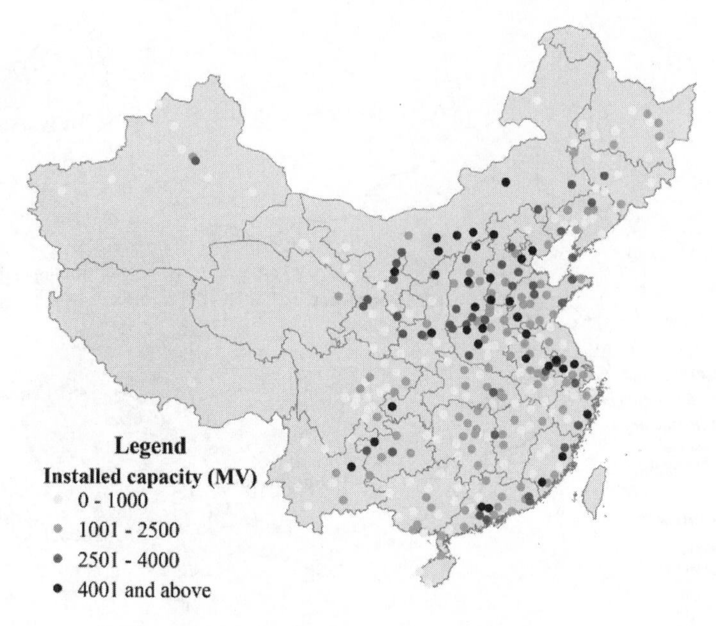

Figure 4. The Installed Capacity of Desulfurization Equipment in Coal-Fired Power Plants (2011).[8]

shown in the case of the USA, if some cities adopt strict regulation while other cities have lax regulation, then this will induce some dirty factories to seek out the lower cost-low regulation city (Henderson, 1996; Greenstone, 2002).

China's central government enacts national environmental protection laws and related policies, makes national environmental protection plans, and defines the control standard of pollution emission. Local (city) governments play the major role in enforcing those policies and plans, and implementing specific regulations. There are two major types of regulation tools: One is administrative interventions, for instance, requiring the installation of specific pieces of emissions control equipment (Xu *et al.*, 2009); and the other is economic incentives, for example, the pollution levy (Wang and Wheeler, 2005; Lin, 2013). In the past, local government officials did not take the central government's environmental laws or policies seriously, and thus they did not actively implement environmental regulations (Deng *et al.*, 2012). Instead, they encouraged industrial pollution in their cities to pursue a higher rate of economic growth (Chow, 2010). Wu *et al.* (2013) also argue that city mayors focus on transportation investment rather than environmental protection because transportation leads to more immediate GDP gains for the city. In recent years, with the environmental performance added into local officials' promotion criteria, they began to change their strategies. The coastal region's environmental regulation has become much stricter than before (Van Rooij and Lo, 2010). Mayors of coastal cities tend to move dirty firms out of their cities, and at the same time, the city governments in underdeveloped area welcomed these firms for economic growth and employment opportunities which are now their 'golden goose'. Those inland city mayors have the incentives to tolerate large firms' heavy pollution in return for generating local tax revenue, creating job opportunities, and promoting economic growth (Jiang *et al.*, 2014; Yu *et al.*, 2013).

Many energy-intensive manufacturing firms relocated or started their new business in inland cities with lower production cost and laxer environmental regulation. This fact suggests the emergence of 'domestic pollution havens'. For instance, Beijing moved out a large amount of polluting firms to nearby cities in the Hebei province before the 2008 Olympic Games.[10] The media has claimed that these factories are a major reason for the aggravated environmental pollution in Hebei in recent years. Foxconn, one of the biggest Taiwanese manufacturers of Apple products, moved its factory from Shenzhen to Henan, which also raised public concerns about pollution growth. A media report shows that 39 of 43 industrial projects with large pollutant emissions were introduced into the Western Region in 2000.[11] Ningxia, a province in the Western Region (see Figure 1), had total exports of 650 million dollars in 2004, 56.9% of which was contributed by energy-intensive and polluting firms.[12] Based on water pollution data, Zheng *et al.* (2013c) conduct a case study on tracing the water pollution transfer associated with industrial transfer between the Yangtze River Delta and Henan province, and find that several pollutants (such as the sulfonamides and steroids) could be detected in the water sample due to this industrial relocation.

In recent years, a common phenomenon is the within-province industrial relocation. For instance, Guangdong province is subsidizing polluting firms in the Pearl River Delta to relocate in the northern part of the province, and Jiangsu province is relocating those firms to the north-Jiangsu (Subei) area. This may be the provincial governments' intended strategy of trying to green the big city by moving dirty activity further from the major population centers and trying to spread income to the poor underperforming areas within the region (Cai *et al.*, 2013; Zheng and Kahn, 2013a).

3.4 *The Local QOL Impact of Industrial Pollution Dynamics*

Industrial emission directly affects a city's air and water pollution levels. Beijing Environmental Protection Agency announced the composition of various sources of local $PM_{2.5}$ concentration in 2011.[13] Coal combustion emissions, local industrial emissions, and imported emissions from nearby industrial hotspots accounted for 16.7%, 16.3%, and 24.5% of the PM_{10} concentration, respectively. Zheng *et al.* (2013a) also estimate the size of this cross-boundary pollution and find that a 10% decrease in imported neighbor pollution is associated with a roughly 1.7% increase in local PM_{10} concentration in 85 Chinese cities.

Industrial pollution has many negative impacts on local QOL, such as lowering worker productivity, hurting children and the elderly, and reducing the desire to outdoor activities. Its negative externality on public health has been well documented (Venners *et al.*, 2003; Chen *et al.*, 2004; Guo *et al.*, 2009; Kan *et al.*, 2012). Ebenstein (2012) finds that industrial activity has led to a severe deterioration in water quality in China's lakes and rivers. He estimates that a deterioration of water quality by a single grade (on a six-grade scale) increases the digestive cancer death rate by 9.7%. Currie *et al.* (2013) review the empirical literature providing both direct and indirect evidence that early childhood exposure to pollution significantly impacts later life outcomes. Chen *et al.* (2013) employ a quasi-experimental approach to provide clear evidence that China's coal-based winter heating policy cut life expectancy by over 5 years in northern China during the period 1981–2000.[14]

The urban QOL literature emphasizes that spatial variation in wages and rents represents a compensating differential for place-based local public goods (Roback, 1982; Rosen, 2002). This revealed preference methodology allows scholars to identify urban households' demand for nonmarket goods, including urban environmental amenities (Gyourko *et al.*, 1999; Albouy,

Table 3. Elasticity Estimates of the Real Estate Capitalization Rates of PM_{10} Concentration.

Period Region	2006–2007 Coastal cities	2006–2007 Inland cities	2008–2009 Coastal cities	2008–2009 Inland cities
Capitalization rate (marginal willingness-to-pay)	−0.493	−0.323	−0.642	−0.466

2008; Albouy and Lue, 2014). In both intracity and intercity studies focusing on China (Zheng and Kahn, 2008; Zheng *et al.*, 2010, 2013a), it is found that home prices are lower in cities or in the locations within a city with higher ambient pollution levels or less green space. Recent research has found in China that the marginal valuation for green amenities is rising over time. Using the same data as that in Zheng *et al.* (2013a), we calculate the capitalization rates of PM_{10} concentration in home prices in China's inland and coastal cities, and their changes over time (Table 3), controlling for a set of city attributes (population, temperature, employment share of manufacturing sector, green space per capita, health care, education, and other urban amenities). In both periods, the richer coastal cities have a higher willingness-to-pay for less PM_{10} pollution than the poorer inland cities, and both numbers are rising over time.

From Table 3, we see that, all else equal, a 1% decrease in PM_{10} concentration is associated with a 0.32–0.64% increase in home price. There is no property tax in Chinese cities, and many cities rely on land sales for a large share of their annual revenues (around 60%) (Cai *et al.*, 2009a). This reliance on land sale revenues in Chinese cities may incentivize local governments to internalize QOL effects because this will increase their land's value (Arnott, 2008). While Chinese cities rely on land sales for revenue today, it is likely that cities will run short of land at some time point in the future. This will encourage such cities to introduce a property tax system. Those cities with high QOL and high real estate prices could enjoy high revenues under this scheme (Zheng and Kahn, 2013a).

4. Conclusion

Any person who has walked into a Walmart Superstore knows that China has been an industrial powerhouse producing many of the goods that consumers seek ranging from computers to American Flags. While China's industrial production has created great wealth, a by-product of such massive production of heavy industry combined with a reliance on coal-fired electricity has been a huge amount of urban pollution. Given that coal is a fossil fuel, this electricity generated for industrial production has also led to soaring greenhouse gas production by China.

This paper has surveyed several literatures to provide a comprehensive overview of the spatial evolution of industrial production, income, pollution, and QOL across China's cities over the last 30 years. The initial concentration of industrial activities in the coastal cities had driven the fast economic growth as well as deteriorated environmental quality there. Many empirical studies document the shifting geography of industrial production toward inland cities since the mid-2000, due to the rising congestion cost of labor and land in the coastal area. This trend has brought pollution and negative QOL impacts to the inland area. Though the scale and composition effects work together to increase the total energy consumption and energy intensity in inland cities, we detect a significant technique effect, which helps the inland cities to reduce their energy intensity and become cleaner. This indicates that the new factories established there may employ more modern engineering technology. This may raise the possibility that the on-going geography dynamics of industrial production will not become a zero-sum pollution game. Instead, it may generate net social benefit as high-density coastal cities deindustrialize and hence reduce their population's exposure to pollution while new factories in inland cities use greener technology. This optimistic view hinges on whether the technique effect (i.e., newer factories opening in the West using relatively low emissions per unit of production) outweighs the scale and composition effects in the long run in inland cities.

The fascinating feature of China's economic geography is that it is determined by a mixture of classic natural advantage features and the strong hand of the local and central governments. The regional balance policies pursued by the central government complements the efforts by inland city mayors to attract economic growth, employment opportunities, and tax revenue. The stricter environmental regulation in richer coastal cities where people have a stronger demand QOL also pushed those dirty firms to the inland cities with laxer environmental regulation.

Throughout this survey, we have discussed a dynamic regional general equilibrium process without writing down a formal general equilibrium model. Future research should consider constructing such a model in which industrial production creates wealth and pollution. Local QOL is a function of per-capita income and pollution. Locations differ with respect to their comparative advantage and alternative uses for manufacturing land. Such research would need to formally model the actions of a strategic national government simultaneously seeking to encourage macrogrowth, environmental progress, and regional income convergence. This survey has demonstrated why such an endeavor is important and how the evolving empirical agenda has quantified many facts relevant for considering the trade-offs that China's industrializing and deindustrializing regions now face.

Acknowledgements

We thank Iris Claus, Les Oxley, Guanghua Wan and anonymous referees for their helpful comments. We thank the National Science Foundation of China (No. 70973065, No. 71273154 and No. 71322307), Program for New Century Excellent Talents in University (NCET-12-0313), and Tsinghua University Initiative Scientific Research Program for research support. We thank the UCLA Ziman center for real estate for generous funding.

Notes

1. *Source*: China Textile Industry Development Report 2010-2011. Published by China Textile & Apparel Press, 2011.
2. All NBSC data in this paper come from China Statistical Yearbook, China Energy Statistical Yearbook, China Environmental Statistical Yearbook and the Web site http://data.stats.gov.cn/index
3. State-owned enterprises (SOEs) lack the flexibility of choosing their locations, but the existing manufacturing SOEs in coastal cities also enjoyed the benefits of a booming economy and expanded, while many in Western and Central Regions had a weak performance and some went bankrupt.
4. There are three categories of tax in China: central taxes (for example, tariffs, tax revenues from railways, banks and insurance companies, and consumption tax), local taxes (for example, business tax, city maintenance tax, etc.), central and local shared taxes (for

example., value-added tax, corporate income tax, individual income tax, etc.). Local city governments can make their own decision on whether they levy business tax and the local share of corporate income tax. To attract FDI and other firms they prefer SEZs, and many local governments offer favorable tax treatments, such as an initial 'two-year exemption and three-year reduction by half' of the above local tax items.

5. In China, by law, urban land is owned by the State. But in practice, the local (city) government controls the use right of the land within its boundary. It can transfer the use right of a land parcel for a certain number of years (industrial land: 50 years; residential land: 70 years) to an entity (a firm or a person) and receive a land transfer fee as its off-budget revenue. The land transfer fee can be determined through negotiation or open auction. For industrial land parcels, since the local government wants to attract certain types of firms, it always negotiates the land transfer fee with those firms and is willing to accept a very low rate.
6. Data set of the First China Pollution Source Census.
7. One reason for rising energy costs is due to the fact that China's government has been reducing energy subsidies in order to discourage the consumption of dirty energy and incentivize more innovation and adoption of energy-efficient products (Zheng and Kahn, 2013a). A second relevant factor is global rising demand for energy.
8. *Source*: http://www.wri.org/blog/can-china%E2%80%99s-air-pollution-action-plan-slow-down-new-coal-power-development
9. *Source*: http://www.chinadaily.com.cn/business/2011--06/18/content_12729071.htm
10. *Source*: http://www.people.com.cn/GB/channel7/498/20000628/121718.html
11. *Source*: http://china.qianlong.com/4352/2005/07/13/2001@2717046.htm
12. *Source*: http://www.readdailynews.com/news-3843243-The-industrial-spray-set-haze-volt-the-PM25-sources-accounted-ranking-after-the-motor-vehicle-exhaust-and-coal-emissions.html
13. China's winter heating policy provides free heating via the provision of coal for boilers in cities north of the Huai River but denied heat to the south.
14. Source: http://www.mep.gov.cn/gkml/hbb/bgg/201104/W020110420407642353906.pdf

References

Albouy, D. (2008) Are big cities really bad places to live? Improving quality-of-life estimates across cities. National Bureau of Economic Research Working Paper No. 14472.

Albouy, D. and Lue, B. (2014) Driving to opportunity: local wages, commuting, and sub-metropolitan quality of life. National Bureau of Economic Research Working Paper No. 19922.

Arnott, R. (2008) Housing policy in developing countries: the importance of the informal economy. In M. Spence, P. Clark Annez and R.M. Buckley (eds.), *Urbanization and Growth* (pp. 167–196). Washington, DC: World Bank.

Atristain, F. (2012) Challenges and opportunities in China's overseas special economic zones: Zambia and Mauritius case studies. Available at http://www.economia.unam.mx/deschimex/cechimex/chmxExtras/documentos/cuadernos/2012/Cuadernos%20del%20Cechimex%202012-7.pdf accessed on January 20, 2014.

Autor, D.H., Dorn, D. and Hanson, G.H. (2013) The China syndrome: local labor market effects of import competition in the United States. *American Economic Review* 103(6): 2121–2168.

Barro, R.J. and Sala-i-Martin, X. (1991) Convergence across states and regions. *Brookings Papers on Economic Activity* 1: 107–182.

Becker, R. and Henderson, J.V. (2000) Effects of air quality regulations on polluting industries. *Journal of Political Economy* 108(2): 379–421.

Bloom, N., Draca, M. and Van Reenen, J. (2011) Trade induced technical change? The impact of Chinese imports on innovation, IT and productivity. National Bureau of Economic Research Working Paper No. 16717.

Broadman, H.G. and Sun, X. (1997) The distribution of foreign direct investment in China. *The World Economy* 20(3): 339–361.

Broda, C., Leibtag, E. and Weinstein, D.E. (2009) The role of prices in measuring the poor's living standards. *Journal of Economic Perspectives* 23(2): 77–97.

Cai, F., Wang, M.Y. and Qu, Y. (2009a) Industrial and labor relocations among Chinese regions. *China Industrial Economics* 8: 5–16. (in Chinese)

Cai, H., Henderson, J.V. and Zhang, Q. (2009b) China's land market auctions: evidence of corruption. National Bureau of Economic Research Working Paper No. 15067.

Cai, H., Chen, Y. and Qing, G. (2013) Polluting thy neighbor: the case of river pollution in china. Working Paper.

Cao, G., Zhang, X., Gong, S., An, X. and Wang, Y. (2011) Emission inventories of primary particles and pollutant gases for China. *Chinese Science Bulletin* 56(8): 781–788.

Chen, J. and Han, X. (2013) The evolution of housing market and its socio-economic impacts in post-reform China: a survey of the literature. Working Paper.

Chen, B., Hong, C. and Kan, H. (2004) Exposures and health outcomes from outdoor air pollutants in China. *Toxicology* 198(1–3): 291–300.

Chen, Y., Ebenstein, A., Greenstone, M. and Li, H. (2013) Evidence on the impact of sustained exposure to air pollution on life expectancy from China's Huai river policy. *Proceedings of the National Academy of Sciences* 110(32): 12936–12941.

Cheng, D. (2012) Product-destination portfolio and dynamics by firm ownership and trade mode: evidence from Chinese industrial exporters. *China and World Economy* 20(5): 21–36.

Chow, G. (2010) China's environmental policy: a critical survey. CEPS Working Paper No. 206.

Copeland, B.R. and Taylor, M.S. (2004) Trade, growth, and the environment. *Journal of Economic Literature* 42(1): 7–71.

Currie, J., Zivin, J.S.G., Mullins, J. and Neidell, M.J. (2013) What do we know about short and long term effects of early life exposure to pollution? National Bureau of Economic Research Working Paper No. 19571.

Deng, H., Zheng, X., Huang, N. and Li, F. (2012) Strategic interaction in spending on environmental protection: spatial evidence from Chinese cities. *China and World Economy* 20(5): 103–120.

Du, J., Lu, Y. and Tao, Z. (2008) FDI location choice: agglomeration vs institutions. *International Journal of Finance and Economics* 13(1): 92–107.

Du, Y. and Yang, C. (2014) Demographic transition and labor market changes: implications to economic development in China. *Journal of Economic Surveys* 28(4): 617–635.

Ebenstein, A. (2012) The consequences of industrialization: evidence from water pollution and digestive cancers in China. *Review of Economics and Statistics* 94(1): 186–201.

Faber, B. (2013) Trade integration, market size and industrialization: evidence from China's National Trunk Highway System. LSE Working Paper. Available at http://cep.lse.ac.uk/pubs/download/dp1244.pdf accessed on January 20, 2014.

Feenstra, R. and Wei, S. (2009) Introduction to "China's Growing Role in World Trade". National Bureau of Economic Research Working Paper No. 14716.

Fisher-Vanden, K., Hu, Y., Jefferson, G., Rock, M. and Toman, M. (2013) Factors influencing energy intensity in four Chinese industries. World Bank Policy Research Working Paper 6551.

Gao, T. (2004) Regional industrial growth: evidence from Chinese industries. *Regional Science and Urban Economics* 34(1): 101–124.

Gao, B., Chen J. and Zou, L. (2012) Housing price's regional differences, labor mobility and industrial upgrading. *Economic Research Journal* (1): 66–79. (in Chinese)

Goldstein, G.S. and Gronberg, T.J. (1984) Economies of scope and economies of agglomeration. *Journal of Urban Economics* 16(1): 91–104.

Greenstone, M. (2002) The impacts of environmental regulation on industrial activity. *Journal of Political Economy* 110(6): 1175–1219.

Guo, Y., Jia, Y., Pan, X., Liu, L. and Wichmann, H. (2009) The association between fine particulate air pollution and hospital emergency room visits for cardiovascular diseases in Beijing, China. *Science of the Total Environment* 407(17): 4826–4830.

Gyourko, J., Kahn. M.E. and Tracy, J. (1999) Quality of life and environmental comparisons. In P. Cheshire and E.S. Mills (eds.), *Handbook of Regional and Urban Economics,* Vol. 3: Applied Urban Economics (pp. 1413–1454). Amsterdam, New York and Oxford: Elsevier Science, North-Holland.

Gyourko, J. and Tracy, J. (1991) The structure of local public finance and the quality of life. *Journal of Political Economy* 91(4): 774–806.

He, K., Huo, H. and Zhang, Q. (2002) Urban air pollution in China: current status, characteristics, and progress. *Annual Review of Energy and the Environment* 27: 397–431.

He, C. and Pan, F. (2013) The trends in geographical agglomeration of Chinese manufacturing industries. In M. Lu, Z. Chen and X. Zhu(eds.), *China's Regional Development: Review and Prospect* (pp. 231–265), New York, NY: Routledge.

Helsley, R.W. and Strange, W.C. (2007) Agglomeration, opportunism, and the organization of production. *Journal of Urban Economics* 62(1): 55–75.

Henderson, J.V. (1996) Effects of air quality regulation. *American Economic Review* 86(4): 789–813.

Jiang, L., Lin, C. and Lin, P. (2014) The determinants of pollution levels: firm-level evidence from Chinese manufacturing. *Journal of Comparative Economics* 42(1): 118–142.

Kahn, M.E. (1997). Particulate pollution trends in the United States. *Regional Science and Urban Economics* 27(1): 87–107.

Kahn, M.E. and Mansur, E.T. (2013) Do local energy prices and regulation affect the geographic concentration of employment? *Journal of Public Economics* 101: 105–114.

Kan, H., Chen, R. and Tong, S. (2012) Ambient air pollution, climate change, and population health in china. *Environment International* 42: 10–19.

Krugman, P. (1991) Increasing returns and economic geography. *The Journal of Political Economy* 99(3): 483–499.

Li, B. and Lu, Y. (2009) Geographic concentration and vertical disintegration: evidence from China. *Journal of Urban Economics* 65(3): 294–304.

Lin, L. (2013) Enforcement of pollution levies in China. *Journal of Public Economics* 98: 32–43.

Long, C. and Zhang, X. (2012) Patterns of China's industrialization: concentration, specialization, and clustering. *China Economic Review* 23(3): 593–612.

Lu, Y., Ni, J., Tao, Z. and Yu, L. (2013) City-industry growth in China. *China Economic Review* 27: 135–147.

Lu, J. and Tao, Z. (2009) Trends and determinants of China's industrial agglomeration. *Journal of Urban Economics* 65(2): 167–180.

Lu, M. and Xiang K. (2013) Break the conflict between efficiency and equality: China's regional development strategy. Working Paper. (in Chinese)

Ma, H., Oxley, L., Xu, X. and Yang, P. (2013) The challenge of synchronous development of the four modernizations in China: current institutions vs. the goals of modernization. Working Paper.

Neary, J.P. (2001) Of hype and hyperbolas: introducing the new economic geography. *Journal of Economic Literature* 39(2): 536–561.

Ogawa, N. and Chen, Q. (2013) End of the first demographic dividend and possible labor market response in China and other Asian countries. *China and World Economy* 21(2): 78–96.

Qi, Y. (2008) Environmental governance in China (Zhongguo Huanjing Jiangguan Tizhi Yanjiu), Shanghai: SDX Joint Publishing Company.

Qi, Y. and Zhang, L. (2014) Local environmental enforcement constrained by central-local relations in China. *Journal of Environmental Policy and Governance* 24(3): 216–232.

Qu, Y., Cai, F. and Zhang, X. (2012) Has the 'flying geese' phenomenon in industrial transformation occurred in China. In H. McKay and L. Song (eds.), *Rebalancing and Sustaining Growth in China* (pp. 93–110). Canberra, Australia: ANU E Press.

Ratcliffe, H.E., Swanson, G.M. and Fischer, L.J. (1996) Human exposure to mercury: a critical assessment of the evidence of adverse health effects. *Journal of Toxicology and Environmental Health* 49(3): 221–270.

Roback, J. (1982) Wages, rents, and the quality of life. *Journal of Political Economy* 90(6): 1257–1278.

Rock, M., Toman, M., Cui, Y., Jiang, K., Song, Y. and Wang, Y. (2013) Technological learning, energy efficiency, and CO_2 emissions in China's energy intensive industries. World Bank Policy Research Working Paper No. 6492. Available at http://www-wds.worldbank.org/external/default/WDSContentServer/WDSP/IB/2013/06/18/000158349_20130618132914/Rendered/PDF/WPS6492.pdf accessed on January 20, 2014.

Rosen S. (2002) Markets and diversity. *American Economic Review* 92(1): 1–15.

Sridhar, K.S. and Wan, G. (2010) Firm location choice in cities: evidence from China, India, and Brazil. *China Economic Review* 21(1): 113–122.

Van Rooij, B. and Lo, C.W. (2010) Fragile convergence: understanding variation in the enforcement of China's industrial pollution law. *Law and Policy* 32(1): 14–37.

Venners, S.A., Wang, B., Xu, Z., Schlatter, Y., Wang, L. and Xu, X. (2003) Particulate matter, sulfur dioxide, and daily mortality in Chongqing, China. *Environmental Health Perspectives* 111(4): 562–567.

Wang, A. (2013) The search for sustainable legitimacy: environmental law and bureaucracy in China. *Harvard Environmental Law Review* 37: 365–440.

Wang, H. and Jin, Y. (2007) Industrial ownership and environmental performance: evidence from China. *Environmental and Resource Economics* 36(3): 255–273.

Wang, H. and Wheeler, D. (2005) Financial incentives and endogenous enforcement in China's pollution levy system. *Journal of Environmental Economics and Management* 49(1): 174–196.

Wen, M. (2004) Relocation and agglomeration of Chinese industry. *Journal of Development Economics* 73(1): 329–347.

World Bank. (2006) Water quality management policy and institutional considerations. Discussion Paper. Washington, DC: The World Bank. Available at http://siteresources.worldbank.org/INTEAPREGTOP-ENVIRONMENT/Resources/China_WPM_final_lo_res.pdf accessed on January 20, 2014.

World Bank. (2007). Cost of pollution in China. Washington, DC: The World Bank. Available at http://siteresources.worldbank.org/INTEAPREGTOPENVIRONMENT/Resources/China_Cost_of_Pollution.pdf accessed on January 20, 2014.

Wu, J., Deng, Y., Huang, J., Morck, R. and Yeung, B. (2013) Incentives and outcomes: China's environmental policy. National Bureau of Economic Research Working Paper No. 18754.

Xu, Y., Williams, R.H. and Socolow, R.H. (2009) China's rapid deployment of SO_2 scrubbers. *Energy and Environmental Science* 2(5): 459–465.

Yu, J., Zhou, L. and Zhu, G. (2013) Strategic interaction in political competition: evidence from spatial effects across Chinese cities. Working Paper. Available at http://zhuguozhong.info/f_research/TournamentCompetition.pdf accessed on January 20, 2014.

Zheng, S. and Kahn, M.E. (2008) Land and residential property markets in a booming economy: new evidence from Beijing. *Journal of Urban Economics* 63(2): 743–757.

Zheng, S., Kahn, M.E. and Liu, H. (2010) Towards a system of open cities in China: home prices, FDI flows and air quality in 35 major cities. *Regional Science and Urban Economics* 40(1): 1–10.

Zheng, S. and Kahn, M.E. (2013a) Understanding China's urban pollution dynamics. *Journal of Economic Literature* 51(3): 731–772.

Zheng, S. and Kahn, M.E. (2013b) China's bullet trains facilitate market integration and mitigate the cost of megacity growth. *Proceedings of the National Academy of Sciences* 110(14): E1248–E1253.

Zheng, S., Cao, J., Kahn, M.E. and Sun, C. (2013a) Real estate valuation and cross-boundary air pollution externalities: evidence from Chinese cities. *The Journal of Real Estate Finance and Economics*. Available at http://link.springer.com/content/pdf/10.1007%2Fs11146-013-9405-4.pdf accessed on January 20, 2014.

Zheng, S., Kahn, M.E., Sun, W. and Luo, D. (2013b) Incentives for China's urban mayors to mitigate pollution externalities: the role of the central government and public environmentalism. *Regional Science and Urban Economics*. Available at http://www.sciencedirect.com/science/article/pii/S0166046213000690 accessed on January 20, 2014.

Zheng, W., Wang, X., Tian, D., Jiang, S., Andersen, M.E., He, G., Crabbe, J.C., Zheng, Y., ZhongY., and Qu, W. (2013c) Water pollutant fingerprinting tracks recent industrial transfer from coastal to inland China: a case study. *Nature Scientific Reports* 3: 1031. Available at http://www.nature.com/srep/2013/130107/srep01031/full/srep01031.html accessed on January 20, 2014.

9

INNOVATION IN CHINA

Peilei Fan
Michigan State University

1. Introduction

China has a long history of pursuing innovation and technological advancement. It is well known that the 'Middle Kingdom' produced the 'four great' inventions: the compass, gunpowder, papermaking, and printing. This ambition for technological supremacy has continued throughout the Maoist Era (1949–1978) and the reform period (1978–present). Though plagued by wars and poverty and under extreme difficulties due to an embargo by western nations, China conducted its first successful atomic bomb test in its northwestern desert in 1964. In recent decades, there have been significant achievements in biotechnology, astronautics and information technology, including: (1) together with four other countries at the forefront of genomic research (the USA, Japan, Germany, and France), China participated in the Human Genome working draft in 2001; (2) China became the third nation to launch a man into space in 2003, following Russia and the U.S.; and (3) China became the third country with supercomputing ability in 2004 and had the fastest supercomputers in the world in 2010 and 2013.

Nevertheless, there is a substantial difference between the pursuit of technological advancement from an historic perspective and the recent launch of an economic development strategy based on innovation. On November 8, 2012, in a report delivered by President Hu Jintao in the 18th National Congress Party, China announced that it would transition into an "innovation-driven economy." Thirty-five years of reform dramatically lifted China out of poverty and positioned the country as the second largest world economy in 2010. However, the growth model it used, which has converted the country into the world's largest factory, producing everything from clothing to electronics, has relied heavily on investments, exports, and a huge low-cost labor force. Currently, China is ready to shift to the next stage, through an economy mainly driven by technological advancement, to address the slow down of its past growth model. Improvements in innovation capability, especially in its industrial sectors, are considered essential to China's sustainable economic growth in the future. Similar to the rest of the world, the importance of innovation to economic growth in China means that innovation should not be treated as merely an element in an economic residual, but rather as a key issue that policy makers should consider as making a positive influence (McCann and Oxley, 2012; Yu *et al.*, 2013).

Against the announcement of China's new economic development strategies driven by innovation are "believer's claims that China is out-innovating the West" and "doubter's claims that China is lagging on the innovation front" (Steinfeld, 2010, p. 34). The common perception is that China's rise in innovation capability poses a threat to U.S. leadership in science and technology.[1]

To unveil the myth of "innovation in China" and its impact on the rest of the world, it is essential to answer the following set of questions: What is the current status of innovation capability in China? How did China improve its innovation capability over the past 35 years? Has any theoretical proposition related to innovation found a resonance in the Chinese context? Further, what can we learn from China's experience, and what are the implications for other emerging countries? In this paper, I address some of the above questions by providing a critical review of innovation in China and related literature. First, I evaluate the current status of China's innovation capability through both the input and output indicators of China's innovation system, such as R&D personnel, R&D expenditure, patents, high-tech and service exports, and scientific and technical journal articles. Further, I underline the contribution of technological progress vis-à-vis labor and capital to China's economic development, indicated by annual GDP growth. I then review China's development of innovation since the economic reform and identify major factors that may explain its evolution, relying on theoretic frameworks of (1) systems of innovation (SI), (2) external linkages, such as global value chains, global production networks, overseas returnees, and R&D globalization, and (3) the dynamics of latecomers' catch-ups. Finally, I review the uneven spatial distribution of innovation capability and analyze possible causes for the inequality, as well as the emerging research in regional innovation systems.

2. Measuring Innovation in China

Innovation capability can be assessed using the input and output measures of the innovation system. The input measures are usually represented by indicators such as the amount of R&D investment and the number of researchers in R&D, whereas output measures are reflected by indicators such as patents, high-tech/service exports, and academic output like scientific and technical journal paper publication. This section will present the evaluation of innovation capability based on these commonly used indicators. It should be noted that one has to exercise caution when using the above-mentioned indicators or any other indicator as an accurate assessment of innovation capability, especially when comparing China's indicators with those of other countries. First, while there are useful guidelines that can make measurements of innovation indicators comparable between most developed countries, such as the OECD countries, China has not been a part of the collective process and thus it is difficult to compare China's indicators with others. Many countries in the OECD have adopted the principles of the Oslo Manual to collect innovation data. Currently, all member states of the European Union (EU) and some candidate countries for the EU[2] have used the community innovation survey (CIS) to standardize their models of innovation surveys (Lopez-Bassols, 2011). Other countries, such as China, Japan, Korea, and Russia, have adopted innovation surveys close to the CIS, but with some adaptations (Lopez-Bassols, 2011; Hong *et al.*, 2012). Although CIS indicators are growing in use, they are still less widely used than the R&D statistics, due to

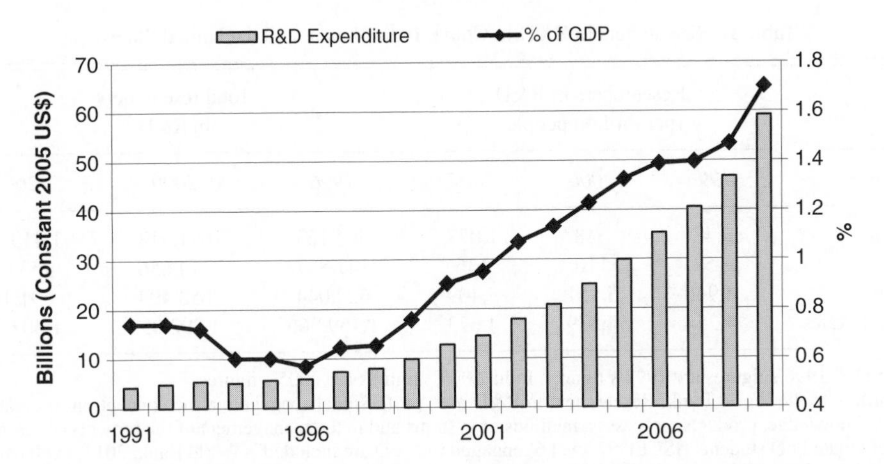

Figure 1. China's R&D Expenditure and Its Percentage of GDP, 1991–2009.

Note: Expenditures for research and development are "current and capital expenditures (both public and private) on creative work undertaken systematically to increase knowledge, including knowledge of humanity, culture, and society, and the use of knowledge for new applications. R&D covers basic research, applied research, and experimental development" (World Bank, 2013, explanation of the definition of Research and development expenditure [% of GDP]).

Source: Figure created by the author based on data from World Development Indicator (World Bank, 2013).

concerns about quality, policy relevance, and international comparability outside of the EU (Lopez-Bassols, 2011). Second, innovation-related data are territory-based and national data does not actually reflect China's innovation due to foreign individuals' and organizations' activities in China, as well as the innovation of Chinese individuals and organizations outside of China (Altenburg *et al.*, 2008).

2.1 *Input indicators*

2.1.1 *R&D Expenditure*

R&D expenditure is considered one of the most important elements in improving the innovation capacity of nations as well as firms (Audretsch and Feldman, 2004). Data analysis on OECD countries such as USA, UK, Japan, France, Italy and Germany, shows that R&D expenditure stimulates innovation and enhances total factor productivity (TFP) (Goto and Suzuki 1989; Hall, 1993; Hall and Mairesse, 1995; Harhoff, 1998; Wakelin, 2001; Griffith *et al.*, 2004; Lang, 2009). A positive and significant relationship has also been found between the R&D expenditure of a firm and its productivity (Griliches and Mairesse, 1984; Griliches, 1986, 1998; Romer 1986, 1990; Lucas, 1988).

Since the mid-1990s, China has invested heavily in R&D and has gradually increased R&D expenditure as a percentage of GDP from around 0.6% in 1996 to 1.7% in 2009 (Figure 1). It is worth noting that the "Decision on Accelerating S&T Development" announced by the state council in 1995 set the ambitious goal of increasing spending on R&D to 1.5% of GDP by 2000, resulting in China's R&D expenditure as a percentage of GDP after 1995 growing

Table 1. Researchers in R&D in China, India, Japan, and the United States.

	Researchers in R&D (per million people)			Total researchers in R&D		
Country	*1996*	*2000*	*2007*	*1996*	*2000*	*2007*
China	447	548	1,077	544,163	691,518	1,419,507
India	152	110	136	147,897	114,656	153,075
Japan	4,946	5,151	5,409	622,044	653,494	691,101
United States	4,254	4,579	4,673	1,159,966	1,292,053	1,407,716

Note: U.S. 1996's figures are 1997's figures. India 2007's figures are 2005's figures.
According to the World Bank, Researchers in R&D are "professionals engaged in the conception or creation of new knowledge, products, processes, methods or systems and in the management of the projects concerned. Postgraduate PhD students (ISCED97 level 6) engaged in R&D are included" (World Bank, 2013, explanation on the definition of Researchers in R&D).

Source: Compiled by the author based on the data from World Development Indicator (World Bank, 2013).

at a much faster pace than in previous years and reaching 1.7% in 2009 (Fan, 2011b). This percentage is still behind that of the OECD countries that, in general, spend on average 2–3% of GDP on R&D. However, considering that China's R&D expenditure increased even faster than its economy, which grew at a remarkable rate of around 10% in the 1990s and 2000s, its R&D expenditure was certainly impressive. The R&D figure expanded from US$4.2 billion in 1991 to US$59 billion in 2009, a 14-fold increase in the space of 18 years. In fact, before China overtook Japan as the second largest economy measured by GDP in 2010, China surpassed Japan to became the second largest nation in R&D expenditure in 2006 (OECD, 2006).

2.1.2 *R&D Personnel*

The number of researchers in R&D reflects the level of human capital for innovation capability and is an important indicator. A comparison of China's data with that of the United States and Japan indicates that the country has improved in this dimension as well (Table 1). The number of researchers in R&D more than doubled, growing from 447 per million in 1996 to 1077 per million in 2007, making China's level around 20% of that of the USA and Japan. However, due to its large population size, when comparing the absolute numbers, China became the leader in terms of the number of total researchers in R&D, slightly surpassing the USA, and more than double that of Japan. In fact, the rich reserve of R&D human resources is one of the major reasons that multinational corporations (MNCs) have chosen to locate their corporate research centers in China. MNCs grew their R&D centers in China fivefold from 2003 to 2007, with 750 foreign R&D centers in China in 2007 (Walsh, 2007), including work to tailor products to the needs of the Chinese market as well as basic R&D (Sun *et al.*, 2008).

2.2 *Output Indicators*

2.2.1 *Patents*

Despite skepticism, the number of patents granted has been accepted as the most appropriate output measure for innovation capability (Mansfield, 1986; Basberg, 1987; Griliches, 1990;

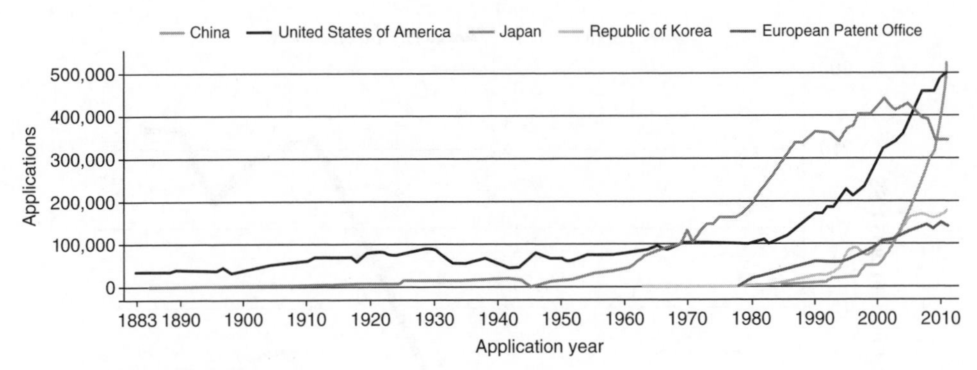

Figure 2. Trend in Invention Patent Application for Top Five Offices.
Source: Neumeyer (2013, Figure 1).

Hagedoorn and Cloodt, 2003). Different indices, such as those tracking R&D inputs, patent counts, paper citations and new product announcements, can all be used as an indicator for output measure of innovation capability. This paper follows Audretsch and Feldman (2004) and uses patent data as the main proxy of output measure of innovation capability. Hagedoorn and Cloodt (2003) found that statistical overlap between various innovativeness indicators is substantial and that any of these indicators, including patents, may be used to measure innovation capability.

Although China adopted modern patent law less than three decades ago in 1984, the number of patents granted to Chinese inventors, in China and worldwide, has been growing exponentially (Figure 2). In 2012, China's State Intellectual Property Office (SIPO) granted 1.26 million patents, a 31% increase over the number granted in 2011 and more than any other patent office in the world. Further, almost 80% of China's patents were awarded to domestic applicants in 2012, while fewer than 50% of all U.S. patents went to U.S. citizens (Neumeyer, 2013).

Worldwide, China has been catching up rapidly in the intellectual property (IP) arena, as illustrated by the decadal data on patents granted by the United States Patent and Trademark Office (USPTO) (Table 2). Compared with other leading Asian inventors excluding Japan,

Table 2. U.S. Patents Granted to Asian Inventors, 1970–2013.

	Total	1970–1979	1980–1989	1990–1999	2000–2009	2010–2013
Taiwan	141,431	57	2,613	22,507	72,365	43,889
S. Korea	127,786	10	646	15,306	58,024	53,800
Hong Kong	11,753	123	886	2,688	5,855	2,201
Singapore	9,967	11	102	957	5,166	3,731
China	37,688	2	178	900	13,219	23,389
India	15,068	81	166	679	5,529	8,613

Note: For 2013, the issue dates are from January 1 to October 30, 2013.

Source: Compiled by the author based on the USPTO Patent Collection Database, website: http://patft.uspto.gov/

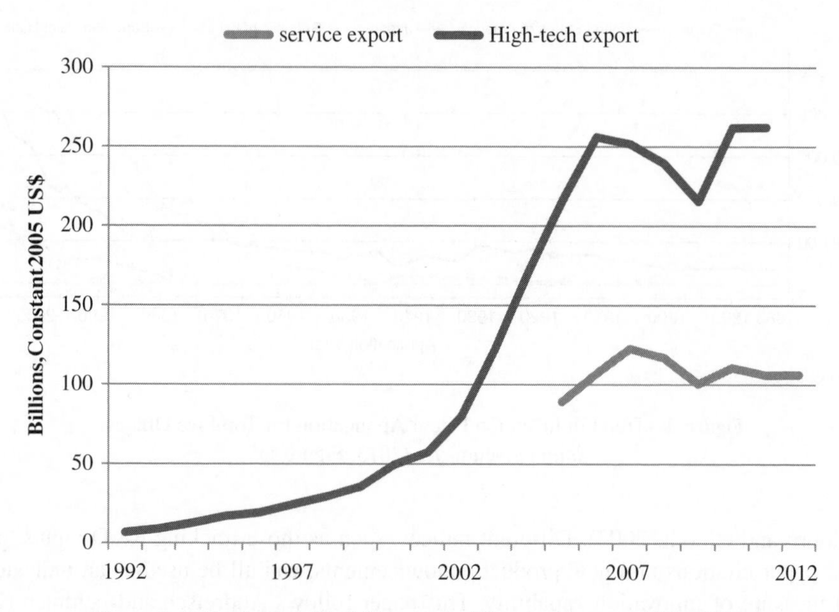

Figure 3. China's High-Tech Exports and Service Exports, 1992–2012.
Source: Figure created by the author based on data from World Development Indicator (World Bank, 2013).

China's progress is hard to dismiss. Although it was behind Hong Kong and Singapore in the 1990s, China's total number of granted patents from the USPTO was more than the sum of those two economies in the 2000s. Further, in the past three years (2010–October 2013), China has substantially increased the number of granted patents, by almost doubling its figures from the 1990s, significantly improving its position vis-à-vis other emerging Asian innovation centers, namely Taiwan and Korea. In 2012, China was listed as No. 9 worldwide in terms of patent applications to the USPTO, trailing after the USA, Japan, Germany, Korea, Taiwan, Canada, the UK and France. However, applications from Chinese inventors increased by 41% over 2011, more than twice the rate of increase of any of those countries (Neumeyer, 2013). In 2012, with 782 U.S. patents granted, a Chinese company, Hong Fu Jin Precision Industry Corp., also became one of top 50 U.S. patent recipients for the first time.

2.2.2 *High-Tech and Service Export*

As its economy has grown, China has also increased the sophistication of its export files, growing particularly in the volume of high-tech and service exports (Figure 3). High-tech exports have gathered momentum and have experienced exponential growth since 2002, whereas the service export area has experienced steady growth since the early 2000s. This evolution pattern is similar to that of the OECD countries (Rodrik, 2006; Schott, 2008; Lai and Li, 2013). However, due to the debate on whether or not growth in high-tech exports can truly reflect improvements in innovation capacity, this paper suggests that readers use this indicator as a complementary reference for China's innovation system. Chinese high-tech exports have been considered as low technology products from high-tech industries (Blustein, 1997) or as the result of the "processing trade": contract manufacturing in China of goods designed elsewhere

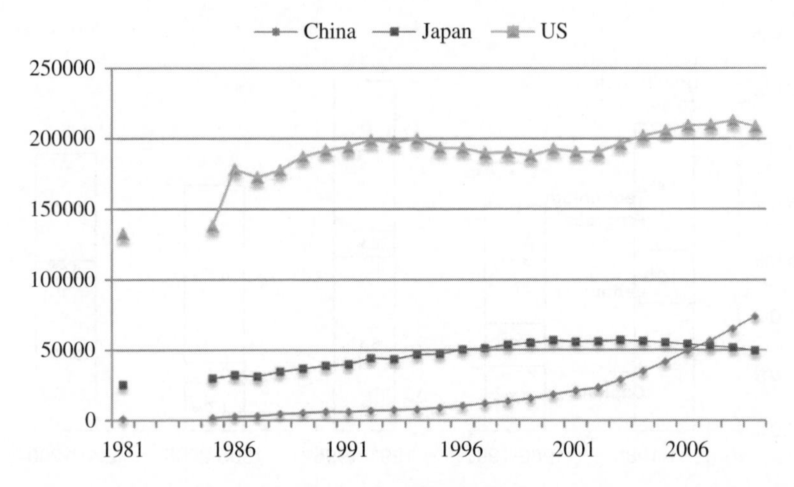

Figure 4. Scientific and Technical Journal Articles Published by China, Japan, and the USA, 1981–2009.
Source: Figure created by the author based on data from World Development Indicator (World Bank, 2013).

(Feenstra and Wei, 2010). In contrast to this negative view, some researchers have emphasized that China has gradually increased the skill content and sophistication of its exports in recent years due to ongoing improvement in human capital and government policies, especially those on tax-favored high-tech zones (Amiti and Freund, 2010; Wang and Wei, 2010; Berger and Martin, 2013).

2.2.3 *Scientific and Technical Journal Articles*

The number of scientific and engineering articles can be used as another output indicator to illustrate the efficiency of the innovation system, especially the more basic and fundamental aspects of innovation. This indicator refers to journal articles published in the following science and technology fields: physics, biology, chemistry, mathematics, clinical medicine, biomedical research, engineering and technology, and earth and space sciences, in journals classified by the Institute for Scientific Information's Science Citation Index (SCI) and the Social Sciences Citation Index (SSCI) (World Bank, 2013). Starting with only 1,100 journal articles in 1981, China surpassed Japan and had around 74,000 scientific and technical journal articles, over a third of that of the USA (208,600), by 2009 (Figure 4).

Finally, through a decomposition analysis, one can assess how much innovation capability actually contributed to the economic development of China (Fan, 2011a) (Figure 5). As GDP growth can be decomposed into the contributions of capital, labor, and technology, the share of technology can be measured by TFP growth (Fan and Watanabe, 2006). The decomposition reveals that technology has significantly influenced China's economic development since the 1980s. It is interesting to note that while capital fluctuated in its contribution to GDP growth in different periods, technological progress made a relatively steady contribution. While at the beginning of the reform era (1981–1985), capital was the leading factor for growth, followed closely by technology, technological progress leaped forward and became the leading growth factor over the next five years (1986–1990) with capital some distance behind. In the 1990s

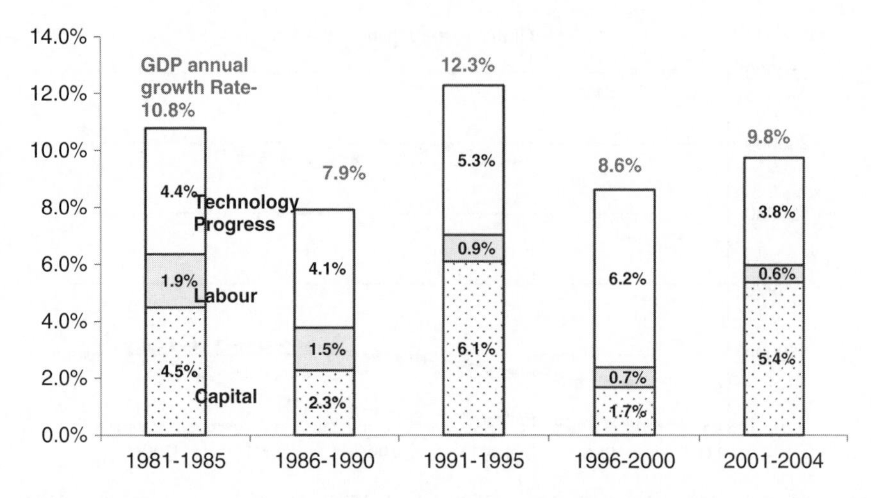

Figure 5. Contribution of Technological Progress to Economic Growth in China, 1981–2004.
Source: Adapted from Fan (2011a, p. 53).

and the early 2000s, technological progress consistently contributed to GDP growth at 4–6% annually, while capital displayed a very unstable pattern, fluctuating from 6.1% (1991–1995) to 1.7% (1996–2000), to 5.4% (2001–2004), reflecting the influences of large injections of capital and the outbreak of the Asian financial crisis.

3. Developing Innovation Capability: The Chinese way

3.1 *The System Approach*

Since Freeman first officially used the term "national system of innovation" (NSI) in his work to analyze technology policy and economic performance in Japan in 1987 (Freeman, 1987), the "SI" approach and its three perspectives, NSI, sectoral system of innovation (SSI), and regional system of innovation (RSI), have been developed and adopted by many researchers as conceptual frameworks to analyze innovation in different contexts (for example, NSI: Freeman, 1987, 1995; Lundvall, 1992; Nelson, 1993; SSI: Breschi and Malerba, 1997; Malerba, 2002, 2004, 2005; Geels, 2004; Malerba and Mani, 2009; RSI: Cooke *et al.*, 1997; Braczyk *et al.*, 1998; Cooke, 2001; Asheim and Isaksen, 2002). As it emphasizes that innovation is to "produce new knowledge or combine existing elements of knowledge in new ways" (Edquist, 2005, p. 184), the "SI" approach distinguishes itself from other approaches that consider technological change and innovation as exogenous (Edquist, 2005).

Due to its holistic and evolutionary perspectives, encompassing product and process innovation, an emphasis on interdependency and nonlinearity, and the role of institutions, the SI approach has also been used by a number of researchers to analyze innovation in China, particularly the evolution of its NSI (Xue, 1997; Gu, 1999; Liu and White, 2001; Fan and Watanabe, 2006; Motohashi and Yun, 2007; Altenburg *et al.*, 2008).[3] Prior to the 1980s, China had a NSI similar to other central planning economies such as the Soviet Union and India, characterized by the complete separation of research activities, education, and manufacturing activities in public research institutes (PRIs), universities, and state-owned enterprises (SOEs), respectively (Xue, 1997). Since the economic reform, the Chinese government has started to actively transform the Soviet model, especially by emphasizing colocating research and manufacturing. The government has used both carrots and sticks to pull and push the R&D institutes to adapt the market environment and to conduct R&D that has industrial implications. For instance, while it reduced institutional funding for PRIs in order to push the PRIs to conduct more market-oriented R&D through industries and universities (Liu and White, 2001), it also offered financial incentives to commercialize R&D results, especially through the Torch Program, a national science and technology program specifically targeting high-tech industrialization, launched in 1988. The government also performed an organizational transformation by advocating mergers of some R&D institutes with enterprises in 1987 and reforming established R&D institutes into entities with economic functions, such as production and consultancy centers, from the 1990s (Gu, 1999; Fan and Watanabe, 2006; Fan, 2011a).

Up to now, Liu and White's (2001) analysis of China's NIS remains the most comprehensive of its kind. They identified five fundamental activities in an innovation system, which extend beyond the R&D system and include inputs to research activity and the use of research outputs. The activities are: "(1) research (basic, developmental, engineering), (2) implementation (manufacturing), (3) end-use (customers of the product or process outputs), (4) linkage (bringing together complementary knowledge), and (5) education" (Liu and White, 2001, p. 1,094). They also coined the term "primary actors," referring to organizations that perform one of the five above-mentioned fundamental activities. Applying this updated framework, they concluded that China's NIS in the transition era had two distinguishing characteristics: the inclusion of new actors for each of the fundamental activities and diversification of the activities of the primary actors. Here, I update their summary of the five fundamental activities in the NSI with some new developments that have occurred in the 2000s.

In the transition era, the most fundamental activity, R&D, has had a significant transformation in both nature and distribution. While the original primary actors, i.e., PRIs, are still among the main actors performing R&D, they were given strong financial incentives to conduct applied research. However, a large amount of direct funding for basic research, particularly in "strategic" high-tech industries such as information technology and biotechnology, is available through national programs such as 863 and 973 (explained in more detail later in this section). The distribution of R&D activities has been extended through colocating R&D and implementation (manufacturing), by either adding in-house R&D to enterprises or inserting the commercial component into research institutes (Liu and White, 2001). Further, new players such as R&D centers for MNCs (Sun *et al.*, 2008), new technology enterprises (Zhou, 2008), and high-tech firms started by overseas returnees (Saxenian, 2002, 2006; Zweig *et al.*, 2006), have entered the scene, while domestic companies started to tap global R&D resources by setting up their R&D units in global hot spots of high-tech development (Fan, 2011b). The business sector quickly rose to become a major contributor to national R&D, with large- and medium-sized enterprises spending RMB 44 billion in 2001, an increase of RMB 14 billion from the 1995 level and accounting for 42% of the national total (Fan and Watanabe, 2006). According to R&D Magazine, in 2004, R&D spending by the industry sector accounted for 61.2% of the national total.

In implementation (manufacturing) activities, many new actors have joined SOEs to become primary actors, including MNCs, joint ventures, township and village enterprises (TVEs), and private companies. In responding to the incentives and freedom to pursue more revenue-generating activities, primary actors in other activities, especially universities and PRIs, have diversified into manufacturing (Gu, 1999), usually in the form of spin-off ventures.

For end-use activities, there is a significant increase in individual and industrial consumers as actors, providing incentives for companies to conduct market-oriented innovation. It is worth mentioning that China's end users, either individuals or organizations, have become more sophisticated as the country's economy has expanded. By understanding, the needs of the end users better and being willing to customize R&D for those end users, some Chinese companies, such as Huawei and ZTE in the telecommunication sector (Fan, 2006a, 2011b), have established competitive advantages compared to the MNCs.

In educational activities, while universities are still the main primary actors, they have extended their activities into R&D and manufacturing. China has rapidly scaled up its higher education sector by expanding existing universities through increased admission and establishing more higher educational institutions, and this has led to a natural increase in graduates with science and technology degrees. Further, the universities have been increasingly pushing for research productivity from their faculties. One such example is the required number of publications for not only promotion of faculty, but also to be allowed to have graduate students to supervise. It is therefore not surprising to see China's gigantic leap in numbers of published journal articles (Figure 4).

Finally, the relationships between the actors have been transformed. While the government was previously in direct control of resource transfer/distribution and coordination of organizations in the innovation system, it is now involved in linking R&D with implementation through a number of measures, including setting up productivity promotion centers to assist firms to implement technologies originating from state R&D institutes and creating incubator centers (Liu and White, 2001). For instance, for basic research, funding from national programs such as Program 973 (explained further below) usually requires the involvement of several research institutes or universities. However, government can directly facilitate the linkage between end users and the implementation sector to promote the R&D results, illustrated by the experience of domestic telecommunication equipment producers (Fan, 2006b).

In addition to reforming its Soviet-style NSI, China has implemented a variety of technology policy initiatives, with a focus on basic research for key areas and research for market needs (Fan, 2011a). Programs for enhancing its basic research include the Key Technologies Research and Development Program in 1982, the High-tech Research and Development Program (Program 863) in 1986, and the National Program for Priority Basic Research and Development (Program 973) in 1997. Policies focusing on high-tech industrialization include the well-known Torch Program, initiated in 1988, which advocated setting up high-tech parks specializing in high-tech innovation, application, and diffusion. The parks are set up to attract foreign high-tech MNCs and to encourage the development of innovative domestic firms. In 2003, about 67% of China's 33,392 high-tech enterprises were located in high-tech parks (Fan, 2011) where they enjoy various benefits for innovation-related activities. For instance, in Zhongguancun Science Park, China's Silicon Valley, benefits for innovation include: (1) a tax cut of up to 15% for key companies in the creative industries, (2) reduction of personal income tax for investors in high-tech R&D to further boost the venture capital sector to aid more tech startups, (3) tax benefits for company income generated by patent transfers, and (4) waiver of the enterprise tax on patents sold at less than 5 million yuan ($820,000) or half the rate of the enterprise tax for higher values.[4]

Although the system approach is very helpful in understanding the internal structure and the evolution of innovation for a specific country/region, it has been criticized for lacking consideration of relationships with key actors outside of the system and for poor understanding of the dynamics of the innovation system, i.e., how structures of interaction develop and change over time (Humphrey and Schmitz, 2002; Bell, 2006). To address these weaknesses, researchers have proposed integrating transborder linkages into the territorially bounded innovation system and analyzing the catch-up in innovation capability, taking into account the changes in technological regimes and the global economic environment (Altenburg *et al.*, 2008; Fan, 2011b). In the following sections, I will focus on analyzing China's innovation along these two dimensions.

3.2 *Global Linkages*

3.2.1 *Interfirm Linkages*

Global linkages, especially those describing relationships between firms, are mostly derived from the literature of interfirm networks, which are considered crucial to fostering innovation inside firms as well as at the regional level. Firms can increase the efficiency of their R&D as interfirm networks allow businesses to leverage their capacity and gain access to external resources, thus reducing the risk and cost of R&D (Hagedoorn and Schakenraad, 1994; Mowery *et al.*, 1996; Ahuja, 2000; Stuart, 2000). Global linkages forged by firms from developing countries are considered particularly helpful for technological upgrading because of the limited resources of local companies in developing countries. The global value chain (GVC) (Humphrey and Schmitz, 2002, 2004; Schmitz, 2004; Gereffi *et al.*, 2005; Sturgeon *et al.*, 2008) and global production network (GPN) (Dicken *et al.*, 2001; Ernst and Kim, 2002; Henderson *et al.*, 2002; Coe *et al.*, 2004; Coe *et al.*, 2008; Yeung, 2009) are two approaches that have emphasized how firms from foreign countries have been instrumental in transferring technology, particularly tacit knowledge, to local companies (Sun and Zhou, 2011). However, several studies have indicated that interfirm networks have limited impact on innovation capability, reflected either by the number of patents (Stuart, 2000), or the novelty or impact of the products (Kotabe and Swan, 1995).

It is widely acknowledged that China's economic development has closely been associated with its incorporation into the GVC or global production network (Enright *et al.*, 2005; Zhou 2008; Lin *et al.*, 2013). But what are the exact impacts of these linkages on firms' innovation capabilities? Altenburg *et al.* (2008) suggested that the opportunity to improve the innovation capabilities of local firms depends on the types of linkages forged and the power constellations within their global partners. For instance, in a captive chain, capability (knowledge-using) that goes with the lead firms' interests will be facilitated and encouraged, whereas capability directed against the interests of the lead firms (knowledge-creating) will have less chance to thrive and may even be discouraged. It is also suggested that while working with lead firms provides access to advanced technology, new design, and process, domestic linkages can be more conducive to the development of innovation capability as there is more opportunity to work with domestic consumers on design, marketing, and branding (Mitsuhashi, 2006; Navas-Alemán, 2006). Based on a large-scale survey of more than 1,000 ICT companies in China, Sun and Zhou (2011) made interesting findings in terms of the impacts of global linkages on innovation in domestic companies compared to the impacts of domestic linkages. First, many Chinese firms (more than half of the surveyed firms) did not have any interfirm linkages, with either domestic or foreign companies. Second, while positive impacts of interfirm linkages on firms' innovation were found, global linkages offered more benefit than domestic linkages, and firms that had both global and domestic linkages benefitted the most. Third, while more intense global linkages led to higher impacts on innovation in local firms, more intense domestic linkages caused overembeddedness and had a negative impact on firms' innovation. Finally, Chinese firms' internal characteristics and local/regional settings also affected linkages, such as: (1) internal R&D did not seem to enhance the positive impact of interfirm technological linkage on firms' innovation; (2) ownership of firms did not seem to have any impact on innovativeness or the use of interfirm linkages for innovation; and (3) the positive impact of technological linkages on innovation in firms remained the same regardless of the types of industrial hubs involved (Sun and Zhou, 2011).

3.2.2 *Global Networks of Professionals and Returnees*

In addition to global linkages in the interfirm network sphere, other linkages, such as global networks of professionals, have increasingly gained attention in explaining the improvement in China's innovation capability, especially after the publication of Saxenian's (2006) work on the development of Bangalore's software and China's computer industry through entrepreneurs, engineers, and scientists who originally came from China but gained substantial work experience in the USA.

In fact, China has a significant advantage in tapping into the global networks of Chinese professionals in the high-tech sector, due to the large number of Chinese students being sent to study in western countries since the economic reforms (Zweig *et al.*, 2004, 2006; Zweig, 2006; Simon and Cao, 2009). Between 1978 and 2013, more than one million Chinese went abroad for study and research (Cao, 2004; MOE, 2013) and the number has been exploding in recent years. The annual number of students who went overseas has risen nearly twenty times, from 20,000 in the late 1990s to nearly 400,000 in recent years (Wang *et al.*, 2009; MOE, 2013). The Chinese government has realized the value of this talent pool and has attempted to entice overseas talent to return to China, in the hope of repeating Taiwan's success story in the electronics industry (Li *et al.*, 2004; Fan and Watanabe, 2006). The government has initiated quite a few programs, from central government level such as the "1000 Talents Programs" and the "1000 Young Talents Program," to local governments, such as Nanjing's "321 Program," Wuxi's "530 Program," and Shenzhen's "Peacock Program." Attracting talent has become a critical task for China and other countries to develop innovative economies (Simon and Cao, 2009; Florida, 2010; Beaverstock and Hall, 2012).

Despite a plethora of literature on returnees, there are some gaps that need to be addressed to improve our understanding of how global professional networks and overseas returnees have contributed to the improvement of the innovation capability of the home countries, such as the strategies and performances of returnee companies vis-à-vis home-grown companies, the specific global linkages that can have significant impact on innovation in returnee companies, and regional (subnational) variations in terms of locating and growing returnee companies. More studies on returnee entrepreneurs and companies that are founded or managed by returnees (returnee companies) are expected to fulfill this need in the near future (Altenburg *et al.*, 2008; Solimano, 2008).

3.2.3 *R&D Globalization*

Along with forging interfirm linkages with global partners, domestic Chinese firms have also started to use R&D globalization as a proactive approach to tap into the resources that global hotspots of innovation have to offer. Examining the locations, purposes, and patterns of R&D globalization has offered important insights concerning innovation by latecomers.

R&D globalization has increasingly been used to improve firms' innovation capability, boost foreign market share, attract talent, and reduce R&D cost (Niosi, 1999; Reddy, 2000; UNCTAD, 2005; Fan, 2011b). Two types of foreign R&D units should be differentiated: home-base-augmenting (HBA) and home-base-exploiting (HBE) units (Kuemmerle, 1997, 1999a, 1999b). While HBA is established "to augment firm-specific capabilities if this mode of augmenting firms' knowledge base offers higher payoffs than licensing in" (Kuemmerle, 1999a, p. 184), HBE units are set up to "exploit firm-specific capabilities if this mode of exploitation offers higher pay-off than licensing out" (Kuemmerle, 1999a, p. 184). The eclectic "ownership-location-internalization" (OLI) theory (Dunning, 1981, 1988) and the internationalization process (IP) theory (Johanson and Vahlue, 1977) are also useful to explain the locations and motivations of R&D by foreign MNCs in China and the R&D globalization of Chinese MNCs as latecomers.

The findings on Chinese firms in the telecom equipment sector indicate that although Chinese firms do not differ from established firms in terms of locations of HBA and HBE R&D units, they differ in the order and pace of development. In contrast to the IP theory, their R&D globalization has progressed simultaneously with, and even ahead of, their globalization of markets and manufacturing. These differences confirm that the R&D globalization of latecomers is not so much about exploiting the existing "ownership" advantages, like the established multinationals, but, rather, to tap into resources and markets that would otherwise be unavailable (Buckley *et al.*, 2007; Li, 2007; Luo and Tung, 2007; Niosi and Tschang, 2009). Further, as these units are particularly attractive to local skilled personnel who originally came from China, the global R&D units represent another way to tap into the global network of Chinese professionals (Fan, 2011b).

3.3 *Dynamics of Catching Up of Latecomers*

Latecomers, in comparison with first movers, are challenged with many disadvantages in developing their innovation capability, such as technological leadership of incumbent firms, preemption of assets, and high buyer switching costs (Lieberman and Montgomery, 1988, 1998; Kardes and Kalyanaram, 1992), but are also blessed with advantages because enhanced information and free-rider effects can save them money and time due to information spillover and learning from the experiences of first movers. Meanwhile, changes in market or consumer tastes and technological regimes, in combination with the resources, people and organization committed by first movers to meet earlier market and technology requirements, can disadvantage first movers and offer opportunities for latecomers to catch up (Richardson, 1996; Cho *et al.*, 1998; Lieberman and Montgomery, 1998). Among the literature on catching-up and technological upgrading strategies of latecomers (e.g., Hobday, 1995; Leonard-Barton, 1995), one can apply Kim's technology learning framework (Kim, 1997) to understand how China catches up in different sectors as a latecomer (Fan, 2011b) and highlight the differences between China and the earlier latecomers such as Japan and the newly industrialized economies (NIEs).

Kim (1997) observed that the technological trajectory of catch-up countries, such as Korea, is in the reverse direction to that of advanced countries. While technology development in advanced countries goes through stages of emergence, consolidation, and maturity, firms in catching-up countries move from imitation, i.e., acquiring, assimilating, and improving mature technologies from advanced countries, to innovation, i.e., eventually accumulating indigenous innovative capability and generating emerging technologies (Kim, 1997). Firms in catching-up countries can rely on three main groups of resources for technological learning: the international community, the domestic community, and in-house efforts.

However, compared to the NIEs, Chinese companies, such as those in the telecom-equipment industry, demonstrated marked differences from their peers in NIEs when they started to catch up (Fan, 2011b; Yu and Li-Hua, 2011; Gao, 2014), mainly due to the changing tradability of knowledge or technological regimes (Altenburg *et al.*, 2008) and the global economic environment.

For instance, while Korean firms initially relied heavily on foreign sources for their catching-up in the automotive, electronics, and semiconductor industries, Chinese firms chose to conduct in-house R&D on switch technology, due to the high cost and unavailability of the existing technology, their lack of understanding of foreign markets and technology, and MNEs' interest in China's market. Further, situated in a dynamic technological regime and a much more integrated global economic environment, in order to compensate for their limited access to global resources, Chinese telecom firms were able to adopt some global technology strategies such as joint collaboration, participation in industrial standards (Gao, 2014), and R&D globalization at a much earlier stage of their catch-up than the Korean firms (Gao *et al.*, 2007; Fan, 2011b).

4. Regional Inequality in Innovation and Regional Innovation System

In stark contrast with the well-researched economic inequality literature, only a few studies, such as those of Li (2009), Liu and White (2001), Sun (2000, 2003), and Fan *et al.* (2012), have assessed regional inequality in innovation capability and its drivers in China.

Using a primary index, a top-five index, a top-10 index and coefficients of variation to indicate spatial patterns of innovation, Sun (2000) found that patents in China were highly clustered in the east–coastal region and the inland provinces, although the degree of spatial concentration declined from 1985 to 1995. When other indicators of innovation, such as new product sales and R&D spending were used, the spatial concentration was found to be on the rise in the 1990s (Sun, 2003).

Using patent numbers from 1985 to 1995, Liu and White (2001) found that economic activity and innovation inputs (i.e., R&D funding and personnel) led to differences in the innovation performance of regions. Also using patent data from 1998 to 2003, Li (2009) illustrated that government support, share of R&D performed by universities and research institutes, and the regional industry-specific innovation environment were significant determinants of innovation efficiency. Li emphasized that the innovation efficiency between regions becomes more disparate when innovation modes are transformed from being university and research institute dominant to being firm dominant.

Fan *et al.* (2012) found that east–central–west interregional inequality increased over time from 1995 to 2006, whereas interprovincial inequality showed a V-pattern until 2003. Using a recently developed decomposition framework, they identified the major factors driving innovation inequality as population, economic development, R&D, location, and openness. The aggravated innovation inequality reflects the growth of China's innovation centers in the eastern region and their admission into the global innovation networks. For instance, 60% of the foreign R&D laboratories in China are located in Beijing, 18% in Shanghai, and 6% in Shenzhen (Yuan, 2005). The fact that R&D is a major factor driving inequality suggests that the efficiency of R&D investment improved in certain regions during the period 1995–2006. Finally, geographic location and openness affect innovation inequality primarily through the coupled evolution of innovation capability and economic development, resulting in first-mover advantages in provinces of the eastern region (Fan *et al.*, 2012).

Worldwide, cities have become the focused locations for economic development and policy intervention (Petrella, 1995; Scott, 2000), facilitated by neoliberal globalization (Harvey, 2005) and the revolution in information and communication technology (ICT) (Castells, 2000–2003). Innovation in the emerging innovative city-regions in China is an exciting field, deserving of more research. For instance, although possessing only 3.2% of the nation's population, Beijing, Shanghai, Shenzhen, and Xian together generated 11% of GDP, 30% of exports, and 24% of the foreign direct investment (FDI) in China. Further, these four city-regions occupy leading positions in the development of high-tech industries, such as ICT and biomedical industries, and they differ in their paths for developing innovation capabilities in these industries. **Beijing** leads in R&D capacity and is the largest base of China's high-tech industries, as it topped other cities in revenue and number of employees in high-tech parks in 2009. Depending little on foreign capital or markets, Beijing's ICT industry features a large number of small- and medium-sized domestic companies focused on software and computer services (Zhou, 2008). **Shanghai** possesses strong manufacturing capacity in the ICT and biotech industries, especially in the integrated circuit (IC) and biomedical sectors, with the largest, most complete, and technologically advanced IC industrial cluster in China. Most of Shanghai's high-tech manufacturing capacity comes from large SOEs and MNCs, with little contribution from nongovernmental firms due to an unsupportive institutional environment for them (Breznitz and Murphree, 2011). **Shenzhen** developed itself from a small fishing village in 1978 to the third largest high-tech industrialization base in China within three decades, featuring mostly domestic firms actively involved in indigenous innovation (Zhou *et al.*, 2011). Accessible venture capital from Hong Kong, the completeness of the ICT industrial value chain, and active private entrepreneurship have been cited as the basis of the prosperity of domestic high-tech firms in Shenzhen (Breznitz and Murphree, 2011). **Xi'an** is the fourth leading city-region in high-tech industrialization in China. While it has mainly relied on SOEs and MNCs (Segal, 2003), in recent years, the government has begun to give more support to the innovation activities of nongovernmental domestic companies.

A number of recent studies have examined industrial and technological development in China's city-regions and how regional systems have interacted with the national system (Segal, 2003; Walcott, 2003; Huang, 2008; Zhou, 2008; Breznitz and Murphree, 2011; Zhou *et al.*, 2011). By studying nongovernmental firms in Beijing, Shanghai, Guangzhou, and Xi'an, Segal (2003) noted regional variations in technological dynamism and argued that different local states accounted for these differences. He further identified the local government of Beijing as the most effective state for the development of nongovernmental firms among the four city-regions. However, his research did not touch upon interactions between MNCs and local firms (Zhou *et al.*, 2011), or the globalization of firms in these city-regions. Walcott (2003) explored the role of policies in developing science and technology parks in Beijing, Shanghai-Suzhou, Shenzhen-Dongwan, and Xi'an. She emphasized that the main differences in policies lay in those promoting MNCs versus those encouraging ties to local research entities. Her work focused on administrative policies and did not examine the technological catching-up of domestic firms through external linkages. Breznitz and Murphree (2011) also investigated the divergent regional systems in Beijing, Shanghai, and Peal-river Delta and how the inherent "structured uncertainty" in China's national and local political systems has contributed to the variations. They argued that these different systems combine to form a unique national system that uses the logic of value creation—focusing on second-generation product and process innovation through specialization in certain production and service stages, enabled by fragmentation of global production and services. Nevertheless, they gave little attention to how successful local firms have actively sought global resources, for instance, through R&D globalization, to improve their innovation capabilities to go beyond second-generation innovation.

More academic research is necessary to address these critical gaps related to the innovation capability of China's emerging city-regions. In this respect, several approaches mentioned by McCann and Oxley (2012) can be considered as appropriate methods to further decode the mystery of innovation and regional development, such as developing conceptual frameworks to analyze the differences between regional and local innovation systems (Crescenzi and Rodríguez-Pose, 2012), computing a composite index to measure the regional degree of exposure to external knowledge sources, thus indicating a region's potential capacity to access nonlocal items of knowledge (Moreno and Miguélez, 2012), and hierarchical or multilevel modeling of under-used firm-level datasets (van Oort *et al.*, 2012).

5. Conclusion

This paper offers a comprehensive and critical review of innovation in China in the postreform era. China's recent progress in innovation capability after the launch of its economic reforms is certainly impressive, illustrated by the dramatic improvement in input and output indicators of innovation systems such as R&D personnel, R&D expenditure, patents, high-tech and service exports, and scientific and technical journal articles. Nevertheless, although improvement in quantity is always the first step in any catch-up scheme, the quality of many indicators has been questioned.

The analysis of China's development of innovation can have implications for others when applying three major theoretic frameworks: (1) system of innovation, (2) global linkages, such as GVCs, global production networks, overseas returnees, and R&D globalization, and (3) the dynamics of latecomers' catch-up processes. While China's evolution of its national innovation system has been the fundamental approach to unleashing the creativity of the "middle kingdom" in postreform years, various global linkages, enabled by the transformation of technological regimes and the global economic environment, have considerably affected China's progress towards becoming a technological superpower. However, we are in need of a better assessment of the impact of these global linkages, i.e., whether these linkages augment or undermine indigenous innovation capability and how. One interesting area that deserves further analysis is how global networks of Chinese professionals and returnees have affected this process. Moreover, being a latecomer, China's catch-up exhibits differences from its predecessors from the NIEs, such as choosing to conduct in-house R&D at an early stage but opting for a much more globally integrated approach later on, as illustrated by the telecom equipment manufacturers. More research would be welcomed in this area to provide policy recommendations for other latecomer countries or regions.

With the rise of emerging nations and the improved innovation capabilities of China and India in particular, one thing is certain: "the long-held monopoly of the west with respect to innovation will be over."[5] After decades of reform, China, along with India, is close to competing on an equal footing with leading OECD countries, such as the USA, Japan, and Germany. In addition to issues at the national level, the uneven spatial distribution of innovation capability of China needs to be taken seriously by the Chinese government, as the increased disparity in innovation capability may significantly affect China's regional economic development in today's knowledge economy. Just like its economic reform, transitioning from "made in China" to "innovated in China" can be a tough national journey with numerous opportunities and challenges unfolding along the way. China may also discover a proper model for its "innovation-driven economy" by learning from the experiences of its various city-regions in experimenting with distinct development pathways for technological upgrading.

Acknowledgment

I thank the editor of the journal, Iris Claus, and two anonymous reviewers for their constructive and helpful comments on an earlier draft of this paper. I also thank friends and colleagues who have been helpful to me during my research on innovation in China. Particularly, I appreciate Guanghua Wan at the Asian Development Bank, Yifei Sun at California State University at Northridge, Denis Simon at Arizona State University, Yu Zhou at Vassar College, and William Lazonick at University of Massachusetts Lowell who provided helpful conversations on China's innovation and economic development on various occasions. Any opinions, findings, conclusions, and recommendations expressed in this paper are solely my own. I am also fully responsible for any errors.

Notes

1. East-West Center. 2011. China not an immediate threat to U.S. technology leadership, expert tells the review commission. Available at http://www.eastwestcenter.org/news-center/east-west-wire/china-not-an-immediate-threat-to-us-tech-leadership-expert-tells-review-commission, accessed on Oct. 30, 2013.
2. As of May 2014, there are five candidate countries for the EU: The former Yugoslav Republic of Macedonia, Iceland, Montenegro, Serbia, and Turkey.
3. In this section, I will focus on NSI and address RSI in Part 4.
4. China Watch. 2013. Tax benefits to fuel innovation, growth. Available at http://chinawatch.washingtonpost.com/2013/11/tax-benefits-to-fuel-innovation-growth.php accessed on Mar. 5, 2014.
5. Kumar, Nirmalya. 2012. India Inside. The emerging innovation threat to the West. Presentation at the London School of Business. Available at http://www.slideshare.net/londonbusinessschool/india-inside-the-emerging-innovation-threat-to-the-west-lbs-professor-nirmalya-kumar accessed on Oct. 30, 2013.

References

Ahuja, G. (2000) The duality of collaboration: inducements and opportunities in the formation of interfirm linkages. *Strategic Management Journal* 21(3): 317–343.

Altenburg, T., Schmitz, H. and Stamm, A. (2008) Breakthrough? China's and India's transition from production to innovation. *World Development* 36(2): 325–344.

Amiti, M. and Freund, C. (2010) An anatomy of China's export growth? In R.C. Feenstra and S. Wei (eds), *China's Growing Role in World Trade*. Chicago: The University of Chicago Press.

Asheim, B.T. and Isaksen, A. (2002) Regional innovation systems: the integration of local 'sticky'and global 'ubiquitous' knowledge. *The Journal of Technology Transfer* 27(1): 77–86.

Audretsch, D.B. and Feldman, M.P. (2004) Knowledge spillovers and the geography of innovation. *Handbook of Regional and Urban Economics* 4: 2713–2739.

Basberg, B.L. (1987) Patents and the measurement of technological change: a survey of the literature. *Research Policy* 16: 131–141.

Beaverstock, J.V. and Hall, S. (2012) Competing for talent: global mobility, immigration and the City of London's labour market. *Cambridge Journal of Regions, Economy and Society* 5(2): 271–288.

Bell, M. (2006) Time and technological learning in industrialising countries: how long does it take? How fast is it moving (if at all)? *International Journal of Technology Management* 36(1/2/3): 25–39.

Berger, B. and Martin, R.F. (2013) The Chinese export boom: an examination of the detailed trade data. *China & World Economy* 21(1): 64–90.

Blustein, P. (1997) Balancing the cost of doing business with Beijing. *Washington Post*, June 19, E01.

Braczyk, H.J., Cooke, P. and Heidenreich, M. (eds) (1998) *Regional Innovation Systems: The Role of Governances in a Globalized World*. London: Routledge.

Breschi, S. and Malerba, F. (1997) Sectoral innovation systems: technological regimes, Schumpeterian dynamics, and spatial Boundaries, In C. Edquist (ed), *Systems of Innovation: Technologies, Institutions and Organizations* (pp. 130–156). London and Washington: Pinter.

Breznitz, D. and Murphree, M. (2011) *Run of the Red Queen: Government, Innovation, Globalization, and Economic Growth in China*. New Haven, CT: Yale University Press.

Buckley, P.J., Clegg, L.J., Cross, A.R., Liu, X., Voss, H. and Zheng, P. (2007) The determinants of Chinese outward foreign investment. *Journal of International Business Studies* 38(4): 499–518.

Cao, C. (2004) Zhongguancun and China's high-tech parks in transition: 'growing pains' or 'premature senility'? *Asian Survey* 44(5): 647–668.

Castells, M. (2000–2003) *The Information Age: Economy, Society and Culture*, 2nd edn, Vols 1, 2 and 3. Oxford: Blackwell.

Cho, D., Kim, D. and Rhee, D. (1998) Latecomer strategies: evidence from the semiconductor industry in Japan and Korea. *Organization Science* 9(4): 489–505.

Coe, N.M., Dicken, P. and Hess, M. (2008) Global production networks: realizing the potential. *Journal of Economic Geography* 8(3): 271–295.

Coe, N.M., Hess, M., Yeung, H.W.C., Dicken, P. and Henderson, J. (2004) 'Globalizing'regional development: a global production networks perspective. *Transactions of the Institute of British Geographers* 29(4): 468–484.

Cooke, P. (2001) Regional innovation systems, clusters, and the knowledge economy. *Industrial and Corporate Change* 10(4): 945–974.

Cooke, P., Gomez Uranga, M. and Etxebarria, G. (1997) Regional innovation systems: institutional and organisational dimensions. *Research Policy* 26(4): 475–491.

Crescenzi, R. and Rodríguez-Pose, A. (2012) An 'integrated'framework for the comparative analysis of the territorial innovation dynamics of developed and emerging countries. *Journal of Economic Surveys* 26(3): 517–533.

Dicken, P., Kelly, P.F., Olds, K. and Wai-Chung Yeung, H. (2001) Chains and networks, territories and scales: towards a relational framework for analysing the global economy. *Global Networks* 1(2): 89–112.

Dunning, J.H. (1981) *International Production and the Multinational Enterprise*. London: Allen & Unwin.

Dunning, J.H. (1988) The eclectic paradigm of international production: a restatement and some possible extensions. *Journal of International Business Studies* 19: 1–31.

Edquist, C. (2005) Systems of innovation perspectives and challenges. In J. Fagerberg, D.C. Mowery and R.R. Nelson (eds), *The Oxford Handbook of Innovation* (pp. 181–208). Oxford: Oxford University Press.

Enright, M.J., Scott, E.E. and Chang, K.M. (2005) *Regional Powerhouse: the Greater Pearl River Delta and the Rise of China* (p. 68). Chichester: Wiley.

Ernst, D. and Kim, L. (2002) Global production networks, knowledge diffusion, and local capability formation. *Research Policy* 31(8): 1417–1429.

Fan, P. (2006a) Promoting indigenous capability: the Chinese government and the catching-up of domestic telecom-equipment firms. *China Review* 6(1): 9–35.

Fan, P. (2006b) Comparative analysis of high-tech parks in Beijing and Shanghai. *Journal of Nanjing University (Nature Science)* 42(3): 242–256.

Fan, P. and Watanabe, C. (2006) Promoting industrial development through technology policy: lessons from Japan and China. *Technology in Society* 28(3): 303–320.

Fan, P. (2011a) Innovation, globalization, and catch-up of latecomers: cases of Chinese telecom firms. *Environment and Planning A* 43(4): 830–849.

Fan, P. (2011b) China and India: innovation capability and economic development. *Economic Change and Restructuring* 44(1–2): 49–73.

Fan, P., Wan, G. and Lu, M. (2012) China's regional inequality in innovation capability, 1995–2006. *China & World Economy* 20(3): 16–36.
Feenstra, R.C. and Wei, S. (eds). (2010) *China's Growing Role in World Trade*. Chicago: The University of Chicago Press.
Florida, R. (2010) *The Flight of the Creative Class: The New Global Competition for Talent*. New York: HarperCollins.
Freeman, C. (1987) *Technology Policy and Economic Performance: Lessons from Japan* (pp. 11–17). London: Pinter Publishers.
Freeman, C. (1995) The 'National System of Innovation'in historical perspective. *Cambridge Journal of Economics* 19(1): 5–24.
Gao, X. (2014) A latecomer's strategy to promote a technology standard: the case of Datang and TD-SCDMA. *Research Policy* 43(3): 597–607.
Gao, X., Zhang, P. and Liu, X. (2007) Competing with MNEs: developing manufacturing capabilities or innovation capabilities. *The Journal of Technology Transfer* 32(1–2): 87–107.
Geels, F.W. (2004) From sectoral systems of innovation to socio-technical systems: insights about dynamics and change from sociology and institutional theory. *Research Policy* 33(6): 897–920.
Gereffi, G., Humphrey, J. and Sturgeon, T. (2005) The governance of global value chains. *Review of International Political Economy* 12(1): 78–104.
Goto, A. and Suzuki, K. (1989) R&D capital, rate of return on R&D investment and spillover of R&D in Japanese manufacturing industries. *The Review of Economics and Statistics* 71(4): 555–564.
Griffith, R., Redding, S. and van Reenen, J. (2004) Mapping the two faces of R&D: productivity growth in a panel of OECD industries. *The Review of Economics and Statistics* 86(4): 883–895.
Griliches, Z. (1986) Productivity R&D and basic research at the firm level in the 1970s. *American Economic Review* 76(1): 141–154.
Griliches, Z. (1990) Patent statistics as economic indicators: a survey. *Journal of Economic Literature* 28(4): 1661–1707.
Griliches, Z. (1998) *R&D and Productivity: The Econometric Evidence*. Chicago: University of Chicago Press.
Griliches, Z. and Mairesse, J. (1984) Productivity and R&D at the firm level. In Z. Griliches (ed), *R&D, Patents, and Productivity* (pp. 339–374). Chicago: University of Chicago Press.
Gu, S. (1999) *China's Industrial Technology*. Tokyo: United Nations University Press.
Hagedoorn, J. and Cloodt, M. (2003) Measuring innovative performance: is there an advantage in using multiple indicators? *Research Policy* 32(8): 1365–1379.
Hagedoorn, J. and Schakenraad, J. (1994) The effect of strategic technology alliances on company performance. *Strategic Management Journal* 15(4): 291–309.
Hall, B.H. (1993) Industrial research during the 1980s: did the rate of return fall? *Brookings Papers on Economic Activity. Microeconomics* 2: 289–343.
Hall, B.H. and Mairesse, J. (1995) Exploring the relationship between R&D and productivity in French manufacturing firms. *Journal of Econometrics* 65: 263–293.
Harhoff, D. (1998) Are there financing constraints for R&D and investment in German manufacturing firms? *Annales d'Economie et de Statistique* 421–456.
Harvey, D. 2005. *A Brief History of Neoliberalism*. Oxford: Oxford University Press.
Henderson, J., Dicken, P., Hess, M., Coe, N. and Yeung, H.W.C. (2002) Global production networks and the analysis of economic development. *Review of International Political Economy* 9(3): 436–464.
Hobday, M. (1995) *Innovation in East Asia*. Cheltenham, UK: Edward Elgar Publishing Ltd.
Hong, S., Oxley, L. and McCann, P. (2012) A survey of the innovation surveys. *Journal of Economic Surveys* 26(3): 420–444.
Huang, Y. (2008) *Capitalism with Chinese Characteristics: Entrepreneurship and the State*. Cambridge: Cambridge University Press.
Humphrey, J. and Schmitz, H. (2002) How does insertion in global value chains affect upgrading in industrial clusters. *Regional Studies* 36(9): 1017–1027.
Humphrey, J. and Schmitz, H. (2004) Chain governance and upgrading: taking stock. In Schmitz, H. (ed), *Local Enterprises in the Global Economy: Issues of Governance and Upgrading* (pp. 349–381). Northampton, MA: Elgar.

Johanson, J. and Vahlne, J.E. (1977) The internationalization process of the firm: a model of knowledge development and increasing foreign market commitments. *Journal of International Business Studies* 8(1): 23–32.

Kardes, F.R. and Kalyanaram, G. (1992) Order-of-entry effects on consumer memory and *judgment*: an information integration perspective. *Journal of Marketing Research* 29: 343–357.

Kim, L. (1997) *From Imitation to Innovation: Dynamics of Korea's Technological Learning*. Boston: Harvard Business School Press.

Kotabe, M. and Scott Swan, K. (1995) The role of strategic alliances in high-technology new product development. *Strategic Management Journal* 16(8): 621–636.

Kuemmerle, W. (1999a) Foreign direct investment in industrial research in the pharmaceutical and electronics industries—results from a survey of multinational firms. *Research Policy* 28: 179–193.

Kuemmerle, W. (1999b) The drivers of foreign direct investment into research and development: an empirical investigation. *Journal of International Business Studies* 30(1): 1–24.

Kuemmerle, W. (1997) Building effective R&D capabilities abroad. *Harvard Business Review* 75: 61–70.

Lai, P. and Li, Q. (2013) Development in China's foreign trade: 2003–2012. *China & World Economy* 21(6): 58–78.

Lang, G. (2009) Measuring the returns of R&D: an empirical study of the German manufacturing sector over 45 years. *Research Policy* 38(9): 1438–1445.

Leonard-Barton, D. (1995) *Wellspring of Knowledge: Building and Sustaining the Sources of Innovation*. Cambridge, MA: Harvard Business School Press.

Li, P.P. (2007) Toward an integrated theory of multinational evolution: the evidence of Chinese multinational enterprises as latecomers. *Journal of International Management* 13(3): 296–318.

Li, X. (2009) China's regional innovation capacity in transition: an empirical approach. *Research Policy* 38: 338–357.

Li, Z., Zhang, J., Wen, K., Thorsteinsdóttir, H., Quach, U., Singer, P.A. and Daar, A.S. (2004) Health biotechnology in China—reawakening of a giant. *Nature Biotechnology*, 22(Supplement): DC13–DC18.

Lieberman, M.B. and Montgomery, D.B. (1988) First-mover advantages. *Strategic Management Journal* 9: 41–58.

Lieberman, M.B. and Montgomery, D.B. (1998) First-mover (dis)advantages: retrospective and link with the resource-based view. *Strategic Management Journal* 19: 1111–1125.

Lin, F., Zhang, C. and Wang, L. (2013) Vertical spillover effects of multinationals on Chinese domestic firms via supplier–customer relationships. *China & World Economy* 21(6): 37–57.

Liu, X. and White, S. (2001) Comparing innovation systems: a framework and application to China's transition context. *Research Policy* 30(7): 1091–1114.

Lopez-Bassols, V. (2011) Innovation surveys and indictors: some experiences from the OECD. CeSTII workshop on the Review of Innovation Measurement in South Africa. Pretoria, South Africa, 8–9 November 2011. Available at http://www.hsrc.ac.za/uploads/pageContent/360/SomeExperiencesZAF_Innovation_Lopez.pdf

Lucas, R.E. (1988) On the mechanics of economic development. *Journal of Monetary Economics* 22: 3–42.

Lundvall, B.-A. (ed) (1992) *National Systems of Innovation: Towards a Theory of Innovation and Interactive Learning*. London: Pinter Publishers.

Luo, Y. and Tung, R.L. (2007) International expansion of emerging market enterprises: a springboard perspective. *Journal of International Business Studies* 38(4), 481–498.

Malerba, F. (2002) Sectoral systems of innovation and production. *Research Policy* 31(2): 247–264.

Malerba, F. (2005) Sectoral systems: how and why innovation differs across sectors. In J. Fagerberg, D.C. Mowery and R.R. Nelson (eds), *The Oxford Handbook of Innovation* (pp. 380–406). Oxford: Oxford University Press.

Malerba, F. (ed) (2004) *Sectoral Systems of Innovation: Concepts, Issues and Analyses of Six Major Sectors in Europe*. Cambridge: Cambridge University Press.

Malerba, F. and Mani, S. (eds). (2009) *Sectoral Systems of Innovation and Production in Developing Countries: Actors, Structure and Evolution*. Cheltenham: Edward Elgar Publishing.

Mansfield, E. (1986) Patents and innovation: an empirical study. *Management Science* 32(2): 173–181.

McCann, P. and Oxley, L. (2012) Innovation, entrepreneurship, geography and growth. *Journal of Economic Surveys* 26(3): 373–376.

Ministry of Education of China (MOE) 2013. Reports on Overseas Students. http://news.sciencenet.cn/htmlnews/2013/2/275135.shtm. Accessed on March 4, 2013.
Mitsuhashi, K. (2006) The furniture value chain from Thailand to Japan: upgrading and the roles of buyers. Doctoral dissertation, University of Sussex.
Moreno, R. and Miguélez, E. (2012) A relational approach to the geography of innovation: a typology of regions. *Journal of Economic Surveys* 26(3): 492–516.
Motohashi, K. and Yun, X. (2007) China's innovation system reform and growing industry and science linkages. *Research Policy* 36: 1431–1442.
Mowery, D.C., Oxley, J.E. and Silverman, B.S. (1996) Strategic alliances and interfirm knowledge transfer. *Strategic Management Journal* 17: 77–91.
Navas-Alemán, L. (2006) *Opportunities and obstacles for industrial upgrading of Brazilian footwear and furniture firms: a comparison of global and national value chains*. Unpublished PhD thesis. Brighton, UK: Institute of Development Studies, University of Sussex.
Nelson, R.R. (ed) (1993) *National Systems of Innovation: A Comparative Study*. New York: Oxford University Press.
Neumeyer, C. (2013) *China's Great Leap Forward in Patents*. Available at http://www.ipwatchdog.com/2013/04/04/chinas-great-leap-forward-in-patents/id=38625/. Accessed on October 15, 2013.
Niosi, J. 1999. Introduction: the internationalization of industrial R&D: from technology transfer to the learning organization. *Research Policy* 28:107–117.
Niosi, J. and Tschang, F.T. (2009) The strategies of Chinese and Indian software multinationals: implications for internationalization theory. *Industrial and Corporate Change* 18(2): 269–294.
OECD (2006) *China will Become World's Second Highest Investor in R&D by End of 2006, Finds OECD*. Paris: OECD. Available from: http://www.oecd.org/science/inno/chinawillbecomeworldssecondhighestinvestorinrdbyendof2006findsoecd.htm. Accessed on October 15, 2013.
Petrella, R. (1995) A global agora vs. gated city-regions. *New Perspectives Quarterly* Winter: 21–22.
Reddy, P. (2000) *Globalization of Corporate R&D: Implications for Innovation Systems in Host Countries*. London and New York: Routledge.
Richardson, J. (1996) Vertical integration and rapid response in fashion apparel. *Organization Science* 7(4): 400–412.
Rodrik, D. (2006) What's so special about China's exports? *China & World Economy* 14(5): 1–19.
Romer, P. (1986) Increasing returns and long-run growth. *Journal of Political Economy* 94(5): 1002–1037.
Romer, P. (1990) Endogenous technological change. *Journal of Political Economy* 98: S71–S102.
Saxenian, A. (2002) Transnational communities and the evolution of global production networks: the cases of Taiwan, China and India. *Industry and Innovation* 9(3): 183–202.
Saxenian, A. (2006) *The New Argonauts: Regional Advantage in a Global Economy*. Cambridge, MA: Harvard University Press.
Schmitz, H. (ed) (2004) *Local Enterprises in the Global Economy: Issues of Governance and Upgrading*. Cheltenham: Edward Elgar Publishing.
Schott, P. (2008) The relative sophistication of Chinese exports. *Economic Policy* 23: 5–49.
Scott, A.J. (2000) *The Cultural Economy of Cities: Essays on the Geography of Image-Producing Industries*. London: Sage Publications.
Segal, A. (2003) *Digital Dragon: High-Technology Enterprises in China*. Ithaca: Cornell University Press.
Simon, D.F. and Cao, C. (2009) *China's Emerging Technological Edge: Assessing the Role of High-End Talent*. Cambridge, UK: Cambridge University Press.
Solimano, A. (ed) (2008) *The International Mobility of Talent: Types, Causes, and Development Impact: Types, Causes, and Development Impact*. New York: Oxford University Press.
Steinfeld, E.S. (2010) *Playing Our Game: Why China's Rise Doesn't Threaten the West*. Oxford: Oxford University Press.
Stuart, T.E. (2000) Interorganizational alliances and the performance of firms: a study of growth and innovation rates in a high-technology industry. *Strategic Management Journal* 21(8): 791–811.
Sturgeon, T., Van Biesebroeck, J. and Gereffi, G. (2008) Value chains, networks and clusters: reframing the global automotive industry. *Journal of Economic Geography* 8(3): 297–321.
Sun, Y. (2000) Spatial distribution of patents in China. *Regional Studies* 34(5): 441–454.

Sun, Y. (2003) Geographic patterns of industrial innovation in China during the 1990s. *Journal of Economic and Social Geography* 94(3): 376–389.
Sun, Y. and Zhou, Y. (2011) Innovation and inter-firm technological networking: evidence from China's information communication technology industry. *Erdkunde* 65(1): 55–70.
Sun, Y., Zedtwitz, M. and Simon, D.F. (eds). (2008) *Global R&D in China*. London: Routledge.
United Nations Conference on Trade and Development (UNCTAD). (2005) *World Investment Report: Transnational Corporations and the Internationalization of R&D*. New York: United Nations.
van Oort, F.G., Burger, M.J., Knoben, J. and Raspe, O. (2012) Multilevel approaches and the firm-agglomeration ambiguity in economic growth studies. *Journal of Economic Surveys* 26(3): 468–491.
Wakelin, K. (2001) Productivity growth and R&D expenditure in UK manufacturing firms. *Research Policy* 30(7): 1079–1090.
Walcott, S. (2003) *Chinese Science and Technology Industrial Parks*. Aldershot: Ashgate Publishing Limited.
Walsh, K. (2007) China R&D: a high-tech field of dreams. *Asia Pacific Business Review* 13(3): 321–335.
Wang, H., Miao, D. and Cheng, X. (2009) *The Report on the Development of Chinese Overseas Educated*. Beijing: China Machine Press. (In Chinese).
Wang, Z. and Wei, S. (2010) What accounts for the rising sophistication of China's export? In R.C. Feenstra and S. Wei (eds), *China's Growing Role in World Trade*. Chicago: The University of Chicago Press.
World Bank. (2013) *World Development Indicators*. Washington, DC: World Bank.
Xue, L. (1997) A historical perspective of China's innovation system reform: a case study. *Journal of Engineering and Technology Management* 14(2): 67–81.
Yeung, H.W.C. (2009) Regional development and the competitive dynamics of global production networks: an East Asian perspective. *Regional Studies* 43(3): 325–351.
Yu, J. and Li-Hua, R. (2011) *China's Highway of Information and Communication Technology*. London: Palgrave Macmillan Publishing.
Yu, W., Hong, J., Wu, Y. and Zhao, D. (2013) Emerging geography of creativity and labor productivity effects in China. *China & World Economy* 21(5): 78–99.
Yuan, Z. (2005) Features and impacts of the internationalization of R&D by transnational corporations: China's case. In UNCTAD (ed), *Globalization of R&D and Developing Countries*, Proceedings of the Expert Meeting Geneva, January 24–26, 2005. New York and Geneva: United Nations, pp. 109–115.
Zhou, Y. (2008) *The Inside Story of China's High-Tech Industry: Making Silicon Valley in Beijing*. Lanham, MD: Rowman & Littlefield.
Zhou, Y., Sun, Y., Wei, Y. and Lin, G.C.S. (2011) De-centering 'spatial fix': patterns of territorialization and regional technological dynamism of ICT hubs in China. *Journal of Economic Geography* 11(1): 119–150.
Zweig, D. (2006) Competing for talent: China's strategies to reverse the brain drain. *International Labour Review* 145(1–2): 65–90.
Zweig, D., Changgui, C. and Rosen, S. (2004) Globalization and transnational human capital: overseas and returnee scholars to China. *The China Quarterly* 179: 735–757.
Zweig, D., Chung, S.F. and Vanhonacker, W. (2006) Rewards of technology: explaining China's reverse migration. *Journal of International Migration and Integration* 7(4): 449–471.

10

CHINA'S SERVICE TRADE

Hejing Chen*
Western University, Canada
John Whalley
Western University, Canada
Centre for International Governance Innovation, Canada
National Bureau of Economic Research, USA

1. Introduction

This paper discusses China's service trade performance over the last three decades, focusing on service subsectors in both the Chinese and the world economy. Since the late 1970s and the onset of high growth in China, the fraction of service trade to GDP has grown steadily from 2% to 7% of GDP today. This expansion of trade in services in the wider economy has reflected China's rapid growth of GDP, and is parallel with the share ratio for other large developed economies including the US and Japan, and compares to that of South Korea and India at earlier stages of their development. This expansion is broad and across most major subsectors: retailing/wholesaling, construction, computer and information services, communications, professional services, and other business services. But despite its high growth rate, China's service trade has been in deficit for decades, and the international competitiveness of major service subsectors remains low. China thus does not exhibit the same maturation in service trade through competitiveness and market power as has occurred with its trade in goods. We calculate openness indices for China's service trade according to China's commitment to WTO/GATS when entering the WTO in 2001. Using two different methodologies, that is, a frequency ratio and a financial ratio, we find the openness index for China's service trade differs across subsectors. Further, we compare China's service trade openness commitments in both their multilateral and regional dimensions.

We then discuss the situation for China's service trade in light of prospective development strategies and assess impacts for the Chinese and global economy. China has adjusted its

*We are grateful to the Ontario Research Fund for financial support.

long-term bias in policies in favor of merchandise manufacturing and heavy industries to encourage high-tech manufacture and services in its far-reaching 12th 5-Year Plan. Based on the guidance of the plan, a series of facilitating policies in terms of tax, finance, land use, and other elements have been launched to boost China's service trade. We also use this discussion as a basis for evaluating the impacts of the current and foreseeable future development of China's service trade. Can service trade have a positive impact on China's economic growth, employment, and technology accumulation? What will happen to international FDI and trade patterns with China's shifting significance towards services? And what are the implications for the international labor market since service trade encompasses the international migration of labor? A resolution of these issues would seem central to China's future growth and development.

Our motivation is to provide a panorama of China's service trade, analyze the forward policy measures needed to promote China's service trade and assess the implications for China and the world. In Section 2, we present some empirical material about the performance of China's service trade and speculate on China's changing comparative advantage, and openness indices within service industries. In Section 3, we analyze development strategies and prospects for China's service trade. Section 4 explores the implications for China's economic development from growth, technology accumulation, and employment perspectives. In Section 5, the implications of China's service trade development for the global economy are examined, and Section 6 concludes.

2. The Performance of China's Service Trade

Since the launch of reforms in 1979 and the subsequent market opening, the promotion of foreign trade has been central to China's efforts to modernize its economy. The policy has met with remarkable success in the merchandise trade. While less well recognized, this has also been the case for China's service trade. Over three decades, China's share of service exports in the world sextupled from 0.6% in 1982 (the date when China's balance of payment accounts first became available) to 3.73% in 2009, while the service import share increased by an order of magnitude, from 0.44% to 4.88% during the same period.[1]

2.1 *The Background to China's Service Trade*

China's opening-up has reflected three stages of development. The first was from 1979 to 1991, during which China opened the door and conducted market-oriented reforms on an experimental basis. Centering on Special Economic Zones (SEZ), Coastal Harbor Open Cities, and Coastal Economic Open Zones in the coastal areas, China opened gradually from south to north and from east to west. Stage two started in 1992 and ran to 2000, with the beginning marked by Deng Xiaoping's "southern tour" during which he spoke in favor of an acceleration of openness and reform. As a result, China's opening region expanded in a broad range from coastal cities to many inland areas including the western region. Stage three was inaugurated by China's entry to the WTO in 2001. Since then, preferential policies as practiced in some regions in the past have lost their impacts. Development in different geographical areas relies now on regional competitiveness, including market environments, the level of industrial development, availability of talented personnel, technical innovation, and quality of government services. In short, over the three decades of openness and reform, China has participated in global

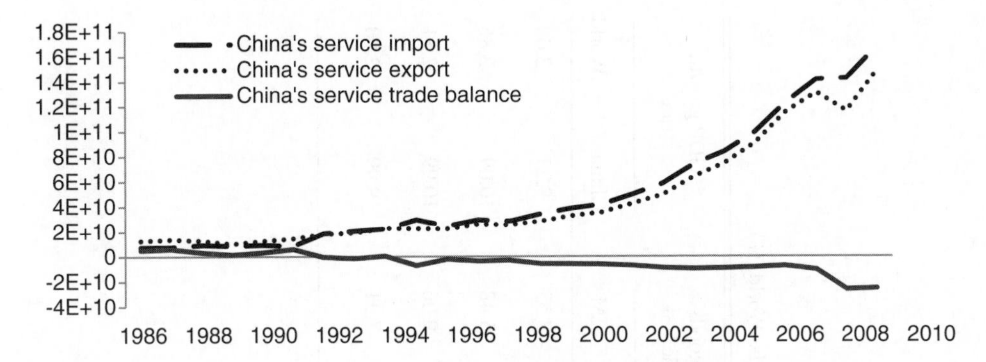

Figure 1. China's Service Trade Flow (2005 US$).
Source: World Bank, World Development Indicators 2012.

competition on a broad scope in both goods and services. This can be seen in the increasing size and accelerated growth rate of service trade as well as its growing contribution to GDP.

During these years, the real value of China's service trade increased more than 15 times, from only US$20.26 billion in 1986 to US$315.77 billion in 2010. In 2009, due to the impact of the financial crisis, China's service trade exports declined 12%, which repeated, but to a larger degree, the history of trade downturns in the Southeast Asian financial crisis of 1998. However, China's service trade resumed and grew rapidly in 2010 both in terms of exports and imports. But unlike the long-standing trade surplus in merchandise trade, China's service trade has experienced trade deficits since 1992. The deficit grew especially in the years 2009 and 2010 (See Figure 1).

From Figure 1, we can see how the size of China's service imports and exports changes with time, which is also coincident with the three stages of opening up. The average annual growth rate of China's GDP and service trade accelerated stage by stage, reflecting China's growing openness and the impact of its promotion on economic growth and trade flows.

However, this accelerating growth trend is distinct from the world goods and services trade, since the latter two display a "V" pattern during these stages. The lower growth rate in the second stage for the world goods and service trade may, in part, result from a series of shocks the world economy experienced, including the disintegration of the Soviet Union, the bursting of the Japanese asset bubble and the following "lost ten years," the Southeast Asian financial crisis, the internet bubble and the 911 affair impacts in 2001. Over the whole period, China's service trade increased at a higher rate than its GDP and world service trade, demonstrating vigor in China's service trade sector. At each stage, China's service imports expanded faster than service exports, and this is reflected in the growing deficit in service trade (see Table 1).

Despite the high growth rate and increased global market share of China's services trade, it still lags behind the development of China's merchandise trade, which can be seen in terms of absolute size, growth rate, and its contribution to the balance of payments. Using relative shares to capture size, the relative share of China's service trade (either exports or imports) in total foreign trade is lower than the world average. The share of world service exports or imports in total exports or imports is consistently around 20%, which indicates world service trade and merchandise trade developing at almost the same rate. For China, however, this share fluctuated over time while always being below 20%.

Table 1. Average Growth Rates of Goods and Services Trade: Comparisons between China and the World (%).

	China's services trade		China's goods trade		World services trade		World goods trade		GDP growth rate	
Stage (Years)	EX	IM	EX	IM	EX	IM	EX	IM	China	World
First stage (1978–1992)	13.92	16.64	12.66	14.33	9.55	8.58	7.52	7.57	9.27	3.08
Second stage (1992–2001)	15.31	17.17	16.07	15.31	4.72	4.56	5.65	5.48	10.09	2.86
Third stage (2001-present)	18.49	19.10	20.77	19.33	10.49	9.66	8.72	9.06	10.99	2.51
Total (1978-present)	15.72	17.54	16.15	16.12	8.19	7.54	7.24	7.31	9.99	2.90

Note: EX and IM denote exports and imports, respectively.
Source: World Bank, World Development Indicators 2011.

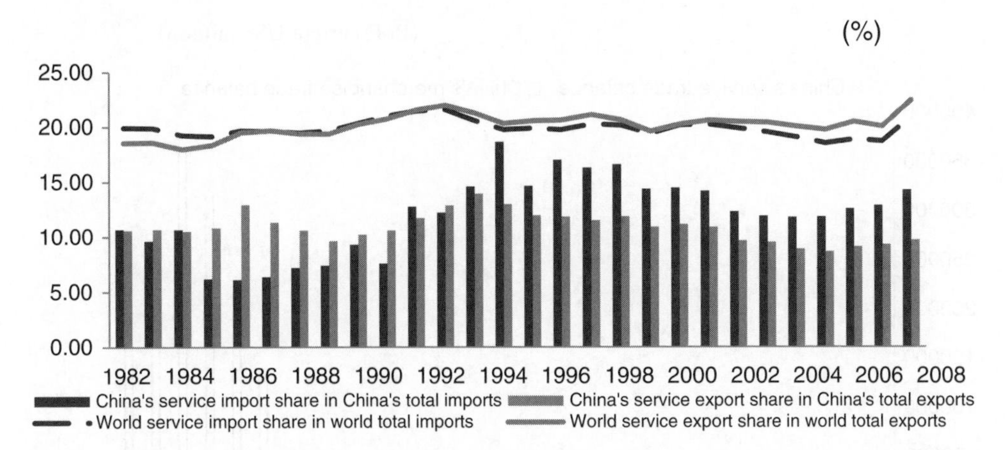

Figure 2. Share of Services in Total Trade: Comparisons between China and the World 1982–2010 (%). *Source:* World Bank, World Development Indicators 2012.

In particular, from the second half of the 1990's onwards, both service import and export shares declined to around 10%. China's service import share has exceeded its export share since 1992, which is reflected in the emerging service trade deficit. The gap between China's service import and export shares since 1992 suggests unbalanced development for China's service trade and merchandise trade. More specifically, it reflects the higher growth rate for merchandise export and service imports relative to service export and merchandise imports (See Figure 2 and Table 1).

As for the contribution to China's balance of payments, from the beginning of opening to the second half of the 1990s, there was no major difference between merchandise trade and service trade, with small trade surpluses in some years and minor deficits in others. However, since the second stage of opening, China's merchandise trade surplus has kept growing while the contribution of services trade to the balance of payments has remained negative. This disparity between China's merchandise trade and service trade intensified in the third stage, when the goods trade surplus increased to historical peaks by dozens of times the average level of the second stage of opening, while the service trade deficit also expanded during the same period (See Figure 3).

2.2 *The Specifics of China's Services Trade*

2.2.1 *China's Services Trade Pattern by Subsector*

It is widely believed that the share of agriculture, manufacturing, and services in GDP and employment is closely related to the level of real GDP per capita. As real income rises, agriculture's share falls, service employment rises, and manufacturing's share rises to a peak at about 3,300 1970 US dollars per capita and then declines. US time series and OECD cross-sections show almost identical patterns for these changes (Fuchs, 1982). Nowadays, services take the place of agriculture and manufacturing as the critical element in the world economy. But there is also change within service sectors, with the importance of traditional services such as travel and transportation gradually declining, and other commercial services involved with

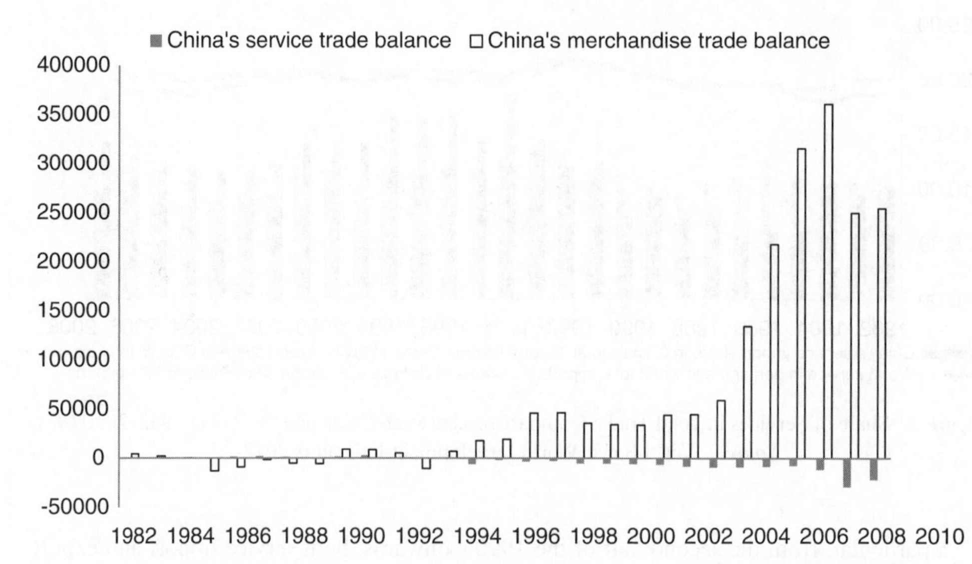

Figure 3. Trade Balance: China's Merchandise and Services Trade 1982–2010 (BoP, current US$ million).
Source: World Bank, World Development Indicators 2012.

the diffusion of new technologies and techniques becoming more critical. Before the second half of the 1990s, traditional services dominated world service trade, while other commercial services have gradually become the more important component of world service trade since the mid-1990s. Within traditional services, the share of travel services has been stable at around 25–30%. It is transportation that has caused the change in the position of traditional services, with its share decreasing by up to ten percentage points both for exports and imports during the three decades (See Figure 4).

The weights allocated to China's three broad categories of services differ a lot between exports and imports and are distinct from world average levels over time. For China's service exports, transportation, travel, and other commercial services in turn dominate in the three opening stages. During the first stage (1982–1992), growth in transportation, as a complementary service, was fostered by the development of China's merchandise trade, which made it the most important component in China's service exports. Travel exports started to increase in the second opening stage, not only resulting from infrastructure construction such as airports, hotels, and restaurants for international tourists, but also the growing recognition of China's friendly environment for international tourists. It was only in the second opening stage that travel exports reached the peak share of 54% with a high average share of nearly 50%. Other commercial services have taken first place in China's service exports in the third stage, and this growth trend has not been adversely affected by the global financial crisis of 2008 (see Figure 5).

For China's service imports, the relative shares of the three categories of services display more volatility, with the range of the shares of transportation, travel, and other commercial services fluctuating among 25%–79%, 3%–37%, and 10%–46%, respectively. There are not

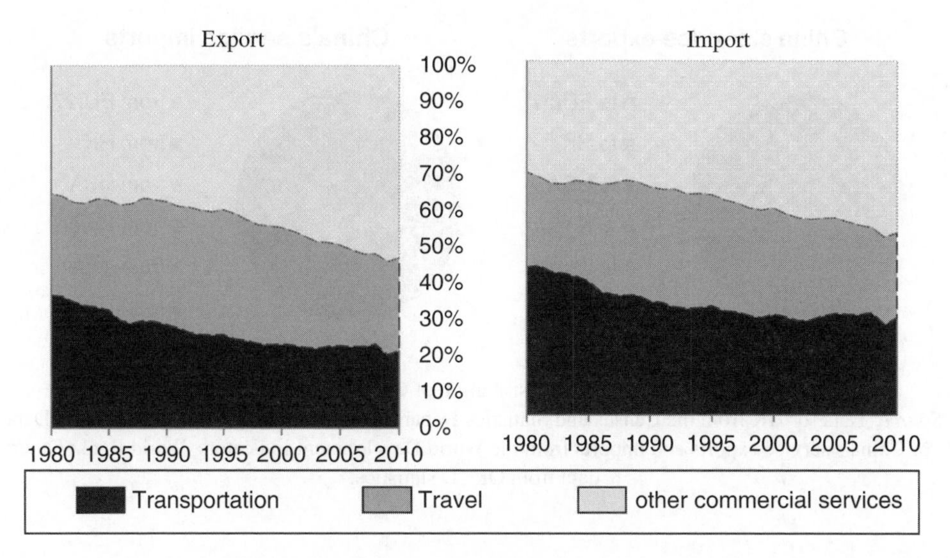

Figure 4. World Commercial Service Trade Composition.
Source: WTO Statistics Database.

the same clearly identified features in each of the three opening stages for imports as exist for exports. However, the general trend of increasing share of other commercial services and decreasing share of traditional services is also the case for China's service imports. Transportation, with a peak share of more than 70%, used to be the most important component in China's services imports from 1982 to 1990. But with the growth of travel and other commercial services, also affected by the negative impact of the Southeast Asian financial crisis

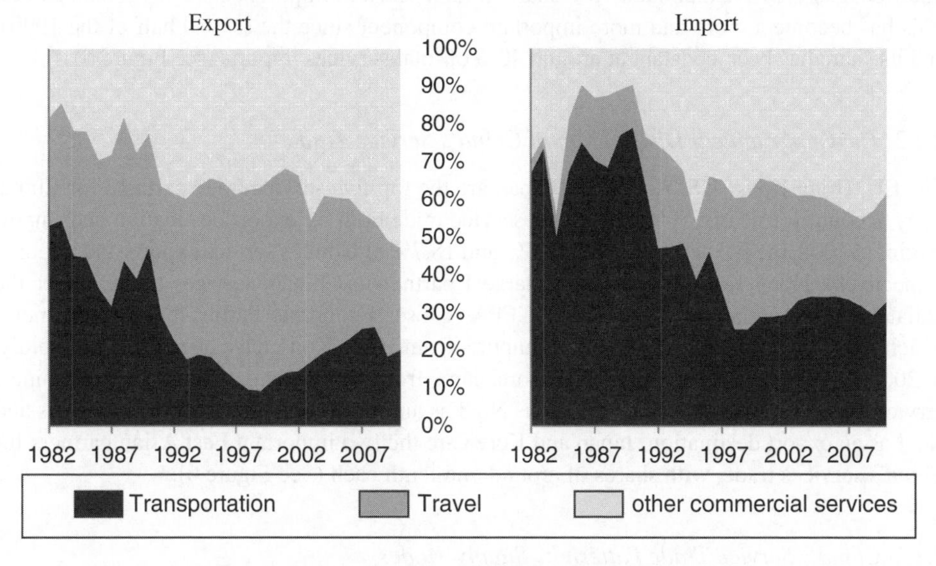

Figure 5. China's Commercial Service Trade Composition.
Note: Government services are excluded in commercial service trade.
Source: WTO Statistics Database.

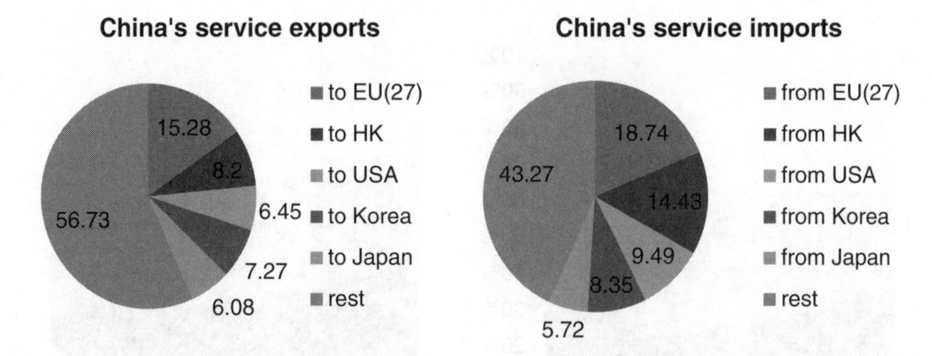

Figure 6. The Geographical Distribution of China's Services Trade: 2008.
Source: Data for HK from the Census and Statistics Department of the Hong Kong government; Data for China's service exports and imports from the World Development Indicators, World Bank; Other data from OECD statistics.

on China's merchandise trade and on transportation service trade, its share fell substantially from 79% to 25% during the period 1991–1998 and then increased a little after 1998. It has been below 35% ever since. At the beginning of China's reforms, China's travel imports were a small share of China's service imports, because of both domestic and international limitations on Chinese resident movements and foreign exchange controls. With a gradual loosening of control over migration and foreign exchange inconvertibility as well as increasing personal disposable income, China's travel imports began to increase steadily except for the years 1989 ("Tiananmen Square") and 2003 ("SARS"). Other commercial services, reflecting a development trend of growing technology and knowledge-intensive services as against traditional services, had about a 10% share in total services imports between 1986 and 1990. This has become a more and more important component since the second half of the 1990s, and its share has been constant at around 40% of total services imports (see Figure 5).

2.2.2 *The Geographical Distribution of China's Service Trade*

The EU, Hong Kong, US, Korea, and Japan are the top five service trade partners for China. They account for nearly 50% of China's service trade both by export destination and import origin. In 2008, the EU accounted for 15.3% and 18.7% of China's service exports and imports, respectively. Hong Kong is the second largest partner in China's services trade. Under the unilateral preferential arrangements of CEPA (Closer Economic Partnership Arrangement) which started in 2004, China's services imports from Hong Kong have been growing rapidly. In 2008, 14.43% of China's services imports came from Hong Kong, while 8.20% of China's service exports went to HK. The US ranks No.3 as an origin for China's services imports and No.4 as an export destination. Japan and Korea are the two important East Asian partners for China's services trade, with shares of around one-tenth each (See Figure 6).

2.2.3 *China's Service Trade Pattern by Supply Modes*

Under the General Agreement on Trade in Services (GATS), trade in services is defined as the supply of a service via four modes, that is, cross-border supply, consumption abroad, commercial presence, and the presence of natural persons. These GATS modes of supply do not match with conventional statistical definitions of trade in services as set out in the Balance of Payments (BOP). This mismatch between the GATS and BOP data is important, as Cave (2002) notes, since BOP data account for most trade under GATS modes of cross-border supply and consumption abroad (under current account-trade-services), a significant amount of that under the presence of natural persons (under current account-income-compensation of employees), but only some of that under commercial presence. The Extended Balance of Payments Services (EBOPS) proposed in the Manual on Statistics of International Trade in Services, 2002 seeks to extend the traditional BOP definition of trade in services by including the value of services provided through foreign affiliates (Foreign Affiliate Trade in Services, FATS).

The Ministry of Commerce of the PRC has recently introduced EBOPS and set up China's services trade statistical system. However, the data released from this source only cover China's inward FATS for the years 2005 and 2006. The annual turnover within China for nonfinancial service foreign affiliates was 73.97 billion US dollars and 91.32 billion US dollars in 2005 and 2006, respectively. The WTO service trade database also shows China's inward FATS sales amounted to 133.96 billion US dollars in 2008, which is close to service imports in the BOP data in the same year. In contrast to the large amount of inward FATS sales, China's outward FATS sales are limited. Though overall data are not available, the illustration of Sino-US bilateral FATS statistics by the US Bureau of Economic Analysis is reflective of the general situation. In 2008, services supplied to China's market by US multinational companies through their majority-owned affiliates in China reached 19.514 billion US dollars, while the counterpart services supplied to the US market by China's multinational companies through their majority-owned affiliates in the US was only 0.432 billion US dollars. If the supply mode of commercial presence is taken into account, China's service trade will thus show larger deficits.

2.3 *China's Service Trade: Competitiveness by Subsectors*

Balassa (1965) suggested that comparative advantage could be inferred from observed trade data and labeled this "revealed comparative advantage" (*RCA*) and proposed calculation of an *RCA* index. This can also be used to assess competitiveness in service trade. Since then there has been a series of revisions and modifications to his *RCA* index. The original *RCA* index that Balassa (1965) proposed is now widely accepted and can be written as follows:

$$RCA_{ij} = RXA_{ij} = \frac{X_{ij}}{\sum\limits_{i=1}^{m} X_{ij}} \Bigg/ \frac{\sum\limits_{j=1}^{n} X_{ij}}{\sum\limits_{i=1}^{m}\sum\limits_{j=1}^{n} X_{ij}}, \tag{1}$$

where X represents exports, i is a country (suppose the number of sample countries is m), j is a commodity or industry (suppose the number of sample industries is n). If country i's share of sample countries exports of j $(X_{ij}/\sum_{i=1}^{m} X_{ij})$ is greater than country i's share of sample countries exports of all the sample industries $(\sum_{j}^{n} X_{ij}/.\sum_{i=1}^{m}\sum_{j-1}^{n} X_{ij})$, then $RCA_{ij} > 1$ and a comparative advantage of country i in commodity/industry j is revealed.

This index, however, may be distorted by the omission of imports, especially where there is a country-size effect. Vollrath (1991) suggested that imports should also be considered by

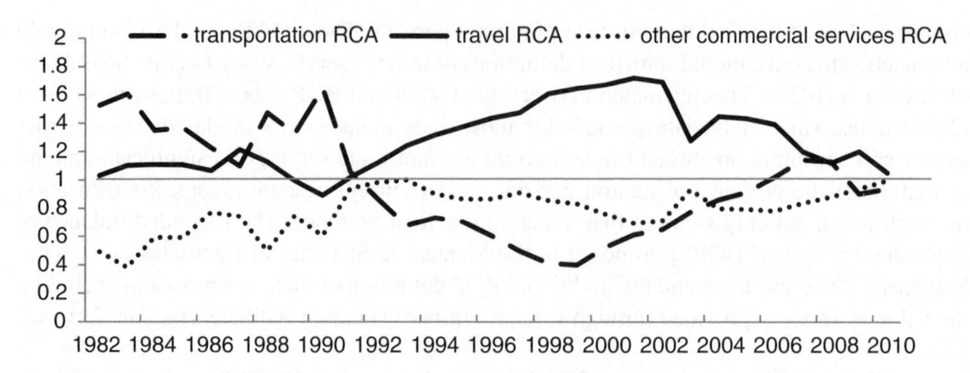

Figure 7. The *RCA* Index of China's Services Trade by Component: 1982–2010.
Source: The WTO statistics database.

offering three alternative ways of measuring a country's *RCA*. These are the relative trade advantage (*RTA*), the logarithm of the relative export advantage (*Ln RXA*), and the revealed competitiveness (*RC*). The *RC* index is the difference between the logarithm of the *RXA* and the logarithm of the relative import advantage (*Ln RXA* – *Ln RMA*). The advantage of presenting the index in logarithmic form is that the index becomes symmetric around zero. Positive values of Vollrath's three alternative measures of *RCA* reveal a comparative/competitive advantage, whereas negative values indicate a comparative/competitive disadvantage (Utkulu and Seymen, 2004). These indices can be adjusted by varying the number of sample countries and sample industries.

Figure 7 displays the original Balassa *RCA* indices for China's service trade at a global level. In most years from 1982 to 2010, the Balassa *RCA* index for China's travel service scores above 1, displaying significant *RCA*. The travel services *RCA* index grew gradually at the beginning of market opening, and decreased below 1 in the years 1989 and 1990. During the second opening stage between 1992 and 2002, the travel services *RCA* index reached its highest level, but dropped afterwards to near the critical level of $RCA = 1$. China's transportation services showed *RCA* in the first opening stage, with its *RCA* index scoring above 1. But since 1992, transportation has displayed comparative disadvantage and its *RCA* index has fallen below 1. The revealed comparative disadvantage of China's other commercial services is also reflected in its low *RCA* indices.

Figure 8 shows the Vollrath *RC* index for China's service trade. The *RC* index is a more comprehensive index than the *RCA* index since imports are taken into account. The formula for the *RC* index is as follows:

$$RC = LnRXA - LnRMA = Ln\left(\frac{X_{ij}}{\sum_{i=1}^{m} X_{ij}} \bigg/ \frac{\sum_{j=1}^{n} X_{ij}}{\sum_{i=1}^{m}\sum_{j=1}^{n} X_{ij}}\right) - Ln\left(\frac{M_{ij}}{\sum_{i=1}^{m} M_{ij}} \bigg/ \frac{\sum_{j=1}^{n} M_{ij}}{\sum_{i=1}^{m}\sum_{j=1}^{n} M_{ij}}\right), \quad (2)$$

where X_{ij} and M_{ij} represent exports and imports, respectively.

Overall, China's travel services have the highest *RC* index among the three categories of services, but the *RC* of China's travel services decreases over time from 2.2 at the beginning of market opening to –0.1 in 2010. The negative *RC* index for China's transportation services

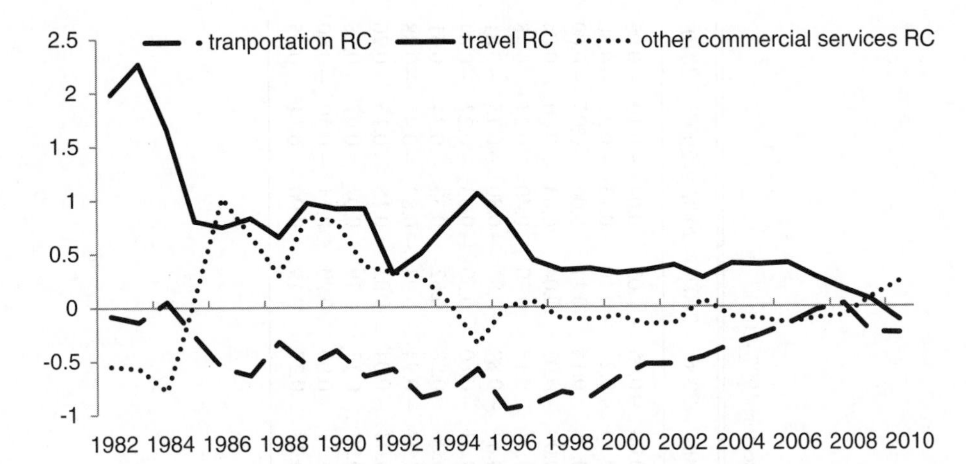

Figure 8. The *RC* Index of China's Service Trade: 1982–2010.
Source: The WTO statistics database.

reveals China's lack of competitiveness in the transportation sector. For other commercial services, the *RC* index fluctuates around zero.

An alternative measure of competitiveness is given by the net trade balance over the total trade volume, expressed as the Trade Competitiveness Index (*TCI*). The formula for the *TCI* for country *i* in commodity/industry *j* is: $TCI_{ij} = {X_{ij} - M_{ij}}/{X_{ij} + M_{ij}}$ where X_{ij} and M_{ij} represent exports and imports for country *i* in commodity/industry *j*, respectively. This index ranges from –1 (when $X_{ij} = 0$) to +1 (when $M_{ij} = 0$). Positive values for the *TCI* suggest competitiveness whereas negative values indicate lack of competitiveness. However, there are ambiguities around zero values (Greenaway and Milner, 1993). Unlike other competitiveness indices, this index makes reference to the "own" country trade performance only.

We use detailed service sector data for China's services trade from 1997 to 2010 to calculate China's services *TCI* (see Table 2). We start from 1997, because that was when China changed the pattern of its balance of payments and adopted the IMF Balance of Payment manual version 5. It is also the first year when detailed information about China's service trade by sector became available. The *TCI* for China's general service trade is negative from 1997 to 2010. The Southeast Asian financial crisis of 1998 and the world financial crisis of 2008 both had a negative effect on China's services trade in the *TCI* in the following years. Among the 12 service sub-sectors, other business services, and travel services display strong competitiveness with a positive *TCI* for most years between 1997 and 2010. The TCI for construction, computer & information, and advertising services grow and remain positive after China's entry to the WTO. However, transportation, insurance, and financial services, as well as royalties and license fees have a negative *TCI* throughout the period, with insurance and royalties and license fees close to –1.

2.4 *International Comparisons of Openness of China's Services Trade*

The share of China's services trade in GDP grew from 2.23% in 1982 to a high point of 7.22% in 2007, while slightly decreasing to 5.79% in 2009. This share can be viewed as an aggregated openness measure for China's service trade. A disaggregated measure of an openness index

Table 2. The Trade Competitive Index (*TCI*) for China's Services Trade by Subsector: 1997–2010.

	1997	1998	1999	2000	2001	2002	2003	2004	2005	2006	2007	2008	2009	2010
Service total	−0.06	−0.05	−0.09	−0.08	−0.08	−0.08	−0.08	−0.07	−0.06	−0.05	−0.03	−0.04	−0.10	−0.06
Transportation	−0.54	−0.49	−0.53	−0.48	−0.42	−0.41	−0.40	−0.34	−0.30	−0.24	−0.16	−0.13	−0.33	−0.30
Travel	0.20	0.16	0.13	0.11	0.12	0.14	0.07	0.15	0.15	0.16	0.11	0.06	−0.05	−0.09
Communication services	−0.03	0.60	0.51	0.70	−0.09	0.08	0.20	−0.03	−0.09	−0.07	0.04	0.03	0.00	0.04
Construction service	−0.34	−0.31	−0.22	−0.25	−0.01	0.13	0.04	0.05	0.24	0.17	0.30	0.40	0.23	0.48
Insurance services	−0.71	−0.64	−0.81	−0.92	−0.85	−0.88	−0.87	−0.88	−0.87	−0.89	−0.84	−0.80	−0.75	−0.81
Financial services	−0.84	−0.72	−0.20	−0.11	0.12	−0.28	−0.21	−0.19	−0.33	−0.80	−0.50	−0.33	−0.27	−0.04
Computer and information services	−0.47	−0.43	0.09	0.15	0.14	−0.28	0.03	0.13	0.06	0.28	0.32	0.33	0.34	0.51
Royalties and license fees	−0.82	−0.74	−0.83	−0.88	−0.89	−0.92	−0.94	−0.90	−0.93	−0.94	−0.93	−0.89	−0.93	−0.88
Consulting services	−0.15	−0.19	−0.30	−0.29	−0.26	−0.34	−0.29	−0.20	−0.08	−0.04	0.03	0.15	0.16	0.20
Advertising services	−0.01	−0.11	0.00	0.05	0.04	−0.03	0.03	0.10	0.22	0.17	0.19	0.07	0.07	0.18
Audio and video services	−0.63	−0.44	−0.67	−0.54	−0.29	−0.53	−0.35	−0.62	−0.33	0.00	0.20	0.14	−0.50	−0.60
Other business services	0.19	0.07	0.02	0.07	0.12	0.28	0.40	0.31	0.29	0.27	0.19	0.06	0.14	0.35

Source: China's Balance of Payments, 1997–2010.

by service sectors can be obtained by quantifying sector barriers with frequency-based, quantity-based, and price-based methodologies. Usually, the frequency ratio, first introduced by Hoekman (1995) in service trade, reflects the nominal trade barrier by examining the commitments to the GATS and/or the services trade related regulations, while quantity and price ratios reflect the tariff equivalent in service trade by estimating the restrictive impact of service trade barriers on import volume and price, respectively.[2] Here, a frequency ratio and a financial ratio (one form of the price-based method) are calculated using China's service trade data.

2.4.1 *A Frequency Method Measure of China's Service Trade Openness*

In its GATS commitment schedule, member countries specify commitments on a sector and on a mode combination basis in terms of both market access and national treatment. Using the GATS commitment schedules of member countries, Hoekman (1995) developed the widely used frequency ratio of service trade openness. Under this, all commitments of each WTO member country are classified into three categories, and are assigned a numerical score as an openness factor for each category.[3] Using these factors, Hoekman calculates three sectoral coverage indicators (hereafter the "Hoekman indices"). The first "unweighted count coverage" is calculated as the number of sector/modes-of-supply combinations where a commitment was made by a country in its GATS schedules and represents the maximum number possible. The second "weighted average coverage" is equal to the sectors/modes listed as a share of the maximum possible, weighted by the openness factors. The third is the share of "no restriction" commitments relative to the maximum possible sectors. The first Hoekman index measures the breadth of commitments, while the second and third indices reflect the depth of commitments. Table 3, from Mattoo (2003), sets out some calculations of these indices for some groups of countries.

China's GATS commitments for service trade cover 10 out of the 12 major GATS service categories and 93 out of the 160 minor categories. From both breadth and depth perspectives, China made substantial openness commitments upon its accession to the WTO as a developing country. Based on international comparisons, the Hoekman index for China's service trade commitments is higher than that for commitments of high-income countries when they became founding WTO members in 1995, except for the share of "no restriction" commitments relative to maximum possible commitments. China has made more specific commitment on national treatment than on market access, which is also the case for most other WTO members (see Table 3).

2.4.2 *China's Service Trade Degree of Openness, Using a Financial Method Based on Listed Company Financial Reports*

Francois and Hoekman (1999) also proposed a measure of service trade openness based on gross operating margins, defined as total sales revenue minus total costs divided by total costs. Data on operating margins provide an indication of the relative profitability of activities, and therefore, the relative magnitude (restrictiveness) of the barriers to entry/exit that may exist. Gross operating margins are calculated using the financial data reported by firms listed on stock exchanges. Hoekman (2000) suggests two methods to gauge the tariff equivalent of service trade restriction through the use of these margins. The first is to use the difference between the average margins of a benchmark "open" country (say, Hong Kong or Singapore)

Table 3. Coverage of China's and Other Countries Specific Commitments to the WTO/GATS (%).

	High-income countries	Low- and middle-income countries	Large developing countries	China
Market Access				
Unweighted average count (sectors-modes listed as a share of maximum possible)	47.3	16.2	38.6	57.4
Average coverage (sectors-modes listed as a share of the maximum possible, weighted by openness factors)	35.9	10.3	22.9	38.1
No restrictions as a share of maximum possible	27.1	7.3	14.9	23.1
National Treatment				
Unweighted average count (sectors-modes listed as a share of maximum possible)	47.3	16.2	38.8	57.4
Average coverage (sectors-modes listed as a share of maximum possible, weighted by openness factors)	37.2	11.2	25.5	45.0
No restrictions as a share of maximum possible	30.8	9.4	20.2	36.5

Note: The breadth and depth of commitments by other countries are understated because their more recent commitments in telecommunications and financial services have not been taken fully into account.

Source: Mattoo (2003).

and the margins of the other countries in the sample. The second employs the difference between manufacturing and service margins, with the margins in manufacturing serving as the benchmark.

Using financial data between 1997 and 2007 reported by firms listed on both the China and Hong Kong stock exchanges, we can calculate the financial ratio for seven service sectors with Hong Kong's data as the benchmark (See Table 4). These seven service sectors are communications, computer & information, construction, finance, recreation, transportation, and travel. We use the ratio of China's specific sector-level gross operating margin to that of Hong Kong instead of their difference to avoid negative measures, and then take the reciprocal of the financial ratio as the openness index. Table 4 suggests that China's finance, computer & information, and construction services are more open than transportation, recreation, communication, and travelling. This relative openness ranking is comparable to the results of Hoekman (2000). However, compared to Hoekman (2000) where China's service openness indices (also with Hong Kong as the benchmark) are less than 0.75 in all the sectors, our results show a general growing trend of openness in China's seven service sectors.

Table 4. The Degree of Openness of China's Services Trade in Seven Sectors Using Financial Measures: 1997–2007.

	Communication	Computer and software	Construction	Finance	Recreation	Transportation	Travelling
1997		1.963		2.159			
1998		1.985		3.953	0.676		0.328
1999		1.549	1.205	3.274	0.478	0.798	1.079
2000	0.213	1.503	1.520	2.554	1.079	0.764	0.695
2001	1.522	1.497	0.425	32.373	0.732	0.679	0.489
2002	1.569	1.218	0.810	1.665	0.755	0.701	0.389
2003	1.199	1.316	0.731	1.099	0.792	0.741	0.529
2004	0.965	1.546	0.725	0.144	0.566	0.867	0.598
2005	1.435	1.571	1.098	0.710	0.713	0.942	0.629
2006	0.963	1.463	1.155	2.393	0.931	0.965	0.726
2007	1.047	1.169	1.498	1.475	1.162	0.891	0.796

Source: Wind Database.

2.5 *FTA Involvement of China's Service Trade*

China considers Free Trade Agreements (FTAs) to be an important and effective supplementary approach to its integration into the global economy and to strengthening its economic cooperation with other economies. As of January 2013, China has 15 FTAs in the process of negotiation with partners in more than 30 economies, of which 10 agreements have been signed already. Nine of these ten FTAs also cover services trade, and are in place with Hong Kong, Macao, ASEAN, Pakistan, Chile, New Zealand, Singapore, Peru, and Costa Rica. The Economic Cooperation Framework Agreement between mainland China and Taiwan[4] also involves commitments on opening services sectors to each other (see Table 5 for the overview of China's service FTAs). Negotiations on FTAs with Australia, Norway, Iceland, Switzerland, and the Gulf Cooperation Council are under way. China signed FTAs with Iceland and Switzerland in April 2013 and July 2013, respectively.

Since all the partners involved with China's service FTAs are WTO members except for one of the ASEAN members, the Lao People's Democratic Republic, China's service commitments to WTO/GATS provide the baseline for these partners with WTO membership. In general, all the service FTAs which have been signed are characterized as GATS+ agreements, that is, following a GATS-type positive list approach with improvements over GATS schedules/offers in relation to bilateral liberalization obligations. However, the extent to which China's service FTAs go beyond its GATS existing commitments varies among individual FTAs.

There are two main ways that regional service trade agreements go beyond GATS: one is by binding commitments in a new service sub-sector (i.e., the sector was not included in the GATS schedule), and the other is by improving upon GATS binding for an existing sub-sector (e.g., removing a limitation and hence providing for binding at a higher level of liberalization). To provide a comprehensive overview of the liberalization commitments of China's service FTAs, we focus on sector coverage, which captures the breadth of open commitments by highlighting the new commitments undertaken, and also identify each sector where improvements to the existing commitments are provided to capture the depth of open commitments.[5]

Table 5. China's Service FTAs Reviewed.

FTA	Date of Signature	Entry into Force	WTO Notification under GATS Art. V	Commitment Structure Type	Supplements
China-Hong Kong, China	29-Jun-2003	29-Jun-2003	27-Dec-2003	Positive list	Supplement I in Oct 2004 Supplement II in Oct 2005 Supplement III in June 2006 Supplement IV in June 2007 Supplement V in July 2008 Supplement VI in May 2009 Supplement VII in May 2010 Supplement VIII in Dec. 2011
China-Macau, China	17-Oct-2003	17-Oct-2003	27-Dec-2003	Positive list	Supplement I in Oct 2004 Supplement II in Oct 2005 Supplement III in June 2006

(*Continued*)

Table 5. *Continued*

FTA	Date of Signature	Entry into Force	WTO Notification under GATS Art. V	Commitment Structure Type	Supplements
China-ASEAN	14-Jan-2007	01-Jul-2007	26-Jun-2008	Positive list	Supplement IV in July 2007 Supplement V in July 2008 Supplement VI in May 2009 Supplement VII in May 2010 Supplement VIII in Dec. 2011 With supplement signed in Nov. 2011, enforced in Jan. 2012
China-New Zealand	07-Apr-2008	01-Oct-2008	21-Apr-2009	Positive list	
China-Chile	13-Apr-2008	01-Aug-2010	18-Nov-2010	Positive list	
China-Singapore	23-Oct-2008	01-Jan-2009	02-Mar-2009	Positive list	
China-Pakistan	21-Feb-2009	10-Oct-2009	20-May-2010	Positive list	
China-Peru	28-Apr-2009	01-Mar-2010	03-Mar-2010	Positive list	
China-Costa Rica	08-Apr-2010	01-Aug-2011	27-Feb-2012	Positive list	

Table 6 highlights China's service subsector coverage for all ten service FTAs China has signed, divided into three categories of unchanged, new and improved. We find that among the ten partners,[6] Hong Kong and Macau have the highest number of both new and improved service subsectors. And among the 11 main service sectors, business services, and transportation services are the two with most value-added (new and improved commitments) over GATS commitments. Some sensitive service sectors/subsectors that have proved difficult to include in multilateral negotiations (e.g., telecom, audiovisual, health, and cultural) now are partially and/or exclusively open to HK and Macau service suppliers. For those services that have already taken on many GATS commitments/offers (e.g., construction, distribution, environmental, and financial), there is only limited space for new service activities, and therefore further improvement based on existing commitments is the main approach through which more liberalization can be achieved.

3. Services Development in China's Wider Development Strategy

The Chinese government currently treats the development of China's service sectors and services trade as part of China's broader development strategy. Not only do services provide the nation with a new source of employment that is critical for absorbing surplus rural labor, but services also provide an important response to many of the sustainability constraints that the Chinese government has long warned of. Unlike resource- and pollution-intensive manufacturing, services are resource-saving and more environment friendly. As a result, transformation of the mode of economic development by shifting to services puts less pressure on worldwide commodity markets and also holds out greater promise for a lighter, greener, and cleaner Chinese GDP.

The 12th 5-Year Plan (2011–2015) sets out an explicit target of increasing the services share of Chinese GDP by four percentage points to 47% by 2015, which can be viewed as an attempt to correct lagged service development. In order to achieve the target, Part IV of the Plan provides an outline for creating the environment necessary for extensive development of the services industry, by accelerating the development of producer services such as financial, logistics, high-tech, and business services, and by developing life services such as business distribution services, tourism services, domestic, and sport services.

For China, a nation lacking a service culture, deregulation of domestic services, and opening up to foreign direct investment and joint ventures seems like a viable option for encouraging large-scale service-led growth and employment. Therefore, promoting service trade is correspondingly a central element of China's 12th 5-Year Plan. According to the Outline of the 12th Five-Year Plan on Trade in Services (hereafter the Outline) drafted and issued jointly by the Ministry of Commerce and 33 other central government departments, the development target for China's service trade is to reach 600 billion US dollars by 2015 at an annual growth rate of 11%, with over 45% of the service export coming from high-value-added services such as computer and IT services, communication, finance, culture, and consultation. The Outline also sets out the target of further opening service trade by increasing the size of commercial presence in communications, finance, computer, information service, and commercial service. Enhancement of international competitiveness in trade in services is set out as another development goal in the Outline. This is to be achieved by expanding the scale of service exports from such sectors as overseas contracting of engineering projects, labor cooperation, transportation, tourism, communication, computing, information services, finance, culture, consultation, distribution, and R&D, by fostering firms with proprietary

Table 6. An Overview of China's Commitments in RTAs: Based on China's GATS Commitments.

Service sectors / subsectors[a]	WTO/ GATS	CEPA with HKG[b]	CEPA with MAC[b]	China-ASEAN FTA[b]	China-CHL FTA[b]	China-NZL FTA[b]	China-SGP FTA[b]	China-PAK FTA[b]	China-Peru FTA[b]	China-CRI FTA[b]	ECFA with TWN[b]
Business (57)	30	34(47)	34(47)	35	21(34)	31	35	38	37	32	6(32)
Unchanged		13	13	19	19	22	19	19	19	19	26
New		17	17	5	4	1	5	8	7	2	2
Improved		17	17	11	11	8	11	11	11	11	4
Communication (37)	24	14(35)	14(35)	24	0(24)	24	24	24	24	24	0(24)
Unchanged		21	21	24	24	24	24	24	24	24	24
New		11	11	0	0	0	0	0	0	0	0
Improved		3	3	0	0	0	0	0	0	0	0
Construction and related engineering (5)	5	5	5	5	5	5	5	5	5	5	0(5)
Unchanged		0	0	5	5	5	5	5	5	5	5
New		0	0	0	0	0	0	0	0	0	0
Improved		5	5	0	0	0	0	0	0	0	0
Distribution (5)	5	4(5)	4(5)	5	5	5	5	5	5	5	0(5)
Unchanged		1	1	2	3	5	2	2	2	2	5
New		0	0	0	0	0	0	0	0	0	0
improved		4	4	3	2	0	3	3	3	3	0
Educational service (5)	5	0(5)	0(5)	5	5	5	5	5	5	5	0(5)
Unchanged		5	5	5	5	5	5	5	5	5	5
New		0	0	0	0	0	0	0	0	0	0
Improved		0	0	0	0	0	0	0	0	0	0
Environmental (7)	7	7	7	7	7	7	7	7	7	7	0(7)
Unchanged		0	0	0	0	0	0	2	7	7	7
New		0	0	0	0	0	0	0	0	0	0
Improved		7	7	7	7	7	7	5	0	0	0
Financial services (18)	14	12(15)	12(15)	14	0(14)	14	14	14	14	0(14)	4(15)
Unchanged		3	3	14	14	14	14	14	14	14	11

(*Continued*)

Table 6. *Continued*

Service sectors / subsectors[a]	WTO/ GATS	CEPA with HKG[b]	CEPA with MAC[b]	China-ASEAN FTA[b]	China-CHL FTA[b]	China-NZL FTA[b]	China-SGP FTA[b]	China-PAK FTA[b]	China-Peru FTA[b]	China-CRI FTA[b]	ECFA with TWN[b]
New		1	1	0	0	0	0	0	0	0	1
Improved		11	11	0	0	0	0	0	0	0	3
Health-related and social services (6)	0	6	6	0	0	0	1	1	0	0	1
Unchanged		0	0	0	0	0	0	0	0	0	0
New		6	6	0	0	0	1	1	0	0	1
Improved		0	0	0	0	0	0	0	0	0	0
Tourism and travel-related services (4)	2	4	4	2	2	2	2	2	2	2	0(2)
Unchanged		0	0	2	2	2	2	1	1	1	2
New		2	2	0	0	0	0	0	0	0	0
Improved		2	2	0	0	0	0	1	1	1	0
Recreation, cultural and sporting services (4)	0	3	3	1	1	1	1	1	1	1	0
Unchanged		0	0	0	0	0	0	0	0	0	0
New		3	3	1	1	1	1	1	1	1	0
Improved		0	0	0	0	0	0	0	0	0	0
Transport services (57)	13	20(26)	19(25)	18	6(17)	14	18	15	14	13	1(13)
Unchanged		6	6	11	11	11	11	13	13	13	12
New		13	12	5	4	1	5	2	1	0	0
Improved		7	7	2	2	2	2	0	0	0	1

Note: [a]the numbers in parentheses represent the maximum number of service subsectors covered based on GATS service sectoral classification (MTN.GNS/W/120) and the innovated service activities in China's service FTAs commitments.
[b]the numbers in parentheses are the effective service subsector coverage for the FTA partner with WTO membership. Country/area code: HKG- Hong Kong, MAC-Macau, CHL-Chile, NZL- New Zealand, SGP-Singapore, PAK-Pakistan, CRI-Costa Rica, TWN-Taiwan.

Source: Authors' calculation.

intellectual property rights and well-known brands to establish the reputation of "Service by China", and by increasing the number of overseas business presence and service outsourcing firms with international qualifications and brands.

In the Plan, exports of services receive more emphasis, with consideration given to balancing China's foreign trade structure. There is stress on expanding and stabilizing exports of traditional service sectors such as tourism and transportation. In the meantime, promoting the export of culture, Chinese medicine, software and information services, logistics in business and trade, financial and insurance services, and other services is seen as in accordance with China's strategy of a new positioning in the international division of labor and international economic cooperation and competition. To enhance the development of service trade, a strategy of developing service outsourcing and establishing service contracting bases is emphasized with a focus on a group of cities along with the accumulation of a human capital and outsourcing network. A wide range of 30 service sectors have been chosen as the key sectors to be cultivated during the 12th 5-year period. These key sectors have been selected to reflect both China's comparative advantage (e.g., tourism) and development trends of global trade in services (e.g., IT service). The Outline also provides detailed development goals and tasks for each key service sector in its annex. All these elements of China's service trade expansion are part of a process which incorporates service trade development into the overall growth strategy.

Policies related to services are to be improved on so as to create a favorable environment for service development. A comprehensive promotion system comprising government departments, chamber of commerce, association, and trade in services firms will be established and will set up a support network for the development of trade in services. The main policies are as follows.

From a tax policy perspective, combined with value-added tax (VAT) reform, the indirect tax system for producer services will be reformed. A pilot scheme aiming to merge business tax (BT) with VAT[7] in transportation and selected modern services sectors was launched in Shanghai on 16 November 2011. According to Circular 111[7] and the Pilot Scheme Implementation Rules, as of 1 January, 2012, businesses registered in Shanghai and engaging in the following sectors ("VAT Taxable Services") will be subject to VAT instead of BT. These service sectors are transportation, leasing of tangible movable assets, R&D and technical services, cultural and innovation services, logistics auxiliary services, attesting, and consulting services. As a result, businesses providing these services are permitted to credit the input VAT on fixed assets, for instance, transportation vehicles, machinery or equipment purchased as capital goods, instead of being levied BT based on turnover. The pilot scheme also provides tax preference for off-shore outsourcing businesses in these service sectors, as well as a zero tax rate (which implies a full export tax rebate) for exports of related services trade.[8] According to the first quarter statistics of the State Administration of Taxation, the pilot scheme affecting 126 thousand enterprises in Shanghai has reduced the tax burden of most involved enterprises,[9] boosted R&D and innovation activities and expanded the export of trade in services. This experience has encouraged Beijing, Tianjin, Shenzhen, Nanjing, and Guangzhou, cities with sound foundations of modern service sectors, to also apply for this pilot scheme. Local Tax Bureaus in various regions also provide tax preferences in terms of corporate income tax, urban land use tax, and property tax to qualified service firms in encouraged sectors.

In addition, other preferential policies involving land supply and financial credit are to be adopted to provide facilitation in trade in services. Service enterprises will have priority over manufacturing in using land at a favorable price, especially in High Technology Parks or Industry Parks. Financing channels for service enterprises will be broadened and the public financing and issuing of bonds of eligible enterprises will be supported. The share of the budget spent on government services procurement will be increased with an expanded range for professional services, technological services, information services, R&D services, transportation and maintenance services, education and training, exhibition, and convention services. Service enterprises' brands and network-building will receive more support from the government. As an international and comprehensive platform for service trade at a state level, the China (Beijing) International Fair for Trade in Services (CIFTIS) hosted by the Ministry of Commerce and organized by the People's Government of Beijing Municipality will be held in Beijing every year starting from 2012.

Chambers of commerce are also making joint efforts to enhance the development of China's service trade. The China Association of Trade in Services, a national nonprofit social body aiming to build a national platform for the coordination and promotion of trade in services and assisting the Government in enhancing the international influence of China's services, was established with the approval of the State Council and under the governance of the Ministry of Commerce in 2007. The Association facilitates communication between government and enterprises as well as information exchange between domestic and international markets by means of a website. Making full use of the platform of fairs such as the China (Dalian) International Software & Information Service Fair, the Hong Kong Trade in Services Fair and the China (Shenzhen) International Cultural Industry Fair, the association also plays an important role in strengthening international communication and cooperation, stimulating corporate dialogue, and helping China's services enterprises participate in professional services fairs.

It is worth emphasizing that the development of China's service trade, as a central part of a wide overall growth strategy, is of major significance for foreign trade growth, enhancing the development of a modern service industry, alleviating employment pressure, driving services consumption growth, upgrading China's soft power, and improving the quality of companies, individuals, and the development of the national economy.

4. Evaluating the Impacts of China's Service Trade Liberalization and Development

We next discuss the impacts of China's service trade liberalization and developments on growth, technology accumulation, and employment. The potential benefits to China are in large part a reflection of estimates of the wider contribution of service trade liberalization to economic growth. We also note the central issue of the extent to which the service liberalization process in China serves as a channel for technology diffusion. We finally discuss the impacts of China's service trade on employment.

4.1 *Impacts on Economic Growth*

A central component in evaluating the effectiveness of service trade policies in China is assessing the impact on economic growth, since service trade liberalization is a route to raising productivity and thus achieving the goal of economic development.

A number of studies demonstrate theoretically that openness in services positively influences long-run growth performance. One of the most important benefits of service trade liberalization comes from more service varieties with higher quality at lower price. Services, especially intermediate or producer services, facilitate transactions through space (transport, telecommunications), or time (financial services) and are important inputs in modern production. Therefore, the greater the variety and quality of services and the larger the reduction in (real) prices associated with greater specialization in services (outsourcing), the greater the impact on productivity (welfare) of firms (households) that buy services (Burgess and Venables, 2004; Mattoo et al., 2006; Hoekman and Mattoo, 2008). Another important benefit, different from that for liberalization of goods, lies in the mobility and scale effects that service trade may involve. The fact that "imports" of services are often locally produced[10] and that liberalization leads to enhanced competition levels both at home and abroad, mean enhanced transmission and diffusion of technology and management skill and thus enhanced possibility for scale economies to generate larger endogenous growth (Rodriguez and Rodrik, 1999).

There are a few empirical studies which include China in the sample of countries analyzed to assess the impact of services liberalization on growth. Using the FTAP and based on their large barrier estimates (a little over 250% as tax equivalent barriers) for the Chinese services sector, Dee and Hanslow (2000) report 130 billion US dollars (or 0.46% of world real income) of gains arising globally from global service trade liberalization under a Doha Round WTO scenario, of which about 90 billion US dollars would accrue from liberalization in China alone (representing about 14.6% of its real GDP). Building on the same model structure and using the same estimates for barriers to trade in services as Dee and Hanslow, Verikios and Zhang (2000) extend their analysis by separately simulating the liberalization of trade in communication services and in financial services. In a scenario of liberalization of trade in communication services, the world is projected to gain about 13 billion US dollars with China capturing 4.4 billion US dollars, and when liberalizing trade in finance, insurance, and business services, the expected global gains are about 3.5 billion US dollars with more than 2 billion going to China.

However, Whalley (2004) argued that the welfare effect of trade liberalization in intermediate services depends on the configuration of initial endowments, consumption patterns, and the volumes of desired transactions, with resource use in transaction costs depending on the pattern of transactions between agents. Chia and Whalley (1997), Ng and Whalley (2004) and Bhattarai and Whalley (2006) constructed numerical examples which highlight features of Chinese services liberalization in areas of banking, insurance, telecoms, and networking. Their results showed that firstly, gains to China need not occur, and secondly that conventional tariff-based analyses of impacts may be misleading, and that country divisions of gains from services liberalization may differ from what is typical for trade in goods.

All the above arguments suggest more work is needed on the mechanisms through which liberalization of China's service trade might lead to higher economic growth.

4.2 *Impacts on Domestic Technology Accumulation via Technology Diffusion*

A further element in the evaluation of China's service trade development is the impact on technology diffusion. There are a number of channels through which the interaction between technology diffusion & accumulation and services may take place. On one hand, technological change, either in the manufacturing sector or services sector, will provide direct stimulus for a higher level of intermediate demand for services as input as well as knowledge flows. Francois (1990) showed that technological change leads to a "splintering" process, by which services (in particular, producer services) spring from the increased technical and social division of labor within production, engendering a strong interdependence between manufacturing and service activities. An expanding service sector will consequently foster the realization of increasing returns due to higher levels of specialization. Liberalization of trade leads to similar results. Tomlinson (2001) also argues that although manufacturing sectors spend more on R&D and generate more patents than service sectors, if technological innovation is understood as affecting marketing, training, and other activities, many services are more technology intensive than generally considered.

On the other hand, technological accumulation via international innovation diffusion depends on liberalization of services. Peri (2004) in his discussion of the theoretical and empirical literature shows that the amount of foreign-produced technology that can be used domestically is limited by two sets of factors: distance, which does not only carry a spatial dimension, and absorption capacity in the receiving country. Liberalization of service trade will play an important role both in the reduction in the cost of technology diffusion resulting from distance and in the enhancement of absorption capacity by promoting harmonization in domestic regulation.

Royalties and license fees, reflecting annual payments for the sale and use of intangible property rights such as patents, industrial processes, trademarks, copyrights, franchises, know-how, and other intellectual property rights, are the most frequently used proxy variable to estimate transfer of technology between countries. This is calculated and reflected in the Balance of Payment Sheet under the title of service trade.

As a relatively backward country, especially from a technology perspective, China remained a technology net importer from 1997 to 2010, the dates for which such data have been reported. In 1997, China's net payments on royalties and license fees were 511.5 million constant US dollars, and this increased 20 times to 10.57 billion constant US dollars in 2010. With such an overwhelmingly large amount and a high growth rate of net payments, China now is the third largest net technology importer, after Ireland and Singapore, in the world. The marked increase in China's net payments reflects the international exploitation of intellectual property which became increasingly important in China's growth process in the globalization era.

Led by international technology diffusion and a surge in domestic R&D intensity,[11] a remarkable increase in the number of patent filings has taken place in China, growing from 8,558 in 1985 to 391,177 in 2010. From a geographical standpoint, China has had the second biggest patent office since 2010. If we take a country of origin standard and only consider the number of patents granted, China ranks third after Japan and the US. The number of patent grants was 84,554 in 2010, accounting for about 30% and 45% of the number for Japan and the US in 2010, respectively. In addition, more than 95% of patents granted to Chinese residents are from the China Patent Office, while these local ratios for the US and Japan are 58% and 66%.

4.3 *Impacts on Employment*

The evaluation of the impacts of China's service trade liberalization and development on employment is another central element in an overall evaluation of the impacts of China's service trade development. The mainstream view among economists is that trade has little, if any, impact on unemployment while it has an impact on the employment pattern across sectors. Standard economic analysis concludes that changes in a country's pattern of trade or direct investment can only temporarily affect its aggregate level of employment, while in the long-run, macroeconomic factors operate to bring employment to a level where unemployment is at its so-called "natural rate" (Baldwin, 1994). Most trade models are full employment models with fully flexible wages. However, there now is a small but growing literature on the relationship between trade and unemployment. Davidson and Matusz (2004) find a negative correlation between job destruction and net exports across sectors (equivalent to a positive correlation between net imports and job destruction). Dutt *et al.* (2009) find that unemployment and trade openness are negatively related. Focusing on cross-country differences in relative factor endowments as the cause of trade and the determinant of relative factor prices, the Heckscher-Ohlin-Samuelson (H-O-S) framework yields clear predictions regarding the effect of trade on employment across sectors, that is, trade results in a redistribution of employment away from the import substitution sector and towards the export sector (Greenaway *et al.*, 1998).

One recent study by Liu and Dai (2007) estimates the relationship between China's service trade and employment using data from 1982 to 2003 based on co-integration tests and Granger causality tests. Co-integration tests show that in the short run, the impact of China's service exports and imports on employment are positive but small (a 1% increase in export and import values for services creates 0.205% and 0.069%, respectively more job opportunities in the service sector), while the impact of service employment on service exports and imports are large but not stable. Granger causality tests indicate that employment in the service sector was a Granger cause of service exports. Another empirical study by Xue and Han (2006) focuses on the effects of China's services FDI on employment. Their findings conclude that the service FDI inflow into China has little influence on the aggregate level of employment, whereas it greatly increases the quality of a country's employment in terms of productivity, skills transfer, and employment structure. Therefore, it is the quality of employment which is of more significance to an employment assessment of China's service liberalization and development.

According to the China Labor Statistical Yearbook, services have been the main source of nonagricultural employment in China. The share of employment in the service sector increased from 27.7% to 34.6% over the decade after China's entry to the WTO, while the commensurate share change for industry employment was from 22.3% to 28.7%. If we further consider the possibility of self-employed and informal employment in the service sector, the share of employment in the service sector will be even higher. The service industry also absorbs most of the labor force with higher education: 75.5%, 81.6%, and 82.3% of the labor force with college, university, and graduate education levels, respectively were employed in service industries in 2010. As a result, the average wage in service sectors is higher than that in the agricultural and industry sectors. For instance, in 2010 the average wage in the agriculture and manufacturing sectors was 16,717 RMB and 30,916 RMB, respectively. With a national wage level at 36,539 RMB, we can infer that it is the high wage in the service sector that creates a national average wage at a higher level than wages in agriculture and the manufacturing sector. Further, the average wage in the top three service sectors, that is, financial intermediation, computer & information services, and scientific research & technical services is 227%, 208%, and 183% of that in the manufacturing sector and 420%, 386%, and 337% of that in the agriculture sector.

5. Potential Global Implications of China's Service Trade Development

In this section, we discuss the potential global implications of China's service trade development. China is now a large entity in the global economy and the liberalization and development of China's service trade also has important implications for the global economy.

5.1 *Global Implications of China's Emerging Competitiveness in Offshore Service Outsourcing*

Beginning in the mid-1990s, cumulative improvements in information and communications technologies (ICT) facilitated an expansion of international trade in services and boosted the growth of offshore service outsourcing. The Gartner Group estimate that the size of the global service outsourcing market grew from $100 billion in 2001 to $893 billion in 2010. Beginning with IT outsourcing (ITO), the form and range of service outsourcing has evolved beyond ITO to encompass entire business process outsourcing (BPO) with higher value added, which is underpinned or enabled by IT. Due to the comprehensive competitiveness of outsourcing in terms of cost (production and transaction cost), labor qualification, and service quality, India is known to be the principal offshore vendor of IT services, claiming at least 80% of the world's business. In 2001, Chinese export revenue in software and IT-enabled services was only 720 million US dollars, less than one-tenth of India's (Qu and Brocklehurst, 2003). However, with a series of promotional policies launched by China's government, China has now become an emerging global base for undertaking offshore service outsourcing contracts. According to the Development Report on China's software and IT service outsourcing released by the Ministry of Industry and Information of China, in 2010 the value of China's service outsourcing reached 275 billion RMB (approximately 40.6 billion US dollars), with ITO and BPO accounting for 56.4% and 43.6%, respectively. Around 5,900 firms are registered to undertake service outsourcing, providing 0.73 million jobs. By September 2010, the number of outsourcing firms with CMM Certification[12] had increased to 1,475, 2.6 times and 86% that of India and the US, respectively.

However, compared to India, the biggest outsourcing destination in the world, China is still significantly behind in terms of competitiveness and maturity in offshore service outsourcing. First, the general scale of India's service outsourcing industry is much larger than that of China's, with aggregate revenues of 88.1 billion US dollars in FY2011, direct employment of nearly 2.5 million, and indirect job opportunities of 8.3 million.[13] Second, Indian service outsourcing has continuously moved up the value chain and proactively driven the adoption of new applications of service outsourcing such as knowledge process outsourcing (KPO). The world KPO industry was estimated to reach 17 billion US dollars by 2010, of which India captures more than 70%. KPO has a high element of intellectual intervention and personal judgment that leverages a combination of academic rigor and expertise. Representing the next wave of high-end services outsourcing, KPO derives its strength from depth of knowledge, experience, and judgment factors. In contrast, ITO and BPO, the main form of service outsourcing China has undertaken, are more about size, volume, and efficiency. Third, India's competitiveness in service outsourcing is also reflected by its companies' rankings in "The Global Outsourcing 100" by IAOP (International Association of Outsourcing Professionals). There are service outsourcing enterprises in India with worldwide reputations for high quality of supply. In 2011, India had 17 companies in the top 100 list, of which 3 were in the top 10 and 5 were in the top 20. Compared to India, there were only 8 companies in China in the list, and none of these ranked in the top 20.

In the global offshore service outsourcing market, China is growing as an important outsourcing destination due to its emerging competitiveness. China may accelerate its pace to challenge India's dominant position in low-end service outsourcing activities such as ITO and BPO. As a result, price competition for deals, particularly for standardized IT outsourcing (ITO) services, will be fierce and providers will need to accept low margins. Nonetheless, India may retain its superiority in the KPO market with a higher growth potential. KPO typically involves a component of ITO, BPO, Research Process Outsourcing (RPO), and Analysis Proves Outsourcing (APO), which may lead to opportunities for cooperation between China and India. The growing relationship between the two countries may take the form of subcontracts (the Indian provider may subcontract the ITO or BPO part of the whole KPO package to China-based companies so as to lower the overall cost) or FDI (Indian providers may set up their presence in China through direct build-out or through merger and acquisition to pursue seamless global delivery). Therefore, competition and cooperation may coexist between China and India and will lead to a high level of specialization and an improved division of labor in the global offshore service outsourcing market. This trend of the two countries racing and partnering to become a global superpower, named "Chindia,"[14] may begin to impact global service strategies.

5.2 *Impacts on Global FDI Flows*

FDI has played an important role in China's economic transformation since China's economic reform in 1978. The development and liberalization of China's service trade has also changed the FDI industry profile in China.

As the largest recipient of FDI in the developing world, China realized 118 billion US dollars FDI inflow in 2011, a 9.72% year-on-year increase compared to 2010. As for the number of FDI projects, 27,712 foreign-invested companies were established in 2011, a 1.12% increase compared to 2010.[15] The most significant trend in 2011 is that the service sector in China has for the first time attracted more FDI than the manufacturing sector. The services sector accounted for 47.62% of the total FDI received in 2011 compared to 44.91% received by the manufacturing sector.

This trend is expected to intensify with the fifth edition of the Catalogue for the Guidance of Foreign Investment Industries in China issued by The National Development and Reform Committee (NDRC) and the Ministry of Commerce at the end of 2011. The revised edition has increased the proportion of service industries in the "encouraged" category by adding nine service industry items, including motor vehicle battery charging stations, venture investment enterprises, intellectual property services, offshore oil pollution clean technology services, and vocational training. Foreign invested healthcare institutions and finance lease companies are moved from the restricted to the permitted category. Further, restrictions on the foreign investment equity ratio are removed in certain sectors – items with equity ratio restrictions are reduced by 11 compared to the 2007 Catalog.

The changing FDI industry structure in China has had spillover effects on other developing countries as an FDI destination. These mainly resulted from the slowing down of FDI in labor-intensive manufacturing due to continuously rising wages and production costs, particularly in coastal regions, as well as government guidance and targeting of shifting FDI inflows towards high-tech industries and services. Some ASEAN member States (such as Indonesia and Viet Nam) and other Asian countries (such as Bangladesh and Sri Lanka) have in contrast gained ground as low cost production locations, especially for low-end manufacturing.

5.3 *Impacts on International Migration of Educated Labor*

The international migration of educated labor is a key element in China's service trade liberalization, and portends future global change. With China's growing economic size and influence on the world and the vigorous development of China's service trade, together with a slump in world labor markets, particularly in advanced countries, triggered by the global financial crisis, China has now become one of the most attractive working locations for overseas Chinese students and foreign experts.

China used to experience a serious brain drain problem: the ratio of returnees to departing Chinese students and scholars was around a quarter from 1978 to 2007. By the end of 2011, this ratio had grown to 36% with a total of 2.25 million overseas Chinese students and 818,400 who migrated back to China. There was a surge in the number of returning overseas Chinese students in 2010 and 2011, with 134,800 and 186,200 overseas Chinese students and scholars returning in 2010 and 2011, respectively, accounting for nearly 40% of total returnees. Most of the returned overseas Chinese students and scholars are now working in high-tech manufacture or service enterprises (mainly in financial services, media services, and IT services), universities, and research institutions.

Foreign experts are currently China's newest import: according to a new program launched by China's State Administration of Foreign Experts Affairs (SAFEA), 1,000 top experts with management experience will be hired in the service industry to train more people in finance, insurance, security, and comprehensive transportation, and five international training bases will be developed in the field of software and integrated circuits for importing high-caliber foreign experts and teams to further global cooperation.

Returned overseas Chinese students and scholars, foreign experts, and senior personnel transferred within MNEs form the talent pool in China to meet the increased demand for educated labor in China's buoyant service industry. A marked increase in international migration of high-end labor is forecast for China, given the prospects for China's trade and FDI in services.

6. Conclusion

In this paper, we document the performance of China's service trade since the early 1980s and assess its domestic and global implications. China's economic development has relied on manufacturing and trade in goods for the first three decades of reform and opening. However, services are now getting more attention in the wider development strategy, as reflected in China's 12th 5-Year Plan. Given the relatively low share in GDP, foreign trade and employment compared to international norms, this leaves space for further development of service industries and service trade in China. Potential major impacts lie in terms of economic growth, employment and labor migration, technology diffusion, and FDI pattern for China and the global economy. These all reflect the increasing global importance of China's service trade and its competitive impacts on global service delivery. The implications are relatively little discussed in the available literature, but will increasingly form a central element in China's integration into the international economy.

Directions for future research might include, though not be limited to, the following issues. First, there is a need to measure the impact of the development of China's service trade on its economic growth. A key challenge here is to devise a model to capture the structural features of the mechanism through which liberalization of China's service trade might lead to higher economic growth. Second, research is needed to examine the potential labor migration and related income distribution effects within service sectors and across industries during the course of liberalization of China's service trade. Third, in China's emerging trend of outward

FDI, the impact of China's service trade on China's economic development and its policy implication on China's FTA negotiation is worth exploring.

Notes

1. Calculated using data from World Development Indicators, World Bank.
2. See Chen and Schembri (2002) for a survey of measurement of service trade barriers.
3. If no restrictions are applied for a given mode of supply in a given sector which could be viewed as fully open, a value of 1 is assigned. If no policies are bound for a given mode of supply in a given sector, a value of 0 is assigned; if restrictions are listed for a given mode of supply in a given sector, then a value of 0.5 is assigned.
4. Based on political considerations, the Economic Cooperation Framework Agreement between mainland China and Taiwan is not defined as a Free Trade Agreement. However, its contents involve tariff concessions on goods, services trade liberalization, investment facilitation as well as industrial and economic cooperation, which make the ECFA work as a de facto FTA. Therefore, in this paper, we treat the ECFA as an FTA.
5. Refer to Roy *et al.* (2006) for the explanation of this methodology.
6. ASEAN is counted as one partner.
7. See red-tape document with code CaiShui [2011] No. 111 ("Circular 111") issued jointly by the Ministry of Finance and the State Administration of Taxation.
8. See red-tape document with code CaiShui [2011] No. 131 for the definition of "export of service trade".
9. The tax burden of transportation enterprises in Shanghai is reported to have increased instead of reduced, which is possibly the result of a higher tax rate being applied (11% rather than 6% for other service sectors).
10. Due to the characteristics of services, that is, the intangibility and the physical proximity of producer and consumer, it is sometimes necessary for the supplier of services to produce locally, which is represented by the supply mode of commercial presence.
11. China's R&D intensity, the gross expenditure on R&D as a percentage of GDP, increased exponentially from 0.71 in 1990 to 1.76 in 2010 despite a spectacular increase in the denominator (GDP).
12. The Capability Maturity Model (CMM), a worldwide certification developed by the Software Engineering Institute of Carnegie Mellon University, is becoming the industry standard in the offshore outsourcing market.
13. See NASSCOM, *Strategic Review 2011: The IT-BPO Sector in India*. Available at http://www.nasscom.in/sites/default/files/researchreports/Exec%20Summary_0.pdf
14. See Gartner (2008).
15. See FDI statistics by Ministry of Commerce. Available at http://www.fdi.gov.cn/pub/FDI_EN/Statistics/FDIStatistics/StatisticsofForeignInvestment/t20120119_140572.htm

References

Balassa, B. (1965) Trade liberalisation and 'revealed' comparative advantage. *The Manchester School* 33(2): 99–123.

Baldwin, R.E. (1994) The effects of trade and foreign direct investment on employment and relative wage. *OECD Economic Studies* 23: 7–51.

Bhattarai, K. and Whalley, J. (2006) The division and size of gains from liberalization in service networks. *Review of International Economics* 14(3): 348–361.

Burgess, R. and Venables, A. J. (2004) Toward a microeconomics of growth. World Bank Policy Research Working Paper No. 3257.

Cave, W. (2002) Measuring International Trade in Services and New Demands on the Family of Classifications 17th Voorburg Group Meeting on Service Statistics, Nantes, 23–27 September 2002.

Chen, Z. and Schembri, L. (2002) Measuring the barriers to trade in services: Literature and methodologies. In J.M. Curtis and D.C. Ciuriak (eds), *Trade Policy Research 2002*. Ottawa, Canada: Department of Foreign Affairs and International Trade.

Chia, N.C. and Whalley, J. (1997) A numerical example showing globally welfare-worsening liberalization of international trade in banking services. *Journal of Policy Modelling* 19(2): 119–127.

Davidson, C. and Matusz, S. J. (2004) *International Trade and Labor Markets: Theory, Evidence, and Policy Implications*. Kalamazoo: WE Upjohn Institute for Employment Research.

Dee, P. and Hanslow, K. (2000) *Multilateral liberalization of services trade. Productivity Commission Staff Research Paper*. Canberra, Australia: Ausinfo.

Dutt, P., Mitra, D. and Ranjian, P. (2009) International trade and unemployment: Theory and cross-national evidence. *Journal of International Economics* 78(1): 32–44.

Francois, J. (1990) Producer services, scale and the division of labor. *Oxford Economic Papers* 42(4): 715–729.

Francois, J. and Hoekman, B. (1999) Market Access in the Services Sectors. Unpublished Manuscript.

Fuchs, V.R. (1982) Economic growth and the rise of service employment. NBER Working Paper No. 486.

Gartner Group (2008) Gartner on outsourcing: 2008–2009. Gartner's Fifth Annual Publication on Outsourcing. Available at http://enea.ro/download/pdf/Gartner%20Why%20Romania%202008.pdf (Last accessed 25 October 2012).

Greenaway, D., Hine, R.C. and Wright, P. (1998) An empirical assessment of the impact of trade on employment in the United Kingdom. Centre for Research on Globalisation and Labour Markets, University of Nottingham Research Paper 98/3.

Greenaway, D. and Milner, C. (1993) *Trade and Industrial Policy in Developing Countries: A Manual of Policy Analysis. Part IV Evaluating Comparative Advantage* (pp.181–208). London: The Macmillan Press.

Hoekman, B. (1995) Tentative first steps: an assessment of the Uruguay round agreement on services. World Bank Policy Research Working Paper No. 1455.

Hoekman, B. (2000) The next round of services negotiations: identifying priorities and options. *Federal Reserve Bank of St. Louis Review* 82(4): 31–48.

Hoekman, B. and Mattoo, A. (2008) Service trade and growth. World Bank Policy Research Working Paper No. 4461.

Liu, Y.L. and Dai, J. (2007) Analysis of services trade and employment in China by co-integration and causality. *Journal of Chongqing University* 6(1): 41–49.

Manual on Statistics of International Trade in Services. (2002) Available at http://unstats.un.org/unsd/publication/Seriesm/Seriesm_86e.pdf, released by the European Commission, IMF, OECD, UNCTAD and WTO.

Mattoo, A., Rathindran, R. and Subramanian, A. (2006) Measuring services trade liberalisation and its impact on economic growth: an illustration. *Journal of Economic Integration* 21(1): 64–98.

Mattoo, A. (2003) China's Accession to the WTO: the services dimension. *Journal of International Economic Law* 6(2): 299–339.

Ngee, C.C. and Whalley, J. (1997) A numerical example showing globally welfare-worsening liberalization of international trade in banking services. *Journal of Policy Modeling* 19(2): 119–127.

Ng, C.-Y. and Whalley, J. (2004) Geographical extension of free trade zones as trade liberalization: a numerical simulation approach. CESifo Working Paper Series No. 1147, Munich.

Peri, G. (2004) Catching-up to foreign technology? Evidence on the "Veblen– Gerschenkron" effect of foreign investments. NBER Working Paper No.10893.

Qu, Z. and Brocklehurst, M. (2003) What will it take for China to become a competitive force in offshore outsourcing? An analysis of the role of transaction costs in supplier selection. *Journal of Information Technology* 18(1): 53–67.

Rodriguez, F. and Rodrik, D. (1999) Trade policy and economic growth: a skeptic's guide to the cross-national literature. NBER Working Paper No. 7081.

Roy, M., Marchetti, J. and Lim, H. (2006) Services liberalization in the new generation of preferential trade agreements (PTAs): how much further than the GATS? WTO Staff Working Paper ERSD-2006–07.

Tomlinson, M. (2001) A new role for business services in economic growth. In D. Archibugi and B.-A. Lundvall (eds), *The Globalizing Learning Economy* (chapter 5, pp. 97–107). Oxford: Oxford University Press.

Utkulu, U. and Seymen, D. (2004) Revealed comparative advantage and competitiveness: evidence for Turkey vis-à-vis the EU/15. European Trade Study Group 6th Annual Conference, ETSG 2004, Nottingham, September 2004.

Verikios, G. and Zhang, X. (2000) Sectoral impacts of liberalising trade in services. Paper presented to the Third Annual Conference on Global Economic Analysis, Melbourne, Australia, June 2000.

Vollrath, T.L. (1991) A theoretical evaluation of alternative trade intensity measures of revealed comparative advantage. *Weltwirtschaftliches Archiv* 130: 265–279.

Whalley, J. (2004) Assessing the benefits to developing countries of liberalization in services trade. *The World Economy* 27(8): 1223–1253.

Xue, J.X. and Han, Y. (2006) The services FDI effects on china's employment. *Nankai Journal* 2: 125–133.

INDEX